THE SMALL BUSINESS BUSINESS PARTNERSHIP KIT

Robert L. Davidson III

John Wiley & Sons, Inc.

New York · Chichester · Brisbane · Toronto · Singapore

Also Available by Robert L. Davidson, III
The Small Business Bankruptcy Kit
The Small Business Incorporation Kit
Contracting Your Services
How to Start Your Own S Corporation

Library of Congress Cataloging-in-Publication Data

Davidson, Robert L., III.
    The small business partnership kit / by Robert L. Davidson, III.
        p.   cm.
    Includes index.
    ISBN 0-471-57653-0 (c) — ISBN 0-471-57654-9 (p)
    1. Partnership—United States—Popular works. I. Title.
KF1375.Z9D38   1992
346.73'0682—dc20
[347.306682]   92-10113

Printed in the United States of America

10 9 8 7 6 5 4 3 2 1

PREFACE

Congratulations! The fact that you are reading this book is evidence of your desire to control your own fate, to start and run a business in which you play a major role. The partnership, the subject of this book, is one of the most popular business forms, with an interesting history dating back into antiquity.

By the time you finish reading this book, you will know more about what a partnership is and how it works than probably 99 percent of Americans. You will know what provisions *can go into* a partnership agreement and what provisions *must go into* a partnership agreement. And you will have insight into the role of your silent partner, the IRS, in the operation of your business.

Where the waters of commerce are murky, namely for the legal niceties and for the tricks of the trade in tax planning, this book will help you select and communicate with professionals, such as lawyers, tax advisors, and CPAs.

Good luck.

ROBERT L. DAVIDSON, III

ABOUT THE AUTHOR

Robert L. Davidson, III, is an attorney and publications consultant in Princeton, New Jersey, where he specializes in author–publisher contracts, small business law, and elder law.

He is author, coauthor, editor, or coeditor of 13 books, the most recent of which are *Contracting Your Services, The Small Business Bankruptcy Kit, The Small Business Incorporation Kit,* and (coauthored with Arnold S. Goldstein) *How to Start Your Own S Corporation,* all published by John Wiley & Sons.

Mr. Davidson holds degrees of Bachelor and Master of Science in Chemical Engineering from the University of Missouri, and a Juris Doctor degree from Fordham University School of Law. He is licensed to practice law in New Jersey, is a member of the American Bar Association and the New Jersey State Bar Association, and of Tau Beta Pi (engineering), Sigma Xi (science), and Alpha Chi Sigma (chemistry) honor societies.

CONTENTS

CHAPTER 1

WHAT "PARTNERSHIP" MEANS

WHAT IS A PARTNERSHIP?

A partnership is a business that is owned by two or more persons who, as co-owners, carry on a trade or business for profit. The idea of partnerships is quite ancient. In 2200 B.C., Hammurabi, King of Babylon, provided for the regulation of partnerships. In ancient Rome, the partnership was called a *societa*.

It was during the Middle Ages in Italy that the laws of partnership, as we know them today, began to develop. Italian merchants often operated as limited partners. Their approach was introduced throughout Europe. But modern partnership law in the United States evolved from English law.

There has been very little change in the laws governing partnerships since the U.S. Congress enacted the Partnership Act in 1890. The most modern version, the Uniform Partnership Act (UPA) was approved in 1914 by the National Conference of Commissioners of Uniform State Laws. Most of the 50 states, the District of Columbia, and several U.S. territories have adopted some version of the UPA. In 1916, the Uniform Limited Partnership Act was approved, and versions of it too have been adopted by most of the 50 states, the District of Columbia, and several U.S. territories.

WHY A PARTNERSHIP?

When you start your business, the most commonly used legal forms from which you can choose are the *sole proprietorship,* the *partnership* (and the *limited partnership*), and the *corporation.* Which form will be best for your business? The fact that you are reading this book indicates that you may favor the partnership form. Even so, it is still important for you to understand what is involved in each form, and their relative advantages and disadvantages.

1

The General Partnership

Although normally just called a partnership, we use the word "general" to show that it is not a limited partnership, which is discussed later.

As already noted, a partnership is a trade or business owned by two or more persons for profit-making purposes. Because it is not incorporated, it has none of the protection of a corporation, but also very few of the disadvantages of a corporation. Each full (or general) partner has the legal right to perform all acts needed to operate the partnership business, unless otherwise agreed.

Legal Requirements   There is no law that requires you to ask official permission to form a partnership, nor do you have to file your partnership agreement with any federal, state, or local governmental agency. Don't be fooled, however, in thinking that there are no legal requirements or controls, as you will see later in this book.

The Partnership Agreement   A written agreement is not a legal requirement to form a general partnership, but a document specifying the details of the agreement is highly recommended. A typical partnership agreement will attempt to cover all major issues that may affect the partnership. It will cover items such who is to contribute what to the partnership, who will provide what functions for the partnership, how partnership profits and losses are to be apportioned, and provisions for continuing the business if a partner leaves or dies.

While your agreement can be as simple as a promise and a handshake, beware. Even if you and your partner or partners are the best of friends and everyone fully agrees on every aspect at the start of the partnership, the human memory is tricky. We all understand and remember things based on our past experiences and our future hopes. These are never identical between any two human beings. Suggestions for what should be in your general partnership agreement are given in Chapters 3 and 4.

Advantages and Disadvantages   The primary advantages of a partnership are its simplicity when compared with a corporation (discussed later), and its use of multiple skills when compared with a sole proprietorship (also discussed later). You will have fewer governmental forms to cope with than for a corporation, and your profits will not be taxed twice, first as the corporation's profits, next as dividends distributed to you by the corporation. Unlike a corporation, a partnership does not have to register as a *foreign* (out-of-state) operation to do business in a state other than the one where it is formed.

Profits and Losses   Partners share profits or losses in proportion to their ownership of the partnership. While the partnership must file an annual tax return, the partnership does not pay taxes.

Profits and losses pass through to the individual partners to be reported on their personal tax returns. This is particularly attractive during the early stages of the partnership where your share of the partnership losses can be applied against your income from other sources.

Coping with Debts   A potential disadvantage with a partnership is the threat of unlimited liability for debts or other claims against the partnership should it become insolvent or involved in expensive legal claims. If the partnership business lacks the money needed to pay a creditor, that creditor can lay claim to your personal assets, and those of your partners, to satisfy the debt. Or, if in conducting partnership business, property is damaged or some person is injured by you or by a partner or by someone employed by your partnership, the partners will be liable.

If all the partners are available and have sufficient personal funds, the debt or court judgment payment will be in relation to the individual percentage ownerships in the partnership. But what if you are the only one with money or property? Or what if the other partners disappear? The claim can be made against you alone. This is called *joint and several liability*.

There are ways to protect yourself. If your personal assets are in an irrevocable trust for the benefit of someone else, such as your children, your spouse, or your parents, your creditors may be held at bay, unless they can prove fraudulent intent to avoid debts when the trust was established. Or you can have a clause in your partnership agreement where your partners agree to indemnify (guarantee you against loss). As to lawsuits, your partnership can have the protection of liability insurance. Whichever way you choose, you will need professional advice and consultation.

When a Partner Is Lost If one of your partners leaves the partnership for any reason, either voluntarily or involuntarily, by law the partnership automatically terminates. This does not mean that the business of the partnership must cease, however, if provisions are included in the partnership agreement for continuing the business.

The Limited Partnership

Limited partnerships are formed by full partners to raise money from investors. Limited partners buy shares of the profits or losses of the partnership, limited to (calculated by) the amounts they invest.

The limited partners have no voice in the management of the partnership, but if there are losses, unpaid debts, or court judgments, their liabilities are no greater than the amounts they have invested. Their personal assets cannot be attacked or attached.

THE SOLE PROPRIETORSHIP

Sole means only or alone. A sole proprietorship is a business owned solely by one person. You, as owner, can hire and fire employees. You may delegate the management of the business to an employee, and you may share profits with employees.

Advantages and Disadvantages

As owner of a sole proprietorship, you are boss. You are the sole decision maker. Success or failure lies on your shoulders alone. You alone are liable for all debts, taxes, and other business liabilities. If one of your employees harms a person or property in connection with his or her duties with your business, you are the one who will be held legally liable.

Taxes and the Sole Proprietorship

As is true for the partnership, the sole proprietorship does not pay taxes. All profits and losses from the business pass through to you, the owner, to be reported on your personal income tax return. If you have income from other sources, you can apply losses from the business against this income.

Ending the Sole Proprietorship

If you, the owner die, the sole proprietorship ends. For this reason, it is important that you make provisions in your will or otherwise either to sell the assets or to transfer them to someone. If your business assets are left by a will, and your heirs want to continue the business, delays in probating your will may harm the business. It may be better to avoid probate and transfer the business assets promptly through use of a *living trust*. Your attorney can advise you on this matter.

WHAT IS A CORPORATION?

A *corporation* is an artificial person with a life of its own, separate from the role or life of any living person. For this reason, a corporation is said to be immortal. It continues to survive the loss of an owner (shareholder) through retirement, death, or sellout.

In contrast to partnerships or sole proprietorships, the corporation must be formed according to the laws of the state in which incorporation takes place. State laws control formation and operation of the corporation; there is no federal corporation law, except in the realm of taxation.

There are three basic types of corporations: the C *corporation* (or regular corporation), the S *corporation* (or Subchapter S corporation), and the *professional corporation* (or personal service corporation).

The C corporation is the most commonly met form. But if you are starting with a small business that will not be immediately profitable, you may wish to elect to convert your C corporation into an S corporation where profits and losses flow directly to you, much as in a partnership. See *How to Start Your Own S Corporation* by Arnold S. Goldstein and Robert L. Davidson, III, (John Wiley & Sons, Inc., 1992) for details on S corporations. If you are a licensed professional, such as a doctor, dentist, lawyer, or architect, you may wish to form a professional corporation where all the owners belong to the same profession.

Starting the Corporation

As noted before, there is no such thing as federal incorporation. Each state has its own laws of incorporation. A corporation is formed by filing *articles of incorporation* with the state. Once the filing is completed, the corporation is ready for business.

Corporation Structure

In general, a corporation comprises three major groups: the owners (or shareholders), the officers who manage the business, and the directors who set policies and direct the business. It is possible for a single person to be a shareholder and an officer, as well as a director.

Advantages and Disadvantages

The most widely known advantage of incorporation is the *corporate shield*, protection of your personal assets from claims by or against the corporation. This protection, also known as *limited liability*, does not exist for partnerships and sole proprietorships.

How important is limited liability? Consider business-debt and lawsuit liabilities. Most liabilities caused by physical or property damage should be covered with appropriate insurance, regardless of your business form. A corporation's limitation of your personal liability will not prevent it from having to pay corporation business debts, even if such payment forces the corporation into insolvency and bankruptcy. But normally, the limited liability protection of a corporation will protect your personal assets, unless you are guilty of some grievous personal illegality in relation to corporation management.

When would limited liability be most helpful for you? It can be valuable if your business is engaged in some high-risk activity that, because of its nature, can create personal or property damage and lawsuits. Or if you cannot find an insurer to cover you, or you cannot afford the insurance premiums.

The other advantage of incorporation is the freedom to transfer ownership through the transfer or sale of your stock. The corporation does not die when an owner dies, as there is always another owner. This is why a corporation is said to be immortal.

The most often mentioned disadvantage of incorporation is the double taxation where corporate profit is first taxed on both federal and local levels; then when distributed to the owners (shareholders) as dividends, what remains is further taxed on personal tax returns.

A seldom mentioned disadvantage of incorporation is what happens if the business fails and it is forced into bankruptcy. In a Chapter 7 liquidation bankruptcy or a Chapter 11 reorganization bankruptcy, the corporation is barred from many of the debt-discharge (cancellation) advantages of the Chapter 12 family-farmer bankruptcy or the Chapter 13 wage-earner bankruptcy. Since most new businesses that do not succeed fail within the first few years, it has been suggested that incorporation should be delayed until the new company is successfully past this critical start-up period.

Another consideration is the paperwork blizzard faced by a corporation. You will have multiple federal and state tax forms and corporate withholding reports (even if you have no profit), and you will have to respond to numerous other bookkeeping demands.

MAKING THE DECISION

Before you decide for or against the partnership form for your business, here are some important questions you should ask yourself:

- Do you need to work with others, or can you do it by yourself? If you need to add other skills or resources to yours, where will you find them? How will you attract them?

- Is there a risk to the business? What is it? What does it mean to you financially? Can you bear the risk?
- Is it important to you to maintain control? Or are you willing to share control with others?
- How will you finance the business? Can you find backing by yourself? Or will you need money or facilities held by others? Will banks or other lenders support you by yourself? Or will you need co-owners to back you?

Finally, but most important, how well do you know yourself? Would you be happiest with a sole proprietorship where you have total control but also total responsibility? How are you at working with others as equals if your business idea needs skills that add to and blend with yours? Are you a plunger by nature, or are you supercautious?

CHAPTER 2

GETTING STARTED

THE IMPORTANCE OF GOOD ADVICE

Should you hire an attorney to help you draft your partnership agreement, or can you do it yourself? Should you pay for an accountant or other tax advisor to help you set up your business- and tax-record bookkeeping system, or do it yourself? The answers to these questions will depend on your personal experience and training, the interrelationships between you and your partners, and the complexity of your business operation.

When to Use a Personal Lawyer

Will your partnership need the advice and services of a lawyer? Perhaps not, if your business has limited legal and financial liabilities. If you are cutting grass or washing windows for a living, you won't be involved in complicated contracts and leases. And you may feel that you do not need a lawyer to help you purchase liability insurance to cover physical or property damage that your activities might cause.

But if you are involved in leasing facilities and equipment, if you are signing high-dollar-amount construction or service contracts, if you are dealing in employee contracts, if you will be dealing with union labor, if you will be facing financial liability claims by creditors or customers, you need the advice and help of a lawyer.

You will meet a dozen or more legal technicalities as you plan and operate your partnership. Some are obvious, others are not. Situations that appear simple to you may be fraught with legal complexities, and you won't know it until it is too late. An innocent failure to observe a simple statute or regulation can cause immense trouble. The simple failure to obtain a certificate of occupancy for the purposes of your business may lead to a fine or penalty, or could close down your operations temporarily, even permanently.

Start to use your personal lawyer with your partnership agreement. You may think it is a simple matter "to agree to agree" with your future partners. Not so. The complexities of even the most simple partnership arrangements can lead to future misunderstandings or ill will, even lawsuits. Without a carefully drafted written agreement, you and your partners may find yourselves working apart instead of together. Without mutual understanding of and agreement for the objectives of the partnership and what each partner will do, you will risk chaos, disorganization, followed by anger, frustration, and eventual disintegration of the partnership.

The clauses and provisions of a relatively simple general partnership agreement are discussed in Chapters 3 and 4. Even with this help, you will be well advised to consult with a lawyer who is well versed in partnership law before you sign on the dotted line.

Continue consulting your lawyer during the operation of your business. You will be signing leases for facilities and equipment. You will be purchasing supplies and furnishings. You will be making deals with customers for your product or service. All these activities entail contracts, and contract law is a world unto itself. If the stakes are too high for you to risk loss, see your lawyer. If there is possible future liability not visible to you at negotiation time, your lawyer can forewarn and advise you. And more.

When to Use a Personal Tax Advisor

If your partnership is a simple operation through which you and your partner or partners merely sell your services, such as consultation or computer programming, and your business expenditures are mainly travel and office supplies, you may feel that a tax advisor, such as a CPA (Certified Public Accountant) is a luxury. Perhaps, but perhaps not.

If you will have employees or will be hiring and paying independent contractors, your business and tax record keeping can become quite complex. You will need to consider withholding taxes, unemployment taxes, social security taxes, worker's compensation insurance, medical and pension benefits, and more. You will be responsible for deductions, exemptions, and credits.

You should seek professional help to set up your system, and then to modify it as your business grows and changes. Your tax advisor can help you prepare your business plan and can show you how to best present your partnership when approaching banks for credit lines or loans.

Tax law is often confusing and opaque. Subchapter K of the Internal Revenue Code (IRC) is notorious, considered by many to be one of the most complicated parts of the IRC. The IRS will look at many factors. Even if you call your business a partnership and have a detailed partnership agreement, the IRS may hold that you have so many operational characteristics in common with a corporation (such as centralized management and freely transferred ownership) that taxwise you will be treated as a corporation.

How to Select Your Advisors

One of the best ways to locate professional advisors for your business is to talk to other businesses (noncompetitive with your business, of course) in your area. Get names of lawyers, accountants, bookkeepers. Get recommendations for those who might fit your needs. Visit these persons. Interview them. Tell them what you will be doing. Explain your needs. Ask them what they can do to assist you.

Don't stop with the first interview. Don't limit yourself to a single person. Most of all, don't be afraid to ask the hard questions: What is their experience? Do they understand your type of business? What will it cost you?

Here are suggestions to keep in mind when selecting your legal and accounting advisors:

1. Find persons you can get along with.
2. Find persons who show an interest in you and your needs.
3. Find persons with experience in the needs of partnerships.
4. Find persons with experience in your type of business.
5. Find persons who will be available when you need them.
6. Find persons you can afford.

Once you have located these individuals, be sure that you have a complete understanding of how you will work with them. What will they do for you? How will they charge you (by the hour, by the job, by retainer)? Under what situations should you contact them? What will you be expected to do in return? What will you do when they are ill or otherwise unavailable? And more.

"TERMS OF ART" GLOSSARY

The legal meanings of words and phrases often contain concepts and hidden connotations that are not immediately obvious from the general dictionary definitions of these words. The following terms, important to the understanding of partnership law, are defined according to their legal usages for partnerships. The words in italic type within definitions are defined elsewhere in this listing.

accrual method [bookkeeping]   financial record-keeping system that credits income when earned or due and expenses when incurred, regardless of actual cash receipts or disbursements (see also *cash method*)

active income   income received as the result of ongoing active efforts (see also *passive income loss*)

adjusted basis   original cost adjusted by additions and depreciation (see also *basis*)

advance notice   notice of an intended action given in advance of the actual action (see also *constructive notice* and *notice*)

appreciation   unearned increase in the value of property due to inflation or other market factors (see also *goodwill*)

arbitration   method for settling a dispute by a quasi-judicial procedure as provided by law or agreement; arbitrator's judgment usually binding on all parties (see also *mediation*)

articles of incorporation   document by which a private corporation is formed under state incorporation laws

assumed business name   name for partnership or sole proprietorship other than the name or names of the owners of the business

auction clause   part of a contract or other agreement that provides for the public sale of property, rights, or other aspects of ownership

balance sheet   financial statement to show the true state of a particular business

basis   in general terms, the initial cost or purchase price (see also *adjusted basis*)

blue-sky laws   laws that provide for the regulation and supervision of investment companies (such as limited partnerships) to protect the public from fraudulent investment schemes

book value [stock]   based on the value of company assets after deducting liabilities

breach of agreement   see *breach of contract*

breach of contract   failure without legal excuse to perform a promise contained in a valid contract, either written or oral

Bulk Sales Act   statute designed to prevent the secret sale in bulk of a business's goods or inventory to defraud creditors

business name   trade name or commercial name used to identify a specific business

business plan   road map for the formation, development, and operation of a business; covers financial, structural, production, business development, and other aspects

bylaws   regulations, ordinances, rules, or laws adopted to govern an association or corporation

C corporation   term used to describe a regular corporation as differentiated from the *S corporation*; see also *corporation*

capital [assets]   actual property or monies invested or undivided assets for the operation of a business

cash method [bookkeeping]   financial record-keeping system relying on actual cash receipts or actual cash disbursements at the time of receipt or disbursement (see also *accrual method*)

commingling of funds   placing of funds for several purposes (such as personal with business, or trust with personal) in a single fund or account

constructive notice   openly available facts or events from which a reasonably alert and aware person should have notice of the existence of a situation (see also *notice*)

contract labor   persons or organizations who are not employees of the hiring business who have contracted to perform specified duties for the hiring business

conveyance of interest   transfer of rights or property free of conditions

copyright   the right of literary property as recognized by law; categorized as *intellectual property*

corporate shield   protection of personal assets from business liabilities through incorporation

corporation   "artificial person" created under the authority of law; normally an association of a number of persons (the *shareholders*) and surviving the resignation or death of any one of the shareholders

DBA   abbreviation for *doing-business-as*, which see

deductions [tax]   business or personal expenses that may be subtracted from gross income to calculate net income

deferred contribution   payments that are either postponed or made in installments

depreciation [tax]   reduction of worth or lessening of value of property from age; calculated by approved IRS formulas

derivative action   legal action by owners (e.g., shareholders or limited partners) against the managers of a business organization charging mismanagement of the business

dissolution [contract]   cancellation or abrogation of an agreement by the affected parties

doing-business-as name used when conducting a partnership or sole proprietorship under a name other than under the owners' names; requires local or state registration; also known as DBA (see also *fictitious business name*)

domicile true, fixed, and permanent home and principal establishment

draft agreement tentative agreement proposal prepared for discussion and amendment before signing

draw term for lawful drawing of money from a business for personal use

EIN see *employer identification number*

employer identification number number issued by state and federal governments to identify a business for tax purposes; also known as EIN

exemptions [tax] items other than business deductions not subject to taxation

family partnerships partnership created with family members only as partners

fictitious business name another way to describe *doing-business-as* or *DBA*

fiduciary duties duties related to the handling of finances or property or other matters for the benefit of another person; implies a high degree of confidence and trust with good faith

fixed assets assets in place and essential to the continued operation of a business

foreign corporation term used to describe a corporation formed in another state; for example, a corporation formed in New Jersey would be considered a foreign corporation in New York, or any of the other 50 states

general partner partner with full rights of participation in management, profits, and losses of a partnership; contrasts with *limited partner*

general partnership business form in which two or more individuals or business organizations agree to operate a business together; principals in the general partnership are general partners

good faith honesty of intention

goodwill value placed on a business that is greater than the combination of capital, stocks, funds, and property; based on a positive attitude toward the business by the business's public

gross income [tax] total income received before deductions for expenses and other expenditures

injunction legal prohibition of a specific act by a person or that person's agent

intangible assets business values such as goodwill, trademarks, copyrights, or franchises

intellectual property general term used to describe *copyright*, *patent*, *trademark*, and *trade secret*

joint and several liability the legal responsibility of one or more or all the parties to a liability (such as partners in a partnership) for the total amount of the liability created by a single party to the liability

joint ventures association of two or more persons or businesses to combine property, monies, effects, skills and/or knowledge to carry out a single business enterprise for profit

Keogh plan tax-deferring retirement savings plan; also known as HR 10

liability potentially subject to an obligation arising from a loss or damage resulting from a contingency, risk, or casualty

license   certificate or document giving permission or authority for a defined action

limited liability   limitation of responsibility for damages or losses; found in *limited partnerships* and through the *corporate shield*

limited partner   investor in a *limited partnership* where profits, losses, and liabilities are limited to the amount invested

limited partnership   special form of *partnership* in which investors (*limited partners*) participate in profits and losses, but management of the partnership is by a *general partner*

liquidation   settling a debt or liability to another party by payment or other form of satisfaction

litigation   contest in a court of law to enforce a right or claim; a lawsuit

living trust   fund established for the benefit of a living person, administered by a trustee, and unavailable for the use of the person or party establishing the trust; for example, parents create a trust for the exclusive benefit of their children

malpractice   bad, wrong, or injudicious performance of professional duties, such as by doctors, lawyers, architects

mediation   action by a disinterested third party to reconcile the differences between disagreeing parties; seeks agreement, but is normally not binding (see also *arbitration*)

mitigation of damages   reductions in a court award of damages because of extenuating circumstances

mortgage   transfer of property as security for a debt, as when a bank holds the deed to property until the purchaser-borrower repays the loan

net profits   the amount remaining from *gross income* after deductions for business expenses and losses

noncompetition clause   agreement that if a person leaves a business, that person will not compete with the business in a prescribed area for a specified period of time

notice   information derived by the senses or the mind, or by communication from another person; knowledge of a fact or state of affairs (see also *constructive notice*)

oral agreements   unwritten ("handshake") contractual agreements between parties; difficult to prove during lawsuits

partnership   see *general partnership*

passive income/loss   income or loss from investments or other sources without active participation (see *active income*)

patent   a grant of specified privilege, property, or authority by a government body, such as the United States Patent and Trademark Office; a form of *intellectual property*

personal service corporation   see *professional corporation*

professional corporation   corporation formed to provide special services, such as by lawyers, physicians, or architects; all corporation shareholders must be licensed or approved as professionals for the stated business purpose; also known as *personal service corporation*

property appreciation   see *appreciation*

property depreciation   see *depreciation*

S corporation   special form of business combining certain aspects of regular corporations with those of partnerships or sole proprietorships; profits and losses pass directly to the shareholders instead of stopping at the corporate level; also known as a *Subchapter S corporation*

sanctions   penalty or punishment to enforce obedience to a law

securities   evidence of debt, rights, or property ownership, such as shares of stock

service business   business formed to provide a service rather than a product

silent partner   partner whose participation in a partnership has not been revealed to the public

sole proprietorship   unincorporated business owned and directed by a single person

spousal interest   continuing interest of a surviving spouse in a business in the event of a divorce from or death of the other spouse

Subchapter S corporation   see *S corporation*

subcontractor   one who takes responsibility for a portion of a contract from a principal contractor or another subcontractor

subpartner   person who agrees with a partnership partner to share in the partner's share of partnership profits or losses by means of a separate agreement

substitute limited partner   purchaser of a limited partner's interest in a limited partnership

trade secrets   plan, process, mechanism, procedure, or information used in business and known only to its owner

trademarks   distinctive mark of authenticity to distinguish one product source from another; can be registered for protection; another form of *intellectual property*

trading partnerships   partnership directly involved in trade, such as a merchant selling a product; examples are theaters, banks, farms, real estate enterprises

trust accounts   money controlled by one party (the trustee) for the benefit of another; see also *fiduciary duties*

Uniform Limited Partnership Act   set of regulations for limited partnerships adopted by most of the 50 states, the District of Columbia, and several U.S. territories with some modifications

Uniform Partnership Act   set of regulations for partnerships adopted by most of the 50 states, the District of Columbia, and several U.S. territories with some modifications

CHAPTER 3

MAKING YOUR PLANS

YOUR BUSINESS PLAN

You wouldn't embark on a cross-country trip without some idea of where you are going and how you will get there. Yet, a surprising number of people start their businesses without a sense of direction and objective, namely a *business plan*.

Business plans come in all shapes and forms, from the very simple to the highly complex. Either way, what is important is that regardless of the type of business you plan, your business plan should answer the following questions:

- *What form should you use?* Since you are reading this book, you are clearly considering the partnership form of business.
- *What should you call your business?* The proper choice of name can help identify your business to potential customers.
- *How will you finance your business?* High hopes or one's piggy bank alone will not be enough. Who will provide the money to hold you over until income equals or exceeds expenses?
- *Where will you house your business?* What facilities will you need to support and operate your business?
- *What is it you will be doing for whom?* Why will they want to buy what you have to offer? How can you identify and find these potential users (customers) of your product or service?
- *How will you approach your potential customers?* What will you do to persuade them to be your customers?
- *Who, what, and where is your competition?* What companies will you be selling against? What products or services will you be trying to replace?

A more complete discussion of business and financial planning and marketing is presented in the author's *Contracting Your Services*, (John Wiley & Sons, Inc.).

SELECTING YOUR PARTNERS

The purpose of a partnership is combine the talents and resources of more than one person to make the intended business work. If your specialty is sales, you may want to team up with a production person and a financial person. Or you may need the facilities and money resources that a partner can bring to the business. There are no foolproof rules to guarantee a perfect partnership, but here are a few essentials to consider when deciding who you want to run a business with you.

How Well Do You Know Your Future Partners?

A partnership is like a marriage, a business marriage. Trust is essential. Not only trust in honesty, but trust in reliability, trust that your partner or partners have the capabilities to perform their shares of the many tasks involved in a growing and prospering business operation.

Why Have You Selected Your Partners?

What skills, experiences, or resources will they bring to the partnership? What can they provide that you can't provide to round out the overall capabilities of the partnership? It wouldn't make good sense for three salesperson types to form a partnership, with no one to produce the product or service and no one to handle financial matters.

Are Your Visions Compatible?

Do you and your partners all see the business in the same way, both at the start, in the near future, and in the long-range future? While you don't want to march in lockstep, you should all travel on the same road and in the same direction.

If you have positive answers to each of the preceding questions, there will be few if any problems that can't be solved and few if any disagreements that can't be resolved.

YOUR PARTNERSHIP AGREEMENT

An agreement is essential. By law, it can be either oral and a handshake, or written and signed. While an oral agreement is legally binding, it relies on the frailties of the human memory and the continuance of good will. As one wag has said, "An oral contract isn't worth the paper it's written on."

Without your own written contract, most states have laws that will control many of the actions of your partnership through the Uniform Partnership Act (UPA) mentioned in Chapter 1, and given in its entirety in Appendix I. Similar material for limited partnerships, called the Uniform Limited Partnership Act (ULPA), is given in Appendix II. Many of the sections of the UPA and the ULPA are mandatory. Others are optional—that is, you can modify them in your written partnership agreement. The trick is to determine what you want to do and how you want to do it, then see what the law will let you do.

Following are some of the more important items you will need to consider when drafting your partnership agreement in Chapter 4. The process starts with the planning and shaping of the partnership goals and operations, and ends though dissolution caused by resignation or death of one of the partners, or the addition of a new partner.

NAMING YOUR PARTNERSHIP

All businesses need to be identified with a name. That is the law. With certain restrictions, you are free to select the name that will best identify your partnership. Many use the names of the partners, such as Smith & Jones. Others are more imaginative, and select a name that describes the business, such as Ace Contractors or Tasty Caterers.

There are limitations. You cannot give your business a name that insinuates that you are an official governmental agency, a bank, an insurance company, a religious organization, or a charity. You cannot give your business a name that would cause confusion of source, such as with DuPont or General Motors. Even if your legal name is Frank Sinatra, the famous Frank can prevent you from using your (his) name for your business. Obviously, you cannot give your business a name that is a profanity or vulgarism. There are other aspects of naming, both business and legal. Your attorney can help you with these.

THE LIFE OF YOUR PARTNERSHIP

How long do you want your partnership to survive? As long as you and your partners are alive or active? Or, if the purpose of the partnership is a specific project with a predictable completion date, you might wish to set a term, such as one or two years, at the end of which the partnership automatically terminates and its assets are liquidated.

BUSINESS PURPOSE

There is no legal requirement that your partnership agreement have a statement of purpose, as is required for incorporation. But it is advisable. The very act of drafting a statement of purpose forces the partners-to-be to communicate on a verbal level. It is while searching for the words to express and communicate your business objectives that you may find unexpected areas of difference, even dangerous disagreement.

This does not mean that you cannot, by agreement of the partners, alter your statement of purpose as your business grows or new areas of opportunity are opened. But it does assure that you all start from the same point, and considering the unreliability of human memory, you will have a reference point to remind all partners of the terms of the original agreement.

WHO WILL CONTRIBUTE WHAT?

The purpose of a partnership instead of a sole proprietorship with a single owner and manager is for each partner to contribute some important skill or asset, and to share in the development and operation of the business. These contributions can come in any of several forms, such as:

- Personal services (based on time, skills, experience);
- Cash or personal credit line (immediately, or deferred);
- Property (equipment, supplies, real estate, patent, copyright).

You will need to decide which partner is to make which contribution, the terms or conditions of the contribution, and how the magnitude or importance of the contribution is related to each partner's ownership interest in the partnership. You will also need to have a clear understanding of what happens if a partner reneges and fails to make a contribution as agreed. There is also the question of future contributions, when allowed, and how they affect partnership ownership interests.

Contributions of property, facilities, or so-called intellectual property (such as patents, trademarks, copyrights) can belong to the entire partnership, or if the partners so agree, they can "loaned" for the use by and benefit of the partnership as long as certain conditions prevail.

Normally, what you contribute to the partnership becomes the property of the partnership. If, for example, you contribute a 10-acre plot of land to the partnership and there are only two partners, you then own 50% of the value of the property, but you do not any longer own any of the land itself, not even 5 acres.

PARTNER FIDUCIARY DUTIES

Each partner has a fiduciary duty to each of the other partners in a partnership. This means, in simple terms, honoring the trust placed in you by others. The importance in understanding fiduciary duty is that the actions of a single partner can be legally binding on all the other partners.

This is the joint and several liability problem discussed earlier. If all the partners cannot be found for payment of a partnership debt or satisfaction of a court judgment, an action for the total amount claimed can be taken against any partner or group of partners who can be found. You won't be allowed to rely on the defense that the partner taking the action did so without the consent of the partnership. If the remiss partner had, to an outsider, the appearances of authority for the partnership, and the outsider relied on this appearance of authority, then the outsider has a strong claim against the partnership (or any one of the partners).

PROFIT AND LOSS DIVISION

How will you handle partnership profits or losses? How will profits be distributed? How will losses be shared? Are all partners actively working at the partnership, and will they receive salaries? How will the salaries be calculated? What if income is insufficient to pay the salaries?

You will need a profit/loss agreement between partners. If there is no profit/loss statement, the Uniform Partnership Act provides for equal sharing of profits and losses, even if initial contributions were quite different. If equal sharing is not the intention, you will need to determine the percentage share for each partner.

In short, the division of partnership profits and losses is a matter of agreement. The methods most often used include (1) fixed percentages, (2) sliding percentages, and (3) variations in accordance with sales, time spent performing partnership business, balances in individual partnership capital accounts, and so on, or (4) a salary or guaranteed minimum.

Losses may be allocated to the "moneymen" of the partnership, those in high tax brackets who will benefit most from the pass-through of losses for their personal tax returns. But the IRS will limit the amount of loss pass-through so that it will not be greater than the partner's interest basis in the partnership.

PROFIT RETENTION FOR BUSINESS GROWTH

For your business to grow, for increased prosperity, you must, of course, plan for the future. You will need new or larger facilities, new equipment, new tools of the trade, advertising, and promotion. It's never too early to anticipate these needs.

If you and your partners withdraw every cent of profit from the partnership, how will you plan for future needs? The answer is, hold back some of the profit. Create a reserve to meet both planned growth and unexpected contingencies. Now is the time to commit to withholding a certain percentage of profits to create this all-important reserve.

But watch out. As you will see in the Chapter 5 discussion of taxes, the IRS will watch to see that you don't hold too large a sum for future needs or that your partnership doesn't earn excessive passive income, such as interest earned by investing the money.

WHO GETS PAID WHAT?

Salaries were mentioned earlier. If all the partners work at the partnership, you will have a salary schedule based on the type of work, the importance of this work to the partnership, the time devoted to the work, and other aspects. Some jobs with the partnership will be more important than others. Some partners will have greater skills than others. Some partners will devote only part of their time to the business of the partnership.

If there are to be salaries, it is essential that you and your partners agree in advance how much each partner is to receive for services to the partnership.

WHO WILL MANAGE THE PARTNERSHIP?

There is a Catch-22 in managing a partnership. By law, each full partner has an equal right to perform all acts needed to operate the partnership business. This means that each partner has the sweeping power to bind the total partnership and each of the other partners. But all partners are not created equal. Not everyone can be boss. Normally, each partner will contribute some specific skill or activity to the partnership. In other words, each will have a specified job with specified responsibilities.

Set up a plan in advance. Decide who will be the overall managing partner, who will handle sales, who will handle accounting and bookkeeping, and so on. Assign specific duties within each of these areas. Does this sound too formal to you? It shouldn't. Without such agreement, things either will not get done, or you will duplicate efforts.

Once the managing partner has been selected, the next step is to define the responsibilities, authorities, and limitations of the position, considering:

- Routine business transactions.
- Daily operating decisions.
- Salary and expenses.
- Check-signing authority.
- Other financial and funds-handling authority.
- Purchase decisions.

NONPARTNERSHIP ACTIVITIES

In many partnerships, particularly during their early years, not all partners will be actively employed in partnership activities. Others will devote a portion of their time to developing other sources of income. Some may have regular jobs. Their contributions will be advisory, provided to the partnership business in the evenings and on weekends. While logical, such an arrangement can, without careful planning and understanding, create conflicts of interest between the needs and goals of the partnership and the needs and goals of the other income source. You will need to agree in advance who can do what. Consider:

- Activities in general that are permitted.
- Specific activities that are permitted.
- Competitive activities that are not permitted.
- Competitive activities that are permitted, but restricted.

WHO OWNS WHAT?

Neither a partner nor a partnership can offer shares to the general public. Capital is obtained through contributions by general partners or investments by limited partners. The question arises—when a partner contributes property to a partnership, who owns it? The partnership? Or the contributing partner?

This problem most often occurs when a partnership is dissolved, as when a partner resigns, retires, or dies, or when the partnership is reconstituted by introducing a new partner. Or when the partnership assets are liquidated.

Unless otherwise stated in the partnership agreement, the property rights of a partner in a partnership are:

- As co-owner with the other partners as a tenant in partnership of specific partnership property.
- As an interest in the partnership itself; that is, a share of the profits and surplus.
- The right to participate in the management of the partnership.
- The right to share in the profits (and losses) of the partnership.

Otherwise, the agreement between partners can control and modify present and future ownership of property or rights. The division of profits, for example, can be on percentages that are different than for losses. Suppose that you contribute a trade secret to the partnership for "as long as I am a partner," or "for long as the partnership survives," then you may claim it back when the partnership terminates. If you contributed a truck or tools or a building under similar conditions, they too are yours exclusively when the partnership terminates.

But what about trade secrets or patents developed by you after the partnership was formed? Are they yours? Or do they belong to the partnership? What about new physical assets purchased for the partnership using partnership-generated income? Answers to these questions depend on the agreement signed by all the partners. Lacking a specific statement otherwise, those things developed for and through the partnership belong to the partnership. On termination of the partnership, they or their value will be distributed to the ex-partners or their estates in accordance with their percentage ownerships of the partnership.

PARTNERS IN, PARTNERS OUT

What happens if, as the partnership continues, there are new needs and new attitudes regarding the relationships between the partners? Can they change their agreement? Yes, but the agreement to change must be unanimous. If one partner holds out against the changes, the partnership can break up and cease to exist. This problem can be avoided if the original agreement contains provisions for amending the agreement with less than unanimous consent.

What happens when a partner leaves the partnership or dies? Or a new partner is added? The partnership no longer exists. It is legally dissolved. It can no longer carry on the business of the old partnership. To continue in business, it must be re-created as a new partnership with a new signing of the existing partnership agreement, or a new agreement.

For the loss of a partner, this necessitates that the partnership agreement have a clearly defined statement for the transfer of the proper share of partnership assets, or their equivalent, to this ex-partner, and the conditions of departure under which this distribution can and will be made.

For the addition of a partner, the partnership agreement must have a clearly defined statement regarding the ownership of existing partnership assets as related to the new partner, the new partner's contribution and role, and the future rights of ownership for the new partner. There will also have to be a written and signed understanding as to the new partner's liability for existing partnership debts or legal judgments.

GETTING OUT OF A PARTNERSHIP

As discussed, the departure of a partner, either voluntarily or involuntarily, from the partnership can have serious consequences, especially if the partnership agreement lacks provisions for the departure.

Transferability of Interest

If you decide to leave the partnership, can you sell your interest in the business to someone outside the partnership? If you die, can you will your interest to your wife or one of your children? If the agreement was carefully written, the answer most likely is no. People form a partnership with those they want to work with. They do not want the sudden injection of a stranger.

Exiting a partnership, voluntarily or otherwise, and transferring your interest in the partnership without the consent of all your partners does not by itself dissolve the partnership, but the rights of the person to whom you assign your partnership rights are limited. The unapproved new owner does not have the right to interfere in the management or administration of the continuing partnership, nor the right to demand information about or an accounting of partnership actions. The new owner has no right to demand an inspection of the partnership books. In fact, all that the transfer does is give the new owner the right to receive the profits (or losses) to which you were entitled before the transfer. Meanwhile, you have not been relieved of liability for partnership debts accrued before you made the transfer.

This situation can be changed by a provision in the partnership agreement, but that too has its perils. It reduces, or perhaps eliminates, the power of the remaining partners to choose those with whom they will work. It means that those who remain active in the partnership may be forced to work with some person or organization they don't know, don't like, don't trust.

If you are one of those remaining in the partnership, you'd be a strong supporter of restricting the sale by one of your partners to an outsider. The solution? Set reasonable terms and conditions of sale so that the departing partner is not trapped, but the remaining partners are not placed in an uncomfortable or impossible position.

The most graceful and acceptable way to exit is to give the other partners a chance to buy your share; the *right of first refusal*. This protects the remaining partners from someone they don't know or don't want in the partnership. What if you have found a ready, willing, and able buyer for your interest, one who will pay you handsomely? Too bad. Unless, of course, the remaining partners like this new person and are willing to accept him or her as a partner.

What if the remaining partners won't or don't have the money to buy your share, and you are prohibited from selling to an outsider? Are you out of luck? Not necessarily. The solution is to dissolve the partnership, sell the business assets, divide the proceeds. The specter of the complete demise of the partnership may encourage the other partners to find a way to purchase your share. But, as for other items of agreement, this must be a clause contained in the signed partnership agreement.

The Buy-Out Clause

If your partnership interest is to be sold, there must be an understanding of how to calculate the worth of your share. There must also be a provision for how you are to be paid: lump sum or over a period of time. And your former partners may want to protect their investment by restricting you from competing with them directly for some designated period of time.

Valuing Partnership Assets   The worth of your interest can be calculated based on the value of existing assets. These include the so-called tangible assets of facilities, equipment, furnishings, and inventory. To these assets, all reasonably collectible accounts receivable are added, along with unbilled but earned fees and work-in-progress payments, plus cash. From the total of the assets and accounts receivables, current debts and liabilities are subtracted. There is another value called *goodwill*, which represents the intangible value of a good business reputation and customer acceptance developed over a period of time.

Partnership Book Value   This is a much simpler method than valuation of assets, but less realistic. Basically, the book-value method takes into consideration the original cost of assets, regardless of what they are worth currently. While vehicles or furniture will depreciate with age and use, real estate normally appreciates in value with time and surrounding development.

Liquidated Value   The simplest method of all is for the partnership agreement to set a specific dollar value on each partner's interest. Such a preset dollar value without regard to growth or decline in the business's value is questionable if a significant portion of the partnership's value is in physical assets. If, however, the business is basically a no-asset operation, such as consulting or computer programming, a preset dollar value can be quite reasonable.

Appraisal Value   The matter of value is easily resolved by laying the responsibility of evaluation onto a third party, such as a business appraiser.

Profitability Value   The first step is to determine what the business's yearly income is, then multiply this figure by a factor, say two or three or more, depending on what kind of business the partnership conducts. The result is then divided according to the partners' shares to determine what your share is worth.

Debts and the Departing Partner

Once a partner, even though you leave, you are not relieved of the responsibility for partnership debts accumulated while you were a partner. The *joint and several* aspect where all partners or any one partner can be liable for the total debt survives. What you can do is arrange in the partnership agreement that if a partner leaves or dies (but is not expelled), the partnership will pay what would otherwise be the departing partner's share of predeparture debt. This does not, however, prevent a creditor from coming after you if for some reason the partnership fails to pay the debt.

Expelling a Partner

Expelling a partner is a drastic move, one seldom seen, particularly among small businesses. Such actions are more common in larger partnerships. Your reasons must be very good, generally more than personal dislike. If there are reasonable grounds for expulsion, they should be stated with specificity in the partnership agreement. For example, a partner in a diet-salon business who becomes grossly overweight may be harmful to partnership interests.

The Uniform Partnership Act and the Uniform Limited Partnership Act provide for expulsion of a general partner who files for personal bankruptcy. The partnership is dissolved if a partner is bankrupt, even if the business itself is still profitable. For this reason, a clause in the partnership agreement in which a partnership can re-form and survive as a business, is well advised.

OTHER ITEMS TO CONSIDER

There are many more things to consider when drafting your partnership agreement. How important they will be to you and the partnership will depend to great extent on the specifics of your operation. Included are:

Noncompetition Clause

This clause prevents a partner who leaves the partnership from competing with the partnership. This must be worded very carefully if you want it to be upheld in a court of law. If it is too restrictive and prevents the other person from a reasonable practice of his or her trade or profession, it will not be allowed.

Compensation

Compensation must be reasonable. It cannot be artificially low to force profits toward a lower-tax-bracket partner, as in a family partnership. Compensation levels should be stated in the agreement. They can always be changed to meet future needs by revising the agreement.

Insurance

What insurance will be carried by the partnership on partner's lives, for income maintenance in case of illness, for medical and health, for partnership liability, to indemnify partners for specified expenses, and so on? This should be specified in the agreement.

Future Changes

When situations arise that call for a revision of an agreement, what are the procedures? Should it require unanimous approval? Or by a mere majority? Or a supermajority? Life will be simpler if this need is anticipated in advance in the agreement.

Debt Responsibility

Will all partners share equally in partnership debt? Or will it be prorated on some other basis, allowing greater responsibility for the major property owners and lesser responsibility for those whose skills are their main assets? If debt responsibility is not to be in line with partnership interest, spell it out.

Termination Agreements

Rather than have the business of the partnership terminate with the loss of a partner, consider a clause that says under what circumstances the partnership will continue in business without a change in name.

Amendments to the Agreement

What happens when partnership needs or objectives change, or when, with experience, you find you don't like some aspect of the original agreement? You can always amend the agreement with unanimous consent of the partners, or you can, in the original agreement, provide for changes with the agreement of a simple majority, or a supermajority, or any other provision.

Partner Disagreements

How will you handle major disagreements between partners? A truly dissatisfied partner can, of course, quit the partnership, perhaps even force termination of partnership business. Or you can have a provision in your agreement to seek *mediation* or *arbitration*, usually through the American Arbitration Association. Mediation normally means that an outsider tries to find grounds of agreement that the disagreeing parties can accept. Arbitration, in contrast, is much like a court trial, although faster and less complex and expensive, with the arbitrator's judgment legally binding on all parties.

CHAPTER 4

DRAFTING THE PARTNERSHIP AGREEMENT

IS A GOOD AGREEMENT DIFFICULT?

No. Building a good general partnership agreement is not difficult. Build your agreement a plank at a time; don't try to do the whole thing in a single afternoon's work session. When one plank is in place, look to the next one. Do as Caesar did when building the Roman Empire: Divide and conquer. Divide the agreement into sections, divide the sections into steps.

Again, we ask: Should there be a written agreement? The answer is an emphatic yes. It is dangerous to rely on an oral understanding and a handshake. At best, you and your partners may remember the terms in the agreement differently, particularly after the passage of time. At worst, you will have no proof to protect your position if the camaraderie of the initial partnership degenerates into charges and countercharges and courtroom litigation.

The written agreement, then, serves four basic and essential functions:

1. The effort taken to reduce the understanding to words will clear the air. It forces everyone involved to be definite and specific. If a point is vague, that vagueness will be seen. If there is a difference in understanding, that too will be seen.
2. Writing "memorializes" the agreement. It is something concrete and definite that you and your partners can refer to to remind yourselves of the specifics of the agreement. It becomes your road map for partner interaction and partnership objectives.
3. And, as a last resort, it provides the basis for protection should partner relations degenerate to the point where legal action is required.
4. It allows you and your partners to spell out in detail the areas where you want (and are allowed by law) to have terms that may differ from those in the UPA or ULPA statutes in your state, which will control how your partnership will be operated unless you specify otherwise.

25

GENERAL PARTNERSHIP AGREEMENTS

A simple general partnership agreement is illustrated and discussed section by section later in this chapter.

In Appendixes I and II, you will find the complete texts of the Uniform Partnership Act (UPA) and the Uniform Limited Partnership Act (ULPA). As mentioned earlier, most of the 50 states, the District of Columbia, and several U.S. territories have adopted versions of both the UPA and ULPA, usually with modifications. While the basic UPA and ULPA can guide you, you will need to refer to your own state's versions for specifics and differences. Your attorney can help you.

While the following section will take you step by step through the development of a relatively noncomplex general partnership agreement, I have not provided such a guide for the much more complicated and demanding limited partnership agreement. Appendix II, which the ULPA is presented in its entirety, discusses key elements in the preparation of a limited partnership agreement.

DRAFTING THE AGREEMENT

The following will guide you step by step through the creation of a general partnership agreement to meet the specific needs of your business objectives. In a number of cases, the following example will seem to duplicate what already exists in the UPA. Such repetition is well advised. It places in writing a convenient and available reminder to each of the partners of the details of your agreement.

In addition, there are a number of "choice" elements in the UPA; that is, the UPA specifies what will control the operation of the general partnership, unless you specify otherwise. Referring to Appendix I, these are:

UPA § 8(2). Conveyance of real property of the partnership.

UPA § 8(4). Conveyances of an estate to the partnership.

UPA § 9(3). Authorization to act for the partnership.

UPA § 15(b). Separate partner obligations.

UPA § 17. Obligations of new partner for past debts.

UPA § 18. Partner rights and duties.

UPA § 19. Keeping of the partnership books.

UPA § 21. Nonpartnership transactions.

UPA § 22. Partner's right to account of partnership affairs.

UPA § 23. Right to continue business after dissolution.

UPA § 25(2). Individual ownership of partnership property.

UPA § 28(2)(b). Interest redemption before foreclosure.

UPA § 36(2). Release from liability upon dissolution.

UPA § 37. Right to wind up partnership after dissolution.

UPA § 38(1). Application of partnership property.

UPA § 38(2). Property rights after wrongful dissolution.

UPA § 40. Property distribution after dissolution.

UPA § 42. Rights of retiring or deceased partner.

UPA § 43. Partner's right to account of his or her interest.

Agreement Preamble

Name selection was discussed in Chapter 3 (see "Naming Your Partnership"). Once you have a name and know the names of the partners, you are ready to prepare the preamble to the agreement:

(Sample Agreement)

GENERAL PARTNERSHIP NAME

The following AGREEMENT is made on this ____ day of _____, 19____, between [name the partners specifically; add addresses if it will help identify them].

The abovenamed persons (hereinafter referred to as PARTNER or PARTNERS) hereby agree to carry on a business as a general partnership (hereinafter referred to as the PARTNERSHIP) under the laws of [name your state], and under the following terms and conditions:

Business Location

You will need an address for your business to include in your partnership agreement. You do not have to conduct all your business from this address, but it must be one where you and the other partners can communicate until such time as you assign another address, or, if a roaring success, create branch offices.

ARTICLE I

Name and Location of Business

(1) The name of the PARTNERSHIP shall be [give name].

(2) The principal place of business for the PARTNERSHIP shall be at [give street address, not P.O. Box number], with other places of business within [name of your state] and other states as agreed by the PARTNERS.

Note that as written, and as would be required by the UPA, to establish other places of business will require a vote of *all* partners, not just a majority. If your partnership is small with only a few partners, this is advisable. On the other hand, a large partnership with a score or more partners might function more smoothly if a majority (or a supermajority, such as two thirds or three fourths) were required.

Partnership Purposes

There is no legal requirement that the purposes of your partnership be included in the agreement, but it is a good idea. By stating your purpose now, you and your partners will be reminded of the original intentions of the partnership. If time and events dictate a modification or radical change, the agreement can be amended. (See "Business Purpose" in Chapter 3.)

ARTICLE II

Partnership Purposes

The purpose of the PARTNERSHIP is to engage in [name or describe your intended business], and other businesses or activities as may be agreed to by the PARTNERS.

Partnership Term of Existence

The term or lifetime of the partnership will to a great extent depend on your business purpose. Are you in for the long haul? If so, the partnership can continue until it is voluntarily terminated by a vote of the partners, or involuntarily terminated by legal action. Or is the partnership designed for a specific project with a foreseeable completion date? Be careful of a specific date. The project may take longer than intended. Consider using the completion of the project as the termination signal. (See "The Life of Your Partnership" in Chapter 3.)

ARTICLE III

Partnership Term

The business of the PARTNERSHIP shall begin on [date] and the PARTNERSHIP shall continue until terminated on [date or condition of termination].

Method of Accounting/Fiscal Year

Is your operation to be simple or complex? Will only the partners be involved, will you have employees or be hiring independent contractors? Will the business require materials and supplies, and create inventories? Will there be credit and installment sales, or only cash transactions? The answers to these questions will determine the type and complexity of your bookkeeping method.

Will you be faced by a seasonal cycle of business, such as summertime sales for beach and swimming pool supplies and equipment, or work depending on the academic school year? Or will your business be relatively steady throughout the calendar year?

The IRS requires that, lacking compelling reasons to the contrary, your fiscal year for tax purposes be the same as the calendar year. But if you do have reasons for a different calendar year, you can apply for the change with the IRS. Your fiscal year requirements are discussed in greater detail in Chapter 5 under "Partnership Tax Year" and "Partnership Tax Year Exceptions."

ARTICLE IV

Accounting Method/Fiscal Year

(1) The PARTNERSHIP tax and business accounting records shall be according to the [name of system] method.

(2) The PARTNERSHIP fiscal year shall be [specify].

Capital Contributions and Accounts

Particular care is needed in describing who will be contributing what to the partnership capital account, such as money, property, or equipment. This description must be in detail and is usually attached to and referenced in the partnership agreement. Note that clause (2) in Article 5 refers to "tax consequences." This is an important consideration. If there is a tax deficit on the contribution, its value as a contribution is decreased.

Once the partner contributions have been made, it is standard procedure to set up a *capital account* (accounting for what has been contributed to the partnership) and a *drawing account* (account into which profits go, and from which a partner can withdraw funds in anticipation of future profits) for each partner. The capital contributions themselves become partnership property and are not to be withdrawn, unless there was some contrary agreement before the contribution was made, such as conditions for the return of patent rights (intellectual property) to the patent holder should the partnership terminate an liquidate. See "Who Will Contribute What?" in Chapter 3.

ARTICLE V

Capital Contributions, Accounts, Withdrawals

(1) Original capital contributed by each PARTNER for the purposes of PARTNERSHIP business development and activities shall comprise the types and amounts shown in detail on Exhibit "A" attached herewith and made a part hereof.

(2) For capital contributions other than money, the contributing PARTNER shall assume the income tax consequences of any difference between the value of said contribution as shown in Exhibit "A" and its adjusted tax basis.

(3) The PARTNERSHIP shall establish and maintain an individual capital account and an individual drawing account for each PARTNER.

(4) The capital contributions of the PARTNERS shall not be subject to withdrawal unless such withdrawal is agreed to by the partners, or upon dissolution of the PARTNERSHIP.

Profit and Loss Sharing

If a single part of the partnership agreement could be considered of primary importance, it is the section that spells out in careful detail who is to get what in the way of shared profit or shared loss, and under what conditions such sharing is to take place. Following is a suggested set of rules to handle the partnership's profit/loss situation where there are three partners.

The usual way to designate rights of profit and loss sharing is by a statement of percent. The percentage in turn can be based on capital contribution, on skills contribution, on intangible values (such as so-called goodwill), or any other basis or combination of bases agreeable to all partners at organization time.

A *draw* is an advance the partner takes from anticipated profits. If the draw exceeds the partner's share of accrued partnership profits at the time it is made, the excess is taken from the partner's capital account and, as such, can affect partnership ownership. As the partner's share of newly accruing partnership profits becomes available, it is first allocated to replenish the capital account, with the overflow going to the drawing account. See "Profit and Loss Division" in Chapter 3.

Although not included in the following example, you may wish to include a clause stating the partner's intention to retain a portion of partnership profits to meet future needs or expansions. Remember, there are limits to what you can hold back before the IRS imposes a penalty.

ARTICLE VI

Profit and Loss Sharing

(1) The net profits or net losses of the PARTNERSHIP during the tax year shall be distributed or charged, as the case may be, to each of the PARTNERS in the following proportions:

_____ [partner #1 name] _____; _____%,
_____ [partner #2 name] _____; _____%, and
_____ [partner #3 name] _____; _____%.

(2) The applicable net profits shall be credited or the net losses shall be charged to each PARTNER's individual drawing accounts as soon as practicable after the close of each fiscal year.

(3) In the event that there is no positive balance in an individual PARTNER's drawing account, net losses accruing to that PARTNER shall be charged to the PARTNER's capital account. When the capital account of a PARTNER has been reduced by the charging of such losses, future profits accruing to that PARTNER shall be credited to the PARTNER's capital account until the reduction for losses has been restored. Thereafter, the PARTNER's share of profits shall be credited to the PARTNER's drawing account.

Managing the Partnership

As mentioned earlier, by law each partner of a partnership has an equal right to make management decisions for the partnership. This is, of course, impractical, and will be adjusted in Article XI of this sample partnership agreement, where duties, responsibilities, and authorities are outlined. See "Who Will Manage the Partnership?" in Chapter 3.

Note in particular three aspects of the following article:

1. You may not wish to require a unanimous vote for partnership decisions if there is a large number of partners.
2. For a small partnership or for the start-up of a new business, it is quite possible that not all partners will devote full time to the partnership. If so, this must be included in specific detail in the agreement.
3. Regarding salaries, if each partner has the same degree of ownership of (interest in) the partnership, and if each partner is to receive the same salary, there is no need for specifying salaries, as each will receive the same amount of profit (or loss) from the partnership.

ARTICLE VII

Partnership Management

(1) Each PARTNER shall have an equal voice in the management of PARTNERSHIP business. All PARTNERSHIP business decisions shall be made by a unanimous vote of the PARTNERS. Each PARTNER shall devote full time and attention to PARTNERSHIP business, and each PARTNER shall receive a salary as agreed upon by the PARTNERS, but the PARTNERSHIP obligation to pay such salaries is limited to PARTNERSHIP assets available for such payment and shall not

be an obligation of the individual PARTNERS. Salaries paid by the PARTNERSHIP to the PARTNERS shall be treated as business expense of the PARTNERSHIP for calculation of net profits and net losses.

Partnership Dissolution

By law, dissolution of a partnership results with a gain or a loss of a partner; any change in the membership of the partnership. This change can be actual, such as by admitting a new partner, or by the retirement, death, or expulsion of a partner. See "Partners In, Partners Out," "Getting Out of a Partnership," and "Who Owns What?" in Chapter 3.

Several major questions arise with such dissolution:

1. How are the accounts handled for the partners?
2. Can the partnership business continue, and, if so, under what conditions?
3. If the partnership continues in business, what are the liabilities of the entering or departing partners regarding past debts or future debts?
4. Do you favor allowing some of the partners to continue the business under the same name?
5. How will the value of the partnership interest of the departing partner be valued? How will the share of the entering partner be calculated?
6. What are the tax implications of payments made to the departing partner?
7. What is the best way to pay a departing partner the value of his or her interest? A lump sum payment may put the surviving partnership out of business. If the payment is to be made on an installment basis, a schedule of payments must be made and adhered to strictly.
8. What if the departing partner sets up a business that is directly competitive with the partnership's business? Should you have a noncompete clause in your agreement to handle this problem? If so, be aware that the courts frown on restrictions that prevent the reasonable use of one's personal skills or experiences to make a living. Your attorney can help you draft an acceptable noncompete clause.
9. Do you want to impose any special conditions for allowing a new partner into the partnership? Skill? Experience? Money? Facilities? Connections? Fame?
10. When accepting a new partner, if you want that person to share responsibility for debts accrued before being accepted, this must be in the agreement.

While the remaining partners of the partnership can agree to pay debts that accrued while the departing partner was active, if for any reason the partnership does not or cannot make payments on these debts, by law the departing partner is still liable for them and can be pursued by the creditor individually or as a part of the larger group (joint and several liability).

Following are suggestions for you to consider. Feel free, however, to modify them according to what you and your partners feel to be most appropriate. A suggestion: As you study this section, consult with your tax advisor as to the tax implications of what follows.

ARTICLE VIII

Partnership Dissolution

The PARTNERSHIP shall be dissolved immediately upon the addition or loss of a PARTNER to the PARTNERSHIP. Loss of a PARTNER can be by retirement, death, bankruptcy, or expulsion.

(1) Any PARTNER may retire from the PARTNERSHIP upon [state number of days] prior notice to the other PARTNERS.

(2) A new PARTNER may be admitted to the PARTNERSHIP by the consent of [state whether unanimous, or what] of the then PARTNERS.

(3) Dissolution of the PARTNERSHIP upon the change in PARTNERS shall be immediate upon the effective date of the retirement, death, insanity, or expulsion of any PARTNER of the PARTNERSHIP.

(4) Upon such dissolution of the PARTNERSHIP, a complete and proper accounting shall be made of each PARTNER's capital account and drawing account, and of the net profit or net loss of the partnership as the date of dissolution.

(5) Upon such dissolution of the PARTNERSHIP, the remaining PARTNERS shall have the right to continue the business of the PARTNERSHIP under the present name, either by themselves or in conjunction with any other person or organization they may select, but they shall pay the value of the departing PARTNER's interest in the PARTNERSHIP as provided hereinafter to the departing PARTNER or to the departing PARTNER's legal representatives. If the remaining PARTNERS desire to continue the business, but not together, the PARTNERSHIP shall be voluntarily dissolved and its assets liquidated as hereinafter provided.

(6) The value of the PARTNERSHIP interest of the departing PARTNER shall be as of the date of the dissolution of the PARTNERSHIP:

(a) The departing PARTNER's unpaid but due salary;

(b) The departing PARTNER's capital account; and

(c) The departing PARTNER's share of accrued profits.

If a net loss has been incurred by the PARTNERSHIP as of the date of dissolution, such net loss shall be deducted from the above amounts.

If there is PARTNERSHIP inventory, it shall be valued at cost or market value, whichever is lower. Other assets shall be valued at book value.

In calculating the value of the departing PARTNER's PARTNERSHIP interest, no value shall be placed on goodwill, going concern, firm name, or similar intangibles.

(7) All amounts payable to the departing PARTNER or the departing PARTNER's legal representatives according to the terms of this section shall constitute payment for the PARTNER's interest in the PARTNERSHIP, and shall be considered to be a distribution under the terms of the Internal Revenue Code, not a payment of income.

Voluntary Dissolution

There may be circumstances other than the departure of a partner where you and your partners wish to dissolve the partnership voluntarily. Perhaps a project has been completed, or a purpose is no longer relevant. Perhaps you all want to go your separate ways. If so, it is advisable to understand in advance just how you will proceed with the voluntary dissolution. Questions you and your partners should consider when drafting this section include:

1. What kind of a majority will be required for the voluntary dissolution of the partnership? Unanimous consent? Simple majority? Supermajority?
2. Do you favor the ability to distribute property in kind instead of a forced sale of all property?
3. Is there any specific item of property where a specific partner should have first-refusal rights for distribution in kind?
4. As for Article VIII, do you favor allowing some of the partners to continue the partnership under the same name?

ARTICLE IX

Voluntary Dissolution of Partnership

(1) Unless otherwise dissolved, as in Section VIII or involuntarily by court action, the PARTNERSHIP shall continue its business activities until dissolved by agreement of the PARTNERS, at which time the affairs of the PARTNERSHIP shall be wound up and the assets of the PARTNERSHIP shall be liquidated as quickly as practicable. Proceeds from such liquidation shall be applied as follows:

(a) To pay liabilities owed to creditors other than PARTNERS;

(b) To pay amounts owed to PARTNERS for unpaid salaries and other debts, and for the credit balances in their respective drawing accounts;

(c) To pay amounts owed to PARTNERS in respect to their individual capital contributions to the PARTNERSHIP; and

(d) To pay amounts owed to PARTNERS for their respective shares of profits.

Gain or loss upon disposition of PARTNERSHIP property during liquidation of the PARTNERSHIP shall be credited or charged to each PARTNER according to that PARTNER's profit or loss interest in the PARTNERSHIP.

Property distributed in kind during the liquidation shall be valued as though sold with the cash proceeds distributed proportionately to the PARTNERS. The difference between the value of property distributed in kind and its book value shall be treated as a gain or loss on the sale of the property, and shall be credited or charged to the receiving PARTNERs in the proportions of their interests in the PARTNERSHIP profits or losses as specified in Article VI of this AGREEMENT.

(2) Upon the voluntary termination of the PARTNERSHIP, any two PARTNERS shall have the right, in lieu of such liquidation, to continue the business activities of the PARTNERSHIP under its present name by themselves or with any other person or organization they may select, upon payment to the withdrawing PARTNER according to Article VIII of this AGREEMENT, or within the provisions of Article VIII and Article IX of this AGREEMENT.

Expelling a Partner

Yes, the day may come when a partner is no longer welcome in or acceptable by the partnership. You may be able to solve the problem through mediation or arbitration (see Article XII), or you may be able to persuade the unwanted partner to resign (see Article VIII). If all else fails, and the presence of the partner in the partnership becomes repugnant, expulsion may be the only recourse open to the partnership. See "Expelling a Partner" in Chapter 3.

But expulsion should not be so easy that it becomes an option to solve every argument or disagreement that arises. The grounds for expulsion should be for grievous behavior that threatens the continued success of the partnership. Examples are:

- The partner is stealing from the partnership.
- The partner has misappropriated partnership property or assets through unpermitted actions.
- The partner has other activities and interests that are competitive to or otherwise harmful to the business interests of the partnership.
- The partner is no longer physically or mentally capable of constructive participation in the activities of the partnership.
- The partner has filed personal bankruptcy, which is immediate grounds for dissolution of the partnership under the UPA.

Whatever grounds you specify, they should be clear, specific, and reasonable, otherwise they will not be supported judicially should the threatened partner appeal the expulsion to a court of law. Advice from your attorney is especially important for this section of the agreement.

You can avoid this section and rely on court action to expel an undesirable partner, with the resulting dissolution of your partnership. Court-action expulsions can be for:

- Personal bankruptcy of a partner, with required expulsion.
- Judicial adjudgment of a partner's mental incompetency.
- A partner's inability to perform according to the partnership agreement.
- The quality of the partner's conduct prejudices partnership business.
- Willful breach of the partnership agreement.
- Failure to contribute urgently needed capital.
- Failure to account for sales and proceeds.
- Use of partnership funds to pay personal debts.
- Constant quarreling.
- Irreconcilable differences.

But lawsuits are best avoided. They can be destructive, both internally and in the public eye. It is best to anticipate potential trouble and have a "bad egg" section in your partnership agreement for expulsion purposes.

ARTICLE X

Expulsion of Partner

(1) A PARTNER may be expelled from the PARTNERSHIP on the grounds of:
   (a) _____ [ground #1] _____;
   (b) _____ [ground #2] _____; or
   (c) _____ [ground #3] _____.

(2) Expulsion of a PARTNER shall require the vote of [specify if unanimous, or some percentage] of the PARTNERS other than the PARTNER against whom the vote is taken.

(3) Expulsion shall become effective upon service of written notice to the expelled PARTNER.

(4) Upon the effective date of the expulsion, the rights of the expelled PARTNER to participate in PARTNERSHIP actions or decisions shall cease.

(5) Upon the effective date of the expulsion, the expelled PARTNER shall no longer share in PARTNERSHIP net profits or net losses.

(6) Upon expulsion, the expelled PARTNER shall be entitled to receive the value of that PARTNER's interest in the PARTNERSHIP as defined in Article VIII, Section 5 of this AGREEMENT.

Partner Powers and Authorities

As discussed earlier, partnership law says that all partners have equal rights in the management of the partnership and in the making of decisions relevant to the activities of the partnership. We all know, however, that in any organization with no designation for whom is to do what, there will be chaos, anarchy, mixed signals, and, most likely, failure. See "Who Will Manage the Partnership?" in Chapter 3.

Now is the time for you and your partners to come to an understanding and to create job descriptions; you should endow each job with certain duties and authorities but control them with certain limitations. Remember, if you find these early decisions do not work as anticipated, the partners can amend the agreement to handle the problem.

Here are some of the questions you and your partners should consider when drafting this section of the agreement:

1. Who will manage the various activities of the partnership, and for each position, what will be the authority, what will be the limitation or control?
2. Will you give borrowing authority to a single partner, a group (such as a committee) of partners, or hold this authority as one requiring unanimous approval by all partners?
3. As for item (1), how will you handle the rights to sell partnership property? Other partnership assets? Products or services produced by the partnership?
4. What constraints will you place on the rights of a partner to commit that partner's share of the partnership to another person or organization?

ARTICLE XI

Partners' Duties and Authorities

Consistent with partnership law under which each and every PARTNER in the PARTNERSHIP has an equal voice in the management of PARTNERSHIP business and financial affairs, and the restrictions and limitations of Sections (2) and (3) of this article, the PARTNERS herein delegate the following:

(1) Duties designation for PARTNERS are:

_____ [PARTNER name] _____; _____ [position] _____: _____ [duties] _____
_____ [PARTNER name] _____; _____ [position] _____; _____ [duties] _____
_____ [PARTNER name] _____; _____ [position] _____: _____ [duties] _____

(2) Checks drawn upon the PARTNERSHIP bank account shall be for PARTNERSHIP purposes only, and shall be signed by [specify which PARTNER or

PARTNERS are authorized, either alone or in combination, to sign PARTNERSHIP checks].

(3) For the following actions on behalf of the PARTNERSHIP or in the name of the PARTNERSHIP, a PARTNER must have the consent of [specify if the full PARTNERSHIP must consent, or some specified majority]:

(a) To borrow or lend money;

(b) To execute any mortgage, bond, or lease;

(c) To assign, transfer, or pledge any debts that are due to the PARTNERSHIP, or to release any debts due the PARTNERSHIP, except when such debt has been paid in full;

(d) To compromise any claim of any nature whatsoever due to the PARTNERSHIP, or to submit to mediation or arbitration any disagreement between the PARTNERSHIP and persons or organizations outside the PARTNERSHIP; or

(e) To sell, assign, pledge, mortgage, or otherwise transfer any or all rights to a PARTNER's interest in the PARTNERSHIP.

Handling Internal Disputes

True, by the time you and your partners have completed considering and drafting the terms of your agreement, all of you will understand and accept these terms, even though you may have had both serious and heated discussions during the planning stages. So now you are confident that all disagreements have been reconciled. That is, reconciled for now. What about the future?

People change, needs change, the economy changes, the business climate changes. Most of the challenges of change can be handled amicably through discussions and compromise. But what about those problems where no agreement can be reached? Does this mean the end of the partnership? Perhaps, but not necessarily, not if you have a mechanism in which you present your disagreements to a disinterested third party, a mediator, or an arbitrator.

To repeat, in mediation you sit down together or separately with someone who is not associated with the partnership, who tries to help you find a suitable middle ground. Arbitration, however, is a formal hearing where the arbitrator (acting much as a judge would act) takes statements and evidence from the disagreeing partners, and makes a judgment. As practiced by the American Arbitration Association, the judgment of the arbitrator is binding. That is, you must accept the arbitrator's ruling, and it cannot be contested or overturned in a court of law. See "Partner Disagreements" in Chapter 3.

Consider the following questions as you review the following article:

1. Do you want to have a way to solve possible future disagreements? Or would you rather just let the partnership break up? If there are only two or a few partners, there is no advantage in one "winning" over another as the end result is anger or hard feelings. If there are a half dozen or more partners, you may feel more free to have a forced settlement.

2. Would you be better off going straight to binding arbitration, or would it be better to use a two-step approach trying mediation first and, if it should fail, going to arbitration?

Either way, remember, the mediation and arbitration services provided by the American Arbitration Association are not free. You must pay for the expense of bringing professional dispute solvers into your internal disagreements.

ARTICLE XII

Dispute Resolution

(1) Should a controversy, claim, or other disagreement arise out of this AGREEMENT that cannot be settled to the satisfaction of the PARTNERS, PARTNERS who are parties to such controversy, claim, or disagreement agree to seek outside mediation to resolve the conflict. Should mediation fail, the PARTNERS involved shall accept the ruling of arbitration in accordance with the then current rules of the American Arbitration Association and the judgment therefrom upon the award may be entered into any court having jurisdiction over the matter.

Miscellaneous Provisions

A number of other less complex provisions should be taken into consideration in the preparation of the partnership agreement. These include banking arrangements, keeping the books open to partners, notices to partners of partnership meetings or actions, and more. There may be other arrangements you will wish to have a part of the agreement. If so, they can be grouped under the "Other Provisions" heading.

ARTICLE XIII

Other Provisions

(1) The PARTNERSHIP banking account shall be maintained in a bank or banks as agreed upon by the PARTNERS.

(2) The account books for all aspects of PARTNERSHIP records shall be open for inspection by any PARTNER or accredited legal representative of said PARTNER during reasonable business hours.

(3) The account books for all aspects of PARTNERSHIP records shall be examined and reviewed at the close of each fiscal year by an independent certified public accountant selected by agreement of the PARTNERS.

(4) Notices to PARTNERS provided for by this AGREEMENT shall be in writing, and shall be considered sufficient if sent by registered or certified mail to the last known address of the PARTNER to whom notice is addressed.

(5) The PARTNERS who are parties to this AGREEMENT further agree that they will execute further documents or perform reasonable actions as may be found necessary for effectively carrying on the business and activities of the PARTNERSHIP.

(6) The PARTNERS herein agree that the law of the State of [specify your state] shall be the effective law for any and all legal actions involving this AGREEMENT, regardless of the state of residence of the PARTNER at the time action is taken.

(7) Should any Article or Section or Subsection thereunder in this AGREEMENT be deemed unenforceable under law, the unenforceability of said Article or Section or Subsection shall have no effect on the validity or legal obligation by any other Article or Section or Subsection of this AGREEMENT.

IN WITNESS WHEREOF, the parties to the PARTNERSHIP have signed this AGREEMENT:

_____ [L.S.]
_____ [L.S.]
_____ [L.S.]

State of _____
                              s.s.:
County of _____

On this ____ day of _____, 19____, before me personally appeared __[PARTNER]__, __[PARTNER]__, and __[PARTNER]__, known to me and known to me to be the persons described in and who executed the foregoing General Partnership AGREEMENT, and they severally acknowledged to me that they executed the same.

_____
Notary Public

EXHIBIT "A"

ADDITIONAL ITEMS FOR THE AGREEMENT

You can, of course, include anything and everything that is relevant to your partnership, as long as it is not illegal or otherwise prevented by statute. Several such possible inclusions are discussed in Chapter 3 under "Other Items to Consider." They include:

- Will you allow nonpartnership activities by partners; if so, what, if any, will be the restrictions?
- Do you want to prevent a partner from leaving the partnership and starting a business that will compete with the business of your partnership?
- How do you want to compensate the partners? Consider those who manage and supervise, those who produce, those who sell, and so on.
- What kind of insurance program will you have? Do you want to have key person insurance to protect partnership income during a period of management transition? Liability insurance? Do you want insurance to cover periods when the business is shut down because of fire or other disaster? Will you have a health insurance and pension program? And so on.

CHAPTER 5

YOUR PARTNERSHIP AND TAXES

YOU AND THE INTERNAL REVENUE SERVICE

The purpose of this chapter is to help you understand the basics of partnership tax law so that you can avoid making serious errors and will be better able to work constructively with your tax advisor. With proper accounting and professional tax planning and preparation, you should gain maximum legal tax-deduction and tax-exemption benefits.

Section K of the Internal Revenue Code (IRC) is well known by certified public accountants (CPAs) and other tax professionals for its complexity. Numerous legal tomes have been authored in the attempt to explain and clarify tax law. What you see in the following pages cannot turn you into an overnight tax expert, but it will shed light on the requirements and procedures for preparing both your partnership and your personal tax returns. What follows is basically a simplification and brief summary of information available in Internal Revenue Service (IRS) Publication 541, *Tax Information on Partnerships*.

DEFINITION OF PARTNERSHIPS

A partnership is the relationship between two or more persons who join together to carry on a trade or business. Each person contributes money, property, labor, or skill, and each expects to share in the profits and losses. *Person* for a partnership means an individual, corporation, trust, estate, or another partnership.

A joint undertaking to share expenses is not of itself a partnership. Mere co-ownership of property that is maintained and leased or rented is not a partnership. However, if the co-owners provide services to the tenants, a partnership exists.

FAMILY PARTNERSHIP TAX RETURNS

When spouses carry on a business together and share in the profits and losses, they may be partners, whether or not they have a formal partnership agreement. As partners, they should report business income or loss as a partnership (Form 1065), not as individuals (Form 1040).

They then carry their shares of partnership income or loss to their Form 1040 (joint or separate). They should then include their respective shares of partnership income or loss on separate Form 1040 Schedules SE (Social Security Self-Employment Tax).

PARTNERSHIP AGREEMENTS

The partnership agreement includes the original agreement and any modifications to it. The modifications must be agreed to by all the partners, or adopted in any other manner provided by the partnership agreement.

For tax purposes, partners can modify the agreement for a particular tax year after the close of the year, but not later than the date for filing the partnership return for the year and not including any extensions of filing time.

In general, a partner's share of income, gain, losses, deductions, or credits is determined by the partnership agreement. However, the agreement or any modification of it will be disregarded by the IRS if the allocations to a partner under the agreement do not have substantial economic effect as defined under "Partnership Distributive Shares," discussed later in this chapter. Where the agreement or any modification of it is silent on any matter, provisions of local law are treated as part of the agreement.

PARTNERSHIP TAX YEAR

The tax year for a partnership usually continues after the death of a partner, the entry of a new partner, or the liquidation, sale, or exchange of a partner's interest.

There are limits to the tax year chosen for a partnership. Generally, the partnership year must conform to the tax years of the partners as follows:

1. *The Majority Tax Year.* Where one or more partners own an interest of more than 50% in partnership profits and capital, the partnership must use the tax year of those partners. The testing day to determine if there is a majority tax year is usually the first day of the partnership's current tax year. If the partnership must change to a majority tax year, it will not be required to do so for two years following the year of change.

2. *Principal Partners' Tax Year.* Where there is no majority tax year, the partnership must use the tax year of all its principal partners, namely those with 5% or greater interest in the partnership's profits or capital.

3. *Least Aggregate Deferral of Income Tax Year.* Where there is not a majority tax year and the principal partners do not have the same tax year, the IRS rule is that the partnership use a tax year that results in the least aggregate deferral of income to the partners.

PARTNERSHIP TAX YEAR EXCEPTIONS

A different tax year can be used if the partnership can establish a business purpose acceptable to the IRS. The mere fact of a tax advantage from income deferral for the partners is not an acceptable reason. See IRS Publication 538, *Accounting Periods and Methods*.

Another exception is found in Section 444 of the IRC. A partnership can make a Section 444 election when it wants to establish a business purpose to get permission for a tax year that is different its required tax year. To make a Section 444 election, you must file Form 8716, *Election to Have a Tax Year Other Than a Required Tax Year*, with the IRS. A copy of the Form 8716 must be attached to the Partnership's Form 1065 partnership tax return for the first year of the election.

PARTNERSHIP INCOME

While your partnership in general computes income and files tax returns as for an individual, there are exceptions requiring certain items of gain, loss, income, and so on to be filed separately.

Most choices for how to compute income are made by the partnership, such as accounting and depreciation methods, accounting for specific items such as depletion or installment sales, nonrecognition of gain on involuntary conversions of property, and amortization of certain partnership organization fees and start-up costs. But each partner chooses how to treat foreign and U.S. possession taxes, certain mining exploration expenses, and income from the discharge of indebtedness.

While the partnership itself does not make estimated tax payments, the partners themselves may have to do so because of income from partnership distributions.

ORGANIZATION/SYNDICATION FEES

No tax deduction is allowed by either the partnership or the partners for expenses for the organization of a partnership, nor is there a deduction for expenses for promoting the sale of the partnership or an interest in the partnership, as in a limited partnership.

The partnership can, however, choose to amortize certain organization fees over a period of not less than 60 months. This applies to expenses related to the creation of the partnership, and expenses chargeable to a capital account. Amortization also applies to start-up expenses, either for the creation of an active trade or business, or to investigate the creation or acquisition of such trade or business.

Regarding syndication, amortization does not apply to commissions, professional fees, and printing costs connected with issuing and marketing interests in the partnership. Such expenses are capitalized, but only if the syndication is successful.

PARTNER'S INCOME TAX RETURNS

Your income as a partner is your distributive share of partnership items, whether or not the share is actually distributed. These items are reported to the partners on Schedule K-1 of Form 1065. For your individual tax return, you then combine deductions or exclusions for income from nonpartnership sources with the partnership distribution. The totals of these two sources are then used to calculate limits you must exceed before making deductions on your Form 1040.

Note that you must treat items on your personal tax return in the same way that they are treated on the partnership return, unless you file Form 8082, *Notice of*

Inconsistent Treatment or Amended Return, with the IRS to explain your reasons for the difference in treatments. If you don't do this, the IRS may make adjustments to your return, with possible penalties.

PARTNERSHIP DISTRIBUTIVE SHARES

Once you have earned a distributive share from your partnership, you must report it on your personal tax return, even if this share was not actually distributed to you. What your distributive share will be (income, gain, loss, deduction, credit) is determined by your partnership agreement, and as reported to you on Form 1065 or Schedule K-1.

Your distributive share will be determined by your interest in the partnership if there are no other provisions in the agreement regarding distribution, or if the allocation does not unfairly affect the distributive shares of the other partners (called "substantial economic effect").

CONTRIBUTED PROPERTY DEPRECIATION

If you or another partner contribute property to the partnership, the partnership's basis to determine depreciation, depletion, gain, or loss for the property is the same for the partnership as the adjusted basis of the property at the time it was contributed. If the fair market value for the property at the time of contribution is greater than (or less than) the adjusted basis, there will be a gain (or loss) that must be allocated among the partners to account for the gain or loss.

ALTERNATIVE MINIMUM TAX

You must include your partnership distributions when computing your alternative minimum tax (IRS Publication 909, *Alternative Minimum Tax for Individuals*).

ACTUAL DISTRIBUTIONS

Partnership distributions as such generally are not taxable since you as a partner must include in your income any share of partnership income, whether or not it is distributed to you. However, a distribution is taxable when treated as a liquidation or as a sale or exchange of all or part of your capital interest in the partnership.

If the partnership distributes borrowed funds to you as a partner, the partnership should list the interest expense of these funds as "interest expense allocated to debt-financed distributions" under "other deductions" on your Schedule K-1. You then deduct on your personal tax return, depending on how you use the funds.

GAIN OR LOSS ON DISTRIBUTIONS

How you treat a distribution or withdrawal from your partnership depends on why the distribution or withdrawal is made, and what it is for.

A distribution of money that is a return of part of your adjusted basis in the partnership (thus, not income generated by the partnership) is not included as income unless it exceeds your adjusted basis. When the partnership distributes property to you, you do not recognize any gain for tax purposes until the sale or other disposition of the property.

You do not recognize a loss unless you dispose of your entire interest in the partnership, and then only if the distribution is in money, unrealized receivables, or inventory items. If you receive any other type of property, you do not recognize a loss. For example, if the adjusted basis of your interest in the partnership is $10,000 and you receive a distribution of $8,000 cash along with land that has a fair market value of $3,000, your basis for the land is $2,000. You do not recognize gain until you sell or otherwise dispose of it.

PARTNERSHIP LOSSES

On your tax return, you cannot recognize a share of partnership loss that is greater than your adjusted-basis interest in the partnership. Your adjusted basis is calculated at the end of the partnership tax year in which the loss occurred, prior to taking the loss into consideration. If your loss is greater than your adjusted basis, it is not deductible for that year.

AT-RISK LOSSES

The *at-risk rules* limit the amount of loss you can deduct so that it does not exceed the amount you have that is considered to be at risk in the activity. Simply stated, you cannot record a tax loss that is greater than what you risk losing if the enterprise is a total loss.

Your at-risk amount is:

- Cash and adjusted basis in property you contributed to the partnership activity.
- Income due you that is retained by the partnership.
- Certain amounts borrowed by the partnership for use in the partnership activity.

In general, you will not be considered to be at risk for borrowed amounts used by the partnership unless you are personally liable for the repayment of these funds or the borrowed amount is secured by your personal (not partnership) property. You are not considered to be at risk for amounts protected against loss through guarantees, stop-loss agreements, or similar arrangements. Nor are you at risk for borrowed amounts if the lender (other than as creditor) has an interest in the activity, or if the lender is related to a person (other than yourself) having such an interest.

PASSIVE ACTIVITIES

Section 469 of the IRC limits losses, deductions, and credits that you as a partner can claim from *passive activities*, although the passive-activity limits do not apply to the partnership itself. Generally, passive activities include those for which you as a partner do not materially participate in the activity, and rental activities, regardless of your participation or lack of it.

FAMILY PARTNERSHIPS

The *family partnership* is a popular way to split income within a family; that is where, for example, a parent shares in the ownership of an interest in the partnership with a younger family member who is in a lower tax bracket. By definition, a family partnership is one in which the members (partners) are closely related through blood or marriage (ancestors, lineal descendants, or spouses, or any trusts for their benefit; but not brothers or sisters).

There are restrictions as to whether or not the IRS will consider a family member to be a partner. The terms you must consider are the *material income-producing factor* and the *capital interest.*

For the IRS to consider a family member to be a bona fide partner, one of the following two requirements must be met:

- The family member must actually own the partnership interest and have actual control over the interest if *capital is a material income-producing factor.*
- The family member must provide substantial or vital services to the partnership if *capital is not a material income-producing factor.*

Capital is considered to be a material income-producing factor if a substantial part of the gross income of the partnership business comes from the use of capital, as when substantial inventories or investments in plant, machinery, or equipment are required. Capital is not a material income-producing factor if the income of the partnership business consists principally of fees, commissions, or other compensation for personal services performed by members or employees of the partnership.

Capital interest in a partnership is an interest in its assets that can be distributed to the owner of the interest if the partner withdraws from the partnership, or the partnership is liquidated. The mere right to share in the earnings and profits of a partnership is not a capital interest in the partnership.

Gift or Purchase of Partnership Interests

When a family member receives a gift of a capital interest in a family partnership in which capital is a material income-producing factor, there are limits to the amount that can be allocated to that member (as donee) as a distributive share of partnership income. But it is also considered to be a gift when an interest in the partnership is purchased by one family member from another member of the family.

The donor of the partnership interest must be allocated an amount of the partnership income generated by the donated interest that represents reasonable compensation for the donor's services to the partnership, as well as what the donor should receive in return for proportionate ownership of the partnership. This requirement is to prevent the donor in a high tax bracket from diverting substantial income to the donee in a lower tax bracket.

For example, you "sell" 50% of your business to your daughter. Profit for the partnership is $60,000. Capital is a material income-producing factor. Reasonable compensation for your services to the partnership is $24,000; your daughter provides no services. The $24,000 compensation must be paid to you, as well as 50% of the remaining $36,000 income due to capital for your 50% ownership in the partnership. Thus, your share of the $60,000 profit is $24,000 plus $18,000, or $42,000; your daughter's share cannot exceed $18,000.

PARTNER DEALINGS WITH PARTNERSHIP

There are special rules for the sales or exchanges of property between partnerships and certain persons:

Losses are not allowed from a sale or exchange of property (other than an interest in the partnership) directly or indirectly between a partnership and a person with greater than 50% direct or indirect interest in the capital or profits of the partnership.

Gains are treated as ordinary income in a sale or exchange of property directly or indirectly between a person and a partnership, or between two partnerships, if more than 50% of the capital or profits interest is directly or indirectly owned by the same persons, and property in the hands of the recipient immediately after the transfer is not a capital asset (i.e., trade accounts receivable, inventory, stock-in-trade, and depreciable or real property used in a trade or business).

The IRS has its own special rules to determine when it considers *constructive ownership* (*constructive* in legal language meaning equivalent or tantamount to actual) to be more than 50%, namely:

1. Ownership of direct or indirect interests are owned proportionately by or for the partners or the partners' beneficiaries, and
2. An individual owns the interest that is directly or indirectly owned by or for the individual's family (brothers and half-brothers, sisters and half-sisters, ancestors, lineal descendants, and spouse), and
3. *Constructive ownership* under rule (1) becomes "actual" ownership under rules (1) and (2); but under rule (2) only, it is not treated as actual ownership so as to make another person the *constructive* owner.

For example, you and a friend along with a trust are equal partners in a partnership. Your wife is the sole beneficiary of the trust. The trust's partnership interest will be attributed to your wife only for the purpose of further attributing the interest to you. This makes you more than 50% partner. Thus, losses on transactions between your wife and the partnership will be disallowed for tax purposes. Any gains will be treated as ordinary gains rather than capital gains.

CONTRIBUTED PROPERTY

In general, neither the partners nor the partnership recognize a gain or loss when contributing property to the partnership in exchange for a partnership interest. This is true for both the formation of a partnership and a partnership already in operation.

CONTRIBUTED SERVICES

It is permissible to acquire an interest in partnership capital as payment for services you perform (or will perform) for the partnership.

BASIS OF PARTNER INTEREST

The *adjusted basis* of your partnership interest normally is figured at the end of the partnership tax year. But when, during the tax year, part of your interest or part of one of your partners' interest has been exchanged or sold, or the entire interest has been liquidated during the tax year, the adjusted basis will be figured on the date of that action.

Calculation of the *adjusted basis* of your interest does not consider capital, equity, or similar accounts shown on the partnership books. For example, assume that you contributed property to the partnership with an adjusted basis of $400, but with a fair market value of $1,000. Further assume that you have a partner who has contributed $1,000 in cash. Since both of you have made contributions in the value of $1,000, you each have a $1,000 capital account in the partnership. But your adjusted basis is only $400, while your partner's is $1,000.

ORIGINAL BASIS OF PARTNERSHIP INTEREST

The *original basis* of your interest, on the other hand, is a combination of the money you contribute plus the basis on any property you contributed. If the property you contributed results in taxable income for you, the income will be included in the basis of your interest. An increase in your individual liabilities because you assume partnership liabilities is also treated as a contribution of money to the partnership.

If you owe money on the property you contribute or if your partner assumes your liabilities, your interest in the partnership is reduced. The liability assumed by your partner is considered a distribution by you of money to your partner, while assumption of the liability by your partner is treated as a contribution of money to the partnership. This means that your basis in the partnership is reduced and your partner's is increased.

For example, assume you purchase a 20% interest in the partnership by contributing property with an adjusted basis to you of $8,000, but with a $4,000 mortgage. The partnership assumes payment of the mortgage. Now your adjusted basis of partnership interest is the $8,000 less your partner's share of the $4,000 mortgage, namely $3,200 (80% of $4,000), leaving you a partnership interest of $4,800 ($8,000 less $3,200).

There are other specific IRS rules for handling basis when you are given or inherit an interest in a partnership (IRS Publication 551), or use a loan to purchase an interest in a partnership (IRS Publication 545).

Original Basis Adjustments

Your original basis is increased by additional contributions to the partnership, your distributive share of both taxable and nontaxable partnership income, and the excess of deduction for depletion that is greater than the depletable property's basis.

Your original basis is decreased by:

- Amount of money and the adjusted basis of property that the partnership distributes to you.
- Your distributive share of partnership income and capital losses.
- Your distributive share of nondeductible partnership expenses that are not capital expenses.
- Your distributive share of deductions for depletion for oil and gas wells.
- Your distributive share of depreciable property placed in service during the year; IRC Section 179 allows a deduction of up to $10,000 for the cost of depreciable property placed in service during the year.

Partnership Liabilities

As a partner, you will have a share of partnership liabilities according to your basis in the partnership when the liability:

- Creates or increases your partnership basis in any of its assets.
- Creates a current deduction to the partnership.
- Decreases your basis in the partnership because it relates to a nondeductible partnership expense that is not a capital expenditure.

Assets as used here includes *capitalized* items that are allocated to future periods (such as organizational expenses). Accrued but unpaid expenses and accounts payable of a cash-basis partnership are not included in partnership liabilities.

When partnership liabilities are increased resulting in an increase in a partner's share of partnership liabilities, the increase is treated as a contribution of money by you to the partnership. When partnership liabilities are decreased resulting in a decrease of your share of partnership liabilities, the decrease is treated as a distribution of money to you by the partnership.

Partnership Share of Liabilities

To determine your share of partnership liabilities, you must determine whether the liability is a recourse or a nonrecourse liability.

A partnership liability is a *recourse liability* to the extent that you or your partner have economic risk of loss for that liability. A liability is a *nonrecourse liability* if neither you nor your partner have economic risk of loss because of that liability. *Economic risk of loss* means you are obligated by law or agreement for payments because of the liability. In a constructive liquidation, all partnership assets including cash are assumed worthless, and all liabilities are due and payable in full. Those partners who must pay off the liabilities have economic risk of loss.

PARTNER'S BASIS OF PROPERTY RECEIVED

The basis of property distributed to you by the partnership is the partnership's adjusted basis immediately preceding the distribution. However, this adjusted basis cannot exceed the adjusted basis of your interest in the partnership, less any money you receive in the same transaction.

For example, if your adjusted basis interest in the partnership is $30,000 and you receive a distribution of property with an adjusted basis of $20,000 plus $4,000 cash, your basis for the property is $20,000. However, if your partnership interest was only $15,000, your basis for the distribution is only $11,000 (your $15,000 interest less the $4,000 cash).

SALES, EXCHANGES, TRANSFERS

If you sell or otherwise exchange your interest in the partnership, the result is a gain or loss, the difference between what you realize (receive) and your adjusted basis interest in the partnership. If, when you sell, you are relieved of partnership liabilities, the amount of these liabilities is included to determine the amount you realize for your interest.

Also to be considered in the calculation are unrealized receivables, as well as substantially appreciated inventory items.

Payments by the partnership to liquidate your interest in the partnership upon your retirement, or to a successor in interest in the event of your death, are treated as distributions to you by the partnership. Amounts paid for unrealized receivables are not considered distributions. Nor are amounts paid for *goodwill* distributions, unless provided for in the partnership agreement.

FILLING IN FORM 1065

Exhibit 5.1 is a sample Form 1065 return prepared by the IRS and illustrated in IRS Publication 541. Referring to Exhibit 5.1, Sample Form 1065, which appears at the end of this chapter:

PAGE 1

Income

The partnership's ordinary income (loss) is shown on lines 1a through 8.

Line 1. Gross sales of $409,465 are entered on line 1a. Returns and allowances of $3,365 are entered on line 1b, resulting in net sales of $406,100, entered on line 1c.

Line 2. Cost of goods sold, $267,641, from Schedule A, line 8 (discussed later), is entered here.

Line 3. Gross profit of $138,459 is shown on this line.

Line 7. Interest income on accounts receivable, $559, is entered on this line. The schedule that must be attached for this line is not shown.

Line 8. Total income, $139,018 (lines 3 through 7), is shown on line 8.

Deductions

The partnership's allowable deductions are shown next on lines 9 through 21.

Line 9. All salaries and wages are included on line 9a, *except* guaranteed payments to partners (shown on line 10). The AbleBee Book Store lists $29,350 on lines 9a and 9c. Because the partnership was not eligible for the jobs credit, no entry is made on line 9b. See Form 5884, *Jobs Credit*, for more information on the jobs credit.

Line 10. Guaranteed payments of $25,000 to partners Able ($20,000) and Brown ($5,000) are entered here. If a guaranteed payment is for interest paid to a partner, enter it here and not on line 12.

Line 11. Rent paid for the business premises, $20,000, is listed on this line.

Line 12. Interest paid to suppliers during the year totaled $1,451. This is business interest, so it is entered on line 12. Interest paid to a *partner* that is not a guaranteed payment is also included on this line. For more information, see Chapter 6 in Publication 535.

Line 13. Deductible taxes of $3,295 are entered on this line.

Line 14. During the year, $250 of amounts owed to the partnership was determined to be worthless. This amount is shown on line 14. If debts previously written off and deducted are collected in later years, the amount collected generally must be included in partnership gross income for the year in which the amount is collected. See Chapter 12 in Publication 535 for more information.

Line 15. Repairs of $1,125 made to partnership equipment are entered on this line. To qualify for the deduction, repairs must not add to the value or appreciably prolong the life of the property repaired.

Lines 16a and 16c. Depreciation of $1,174 from Form 4562, *Depreciation and Amortization,* is entered here. Any amount on line 16b is also from Form 4562. The partnership must use Form 4562 to report the depreciation expense claimed on this line and elsewhere on the partnership return. A filled-in Form 4562 is not shown in this example.

Line 20. Other allowable deductions of $8,003 that are not claimed elsewhere on the return or for which a separate line is not provided on page 1 are included on this line. The partnership attaches a schedule that lists each deduction and its amount that is included on line 20. This schedule is not illustrated.

Line 21. The total of all deductions, $89,648 (lines 9c through 20), is entered on this line.

Line 22. The amount on line 21 is subtracted from the amount on line 8. The result, $49,370, is entered on line 22 of page 1 and is allocated to each partner on line 1 of Schedule K-1. The total is shown on line 1 of Schedule K.

Signatures

The return must be signed by a general partner. Also, any person, firm, or corporation that prepares the return for compensation, other than a full-time employee of the partnership, must sign it. The AbleBee Book Store did not have a paid preparer who was required to sign the return.

PAGE 2

SCHEDULE A

Schedule A is the computation of cost of goods sold. Beginning inventory, $18,125 (entered on line 1), is added to net purchases, $268,741, and is entered on line 2. The total, $286,866, is entered on line 6. Ending inventory, $19,225 (entered on line 7), is subtracted from the amount on line 6 to arrive at cost of goods sold, $267,641 (entered on line 8 and on page 1, line 2).

The partnership answered all applicable questions for item 9.

SCHEDULE B

Schedule B contains 11 questions pertaining to the partnership. Answer these questions by marking the "yes" or "no" boxes.

Question 5 asks if the partnership meets all the requirements listed in the instructions for Question 5. These requirements are:

1. The partnership's total receipts are less than $250,000; and
2. The partnership's total assets are less than $250,000; and
3. Schedules K-1 are filed with the return and furnished to the partners on or before the due date of the partnership return (including extensions).

If all three of these requirements are met, mark the "yes" box to Question 5 and the partnership is not required to complete Schedules L, M-1, and M-2.

PAGE 3

SCHEDULE K

Schedule K must be completed by all partnerships. It lists the total of all partners' shares of income, deductions, credits, etc. The partnership agreement can provide for the manner in which the partners will share each item of income, gain, loss, deduction, or credit, etc., of the partnership. If the main purpose of any provision in the partnership agreement, regarding a partner's share of any item, is to evade or avoid federal income tax, the provision will be disregarded.

Each partner is allocated his or her distributive share of any item from the partnership if a different income tax liability will result from the item being distributable to the partner separately, rather than being distributable to the partner as part of the partnership's income or loss (line 22, page 1).

Each partner's distributive share of income, deductions, credits, etc., should be reported on Schedule K-1. The line items for Schedule K are discussed in combination with the Schedule K-1 line items, later.

PAGE 4

SCHEDULES L, M-1, AND M-2

Partnerships do not have to complete Schedules L, M-1, or M-2 if all of the tests listed in the instructions for Question 5 are met and Question 5 on page 2 is marked "Yes." The AbleBee Book Store does not meet all of the tests, so these schedules must be completed.

Schedule L

Schedule L contains the partnership's balance sheets at the beginning and end of the tax year. All information shown on the balance sheets for the AbleBee Book Store should agree with its books of account. Any differences should be reconciled and explained in a separate schedule attached to the return.

The entry for total assets at the end of the year, $45,391, is carried to Item F at the top of page 1 if Item F is required to be completed. See the instructions for Form 1065 for more information.

Schedule M-1

Schedule M-1 is the reconciliation of income per the partnership books with income per Form 1065.

Line 1. This line shows the net income per the books of $48,920. This amount is from the profit and loss account (not shown in this example).

Line 2. This line includes the guaranteed payments to partners.

Line 4. This is the total of lines 1 through 3 of $73,920.

Line 5. Included in line 5 is the $50 tax-exempt interest income from municipal bonds that is recorded on the books but is not included on Schedule K, lines 1 through 7. Each partner's share of this interest is reported on his or her Schedule K-1 on line 20.

Line 8. This line is the same as Schedule K, line 20a. It is also the same as line 4 less line 7, $73,870.

Schedule M-2

Schedule M-2 is an analysis of the partner's capital accounts. It shows the total equity of all partners in the partnership at the beginning and end of the tax year and shows the adjustments that caused any increase or decrease. The total of all the partners' capital accounts is the difference between the partnership's assets and liabilities shown on Schedule L. A partner's capital account will not necessarily represent the tax basis for an interest in the partnership.

Line 1. As of January 1, the total of the partners' capital accounts was $27,550 (Mr. Able—$14,050; Mr. Brown—$13,500). This amount should agree with the beginning balance shown on Schedule L for the partners' capital accounts.

Line 3. This is the net income per the books.

Line 5. This is the total of lines 1 through 4.

Line 6. Each partner withdrew $26,440 (totaling $52,880) from the partnership. The partners' guaranteed payments, which were actually paid, are not included in this column because they were deducted in arriving at the amount shown in line 3. Any other distributions to the partners, in cash or property other than cash, would also be included here.

Line 9. This shows the total equity of all partners as shown in the books of account as of December 31. This amount should agree with the year-end balance shown on Schedule L for the partners' capital accounts.

Item J on Schedule K-1 reflects each partner's share of the amounts shown in lines 1 through 9 of Schedule M-2.

SCHEDULE K-1

Schedule K-1 lists each partner's share of income, deductions, credits, etc. It also shows where to report the items on the partner's individual income tax return.

Illustrated is a copy of the Schedule K-1 for Frank W. Able. All information asked for at the top of Schedule K-1 must be supplied for each partner.

Since all line items on Schedule K-1 are not applicable to every partnership, a substitute Schedule K-1 may be used. See the instructions for Form 1065 for more information.

Allocation of Partnership Items

The partners' shares of income, deductions, etc., are shown next in lines 1 through 19, Schedule K, and lines 1 through 20, Schedule K-1.

Income (Loss)

Line 1. This line on Schedule K-1 shows Able's share, $24,685, of the income from the partnership shown on line 22, page 1. The total amount of income is shown on line 1, Schedule K.

Line 4b. Dividends are among the items that must be separately stated and not included in the income (loss) of the partnership on Form 1065, page 1, line 22. This line on Schedule K-1 shows Able's share, $75. This line on Schedule K shows the total dividends of $150.

Line 5. This line on Schedule K-1 should show only the guaranteed payments to Able of $20,000. This line on Schedule K shows the total guaranteed payments, to all partners, of $25,000.

Deductions

Line 8. During the year, the partnership made a $650 contribution to the American Lung Association. Each partner can deduct all or part of his or her share of the partnership's charitable contributions on his or her individual income tax return, if the partner itemizes deductions. Able's share of the contribution, $325, is entered on line 8, Schedule K-1. This line on Schedule K shows the total contribution. For more information, see Publication 526, *Charitable Contributions.*

Investment Interest

Lines 12a–12b. The partnership's total interest on investment debt, and items of investment income and expenses, are entered on the applicable lines of Schedule K, and each partner's share is entered on Schedule K-1. For more information, see Publication 550, *Investment Income and Expenses,* and the instructions for Form 1065. This partnership did not have any investment interest expense or other investment expenses. It did have investment income as shown on line 4b, Schedule K. The total of all portfolio income, lines 4a through 4f, is shown on line 12b(1), Schedule K, and the partner's share is shown on line 12b(1), Schedule K-1.

Self-Employment Tax

Line 15a. Net earnings (loss) from self-employment are entered on Schedule K, and each individual partner's share is shown on his or her Schedule K-1. Guaranteed payments are included in net earnings from self-employment. Each partner uses his or her share to figure his or her self-employment tax on Schedule SE (Form 1040), *Self-Employment Tax*.

Analysis

Lines 20a–20b (Schedule K only).   An analysis must be made of the distributive items on Schedule K. This analysis is based on the type of partner. Since the AbleBee Book Store has two persons, both of whom are general partners, the entries are $73,870 on lines 20a and 20b(1), column (b)i.

EXHIBIT 5.1   Sample Form 1065

Form 1065
Department of the Treasury
Internal Revenue Service

U.S. Partnership Return of Income

For calendar year 1991, or tax year beginning ...., 1991, and ending............, 19.....
▶ See separate Instructions.

OMB No. 1545-0099

1991

A Principal business activity Retail	Use the IRS label. Other-wise, please print or type.
B Principal product or service Books	
C Business code number 5942	

10-9876543   DEC91   D71
AbleBee Book Store
334 WEST MAIN STREET
ANYTOWN   MD   20904

I R S

D Employer identification number
10-9876543
E Date business started
10/1/78
F Total assets (see Specific Instructions)
$ 45,391

G Check applicable boxes: (1) ☐ Initial return   (2) ☐ Final return   (3) ☐ Change in address   (4) ☐ Amended return
H Check accounting method: (1) ☐ Cash   (2) ☑ Accrual   (3) ☐ Other (specify) ▶ ....
I Number of partners in this partnership. .... ▶ 2

Caution: Include only trade or business income and expenses on lines 1a through 22 below. See the instructions for more information.

Income

1a Gross receipts or sales	**1a** 409,465		
b Less returns and allowances	**1b** 3,365	**1c**	406,100
2 Cost of goods sold (Schedule A, line 8)		**2**	267,641
3 Gross profit. Subtract line 2 from line 1c		**3**	138,459
4 Ordinary income (loss) from other partnerships and fiduciaries *(attach schedule)*		**4**	
5 Net farm profit (loss) *(attach Schedule F (Form 1040))*		**5**	
6 Net gain (loss) from Form 4797, Part II, line 18		**6**	
7 Other income (loss) (see instructions) *(attach schedule)*		**7**	559
8 Total income (loss). Combine lines 3 through 7		**8**	139,018

Deductions (see instructions for limitations)

9a Salaries and wages (other than to partners)	**9a** 29,350		
b Less jobs credit	**9b**	**9c**	29,350
10 Guaranteed payments to partners		**10**	25,000
11 Rent		**11**	20,000
12 Interest		**12**	1,451
13 Taxes		**13**	3,295
14 Bad debts		**14**	250
15 Repairs		**15**	1,125
16a Depreciation (see instructions)	**16a** 1,174		
b Less depreciation reported on Schedule A and elsewhere on return	**16b**	**16c**	1,174
17 Depletion (Do not deduct oil and gas depletion.)		**17**	
18 Retirement plans, etc.		**18**	
19 Employee benefit programs		**19**	
20 Other deductions *(attach schedule)*		**20**	8,003
21 Total deductions. Add the amounts shown in the far right column for lines 9c through 20		**21**	89,648
22 Ordinary income (loss) from trade or business activities. Subtract line 21 from line 8		**22**	49,370

Please Sign Here

Under penalties of perjury, I declare that I have examined this return, including accompanying schedules and statements, and to the best of my knowledge and belief, it is true, correct, and complete. Declaration of preparer (other than general partner) is based on all information of which preparer has any knowledge.

▶ *Frank W. Able*   ▶ 3/27/92
Signature of general partner   Date

Paid Preparer's Use Only

Preparer's signature ▶	Date	Check if self-employed ▶ ☐ Preparer's social security no.
Firm's name (or yours if self-employed) and address ▶		E.I. No. ▶ ZIP code ▶

For Paperwork Reduction Act Notice, see page 1 of separate instructions.   Cat. No. 11390Z   Form **1065** (1991)

EXHIBIT 5.1 (Continued)

Form 1065 (1991)   Page **2**

Schedule A Cost of Goods Sold

1	Inventory at beginning of year	**1**	*18,125*
2	Purchases less cost of items withdrawn for personal use	**2**	*268,741*
3	Cost of labor	**3**	
4	Additional section 263A costs (see instructions) *(attach schedule)*	**4**	
5	Other costs *(attach schedule)*	**5**	
6	**Total.** Add lines 1 through 5	**6**	*286,866*
7	Inventory at end of year	**7**	*19,225*
8	**Cost of goods sold.** Subtract line 7 from line 6. Enter here and on page 1, line 2	**8**	*267,641*

9a Check all methods used for valuing closing inventory:
- **(i)** ☐ Cost
- **(ii)** ☑ Lower of cost or market as described in Regulations section 1.471-4
- **(iii)** ☐ Writedown of "subnormal" goods as described in Regulations section 1.471-2(c)
- **(iv)** ☐ Other (specify method used and attach explanation) ▶ ....

b Check this box if the LIFO inventory method was adopted this tax year for any goods *(if checked, attach Form 970)* . . ▶ ☐

c Do the rules of section 263A (for property produced or acquired for resale) apply to the partnership? . . ☐ Yes ☑ No

d Was there any change in determining quantities, cost, or valuations between opening and closing inventory? ☐ Yes ☑ No
  If "Yes," attach explanation.

Schedule B Other Information

		Yes	No
1	Is this partnership a limited partnership?		✓
2	Are any partners in this partnership also partnerships?		✓
3	Is this partnership a partner in another partnership?		✓
4	Is this partnership subject to the consolidated audit procedures of sections 6221 through 6233? If "Yes," see **Designation of Tax Matters Partner** below		✓
5	Does this partnership meet **all** the requirements shown in the instructions for **Question 5?**		✓
6	Does this partnership have any foreign partners?		✓
7	Is this partnership a publicly traded partnership as defined in section 469(k)(2)?		✓
8	Has this partnership filed, or is it required to file, **Form 8264,** Application for Registration of a Tax Shelter? .		✓
9	At any time during the tax year, did the partnership have an interest in or a signature or other authority over a financial account in a foreign country (such as a bank account, securities account, or other financial account)? (See the instructions for exceptions and filing requirements for form TD F 90-22.1.) If "Yes," enter the name of the foreign country. ▶		✓
10	Was the partnership the grantor of, or transferor to, a foreign trust which existed during the current tax year, whether or not the partnership or any partner has any beneficial interest in it? If "Yes," you may have to file Forms 3520, 3520-A, or 926		✓
11	Was there a distribution of property or a transfer (for example, by sale or death) of a partnership interest during the tax year? If "Yes," you may elect to adjust the basis of the partnership's assets under section 754 by attaching the statement described under **Elections** on page 5 of the instructions		✓

Designation of Tax Matters Partner (See instructions.)

Enter below the general partner designated as the tax matters partner (TMP) for the tax year of this return:

Name of
designated TMP ▶ _____   Identifying
                                                 number of TMP ▶ _____

Address of
designated TMP ▶ _____

EXHIBIT 5.1 (Continued)

Form 1065 (1991)   Page **3**

Schedule K — Partners' Shares of Income, Credits, Deductions, Etc.

	(a) Distributive share items		(b) Total amount
Income (Loss)	1 Ordinary income (loss) from trade or business activities (page 1, line 22)	1	49,370
	2 Net income (loss) from rental real estate activities *(attach Form 8825)*	2	
	3a Gross income from other rental activities 3a		
	b Less expenses *(attach schedule)* 3b		
	c Net income (loss) from other rental activities	3c	
	4 Portfolio income (loss) (see instructions):		
	a Interest income	4a	
	b Dividend income	4b	150
	c Royalty income	4c	
	d Net short-term capital gain (loss) *(attach Schedule D (Form 1065))*	4d	
	e Net long-term capital gain (loss) *(attach Schedule D (Form 1065))*	4e	
	f Other portfolio income (loss) *(attach schedule)*	4f	
	5 Guaranteed payments to partners	5	25,000
	6 Net gain (loss) under section 1231 (other than due to casualty or theft) *(attach Form 4797)*	6	
	7 Other income (loss) *(attach schedule)*	7	
Deductions	8 Charitable contributions (see instructions) *(attach list)*	8	650
	9 Section 179 expense deduction *(attach Form 4562)*	9	
	10 Deductions related to portfolio income (see instructions) (itemize)	10	
	11 Other deductions *(attach schedule)*	11	
Investment Interest	12a Interest expense on investment debts	12a	
	b (1) Investment income included on lines 4a through 4f above	12b(1)	150
	(2) Investment expenses included on line 10 above	12b(2)	
Credits	13a Credit for income tax withheld	13a	
	b Low-income housing credit (see instructions):		
	(1) From partnerships to which section 42(j)(5) applies for property placed in service before 1990	13b(1)	
	(2) Other than on line 13b(1) for property placed in service before 1990	13b(2)	
	(3) From partnerships to which section 42(j)(5) applies for property placed in service after 1989	13b(3)	
	(4) Other than on line 13b(3) for property placed in service after 1989	13b(4)	
	c Qualified rehabilitation expenditures related to rental real estate activities *(attach Form 3468)*	13c	
	d Credits (other than credits shown on lines 13b and 13c) related to rental real estate activities (see instructions)	13d	
	e Credits related to other rental activities (see instructions)	13e	
	14 Other credits (see instructions)	14	
Self-Employment	15a Net earnings (loss) from self-employment	15a	74,370
	b Gross farming or fishing income	15b	
	c Gross nonfarm income	15c	
Adjustments and Tax Preference items	16a Accelerated depreciation of real property placed in service before 1987	16a	
	b Accelerated depreciation of leased personal property placed in service before 1987	16b	
	c Depreciation adjustment on property placed in service after 1986	16c	
	d Depletion (other than oil and gas)	16d	
	e (1) Gross income from oil, gas, and geothermal properties	16e(1)	
	(2) Deductions allocable to oil, gas, and geothermal properties	16e(2)	
	f Other adjustments and tax preference items *(attach schedule)*	16f	
Foreign Taxes	17a Type of income ▶ .... b Foreign country or U.S. possession ▶		
	c Total gross income from sources outside the U.S. *(attach schedule)*	17c	
	d Total applicable deductions and losses *(attach schedule)*	17d	
	e Total foreign taxes (check one): ▶ ☐ Paid ☐ Accrued	17e	
	f Reduction in taxes available for credit *(attach schedule)*	17f	
	g Other foreign tax information *(attach schedule)*	17g	
Other	18a Total expenditures to which a section 59(e) election may apply	18a	
	b Type of expenditures ▶		
	19 Other items and amounts required to be reported separately to partners (see instructions) *(attach schedule)*		
Analysis	20a Income (loss). Combine lines 1 through 7 in column (b). From the result, subtract the sum of lines 8 through 12a, 17e, and 18a	20a	73,870

b Analysis by type of partner:	(a) Corporate	(b) Individual i. Active	(b) Individual ii. Passive	(c) Partnership	(d) Exempt organization	(e) Nominee/Other
(1) General partners		73,870				
(2) Limited partners						

EXHIBIT 5.1 (Continued)

Form 1065 (1991)   **Page 4**

Caution: *Read the instructions for **Question 5** of Schedule B on page 14 of the instructions before completing Schedules L, M-1, and M-2.*

Schedule L — Balance Sheets

Assets	Beginning of tax year (a)	(b)	End of tax year (c)	(d)
1 Cash		3,455		3,350
2a Trade notes and accounts receivable	7,150		10,990	
b Less allowance for bad debts		7,150		10,990
3 Inventories		18,125		19,225
4 U.S. government obligations				
5 Tax-exempt securities		1,000		1,000
6 Other current assets (attach schedule)				
7 Mortgage and real estate loans				
8 Other investments (attach schedule)		1,000		1,000
9a Buildings and other depreciable assets	15,000		15,000	
b Less accumulated depreciation	4,000	11,000	5,174	9,826
10a Depletable assets				
b Less accumulated depletion				
11 Land (net of any amortization)				
12a Intangible assets (amortizable only)				
b Less accumulated amortization				
13 Other assets (attach schedule)				
14 **Total assets**		41,730		45,391
Liabilities and Capital				
15 Accounts payable		10,180		10,462
16 Mortgages, notes, bonds payable in less than 1 year		4,000		3,600
17 Other current liabilities (attach schedule)				
18 All nonrecourse loans				
19 Mortgages, notes, bonds payable in 1 year or more				7,739
20 Other liabilities (attach schedule)				
21 Partners' capital accounts		27,550		23,590
22 **Total liabilities and capital**		41,730		45,391

Schedule M-1 — Reconciliation of Income per Books With Income per Return

1 Net income per books	48,920	5 Income recorded on books this year not included on Schedule K, lines 1 through 7 (itemize):		
2 Income included on Schedule K, lines 1 through 7, not recorded on books this year (itemize): *Guaranteed Payments*		a Tax-exempt interest $ *50*		50
	25,000	6 Deductions included on Schedule K, lines 1 through 12a, 17e, and 18a, not charged against book income this year (itemize):		
3 Expenses recorded on books this year not included on Schedule K, lines 1 through 12a, 17e, and 18a (itemize):		a Depreciation $		
a Depreciation $				
b Travel and entertainment $				
		7 Total of lines 5 and 6		50
4 Total of lines 1 through 3	73,920	8 Income (loss) (Schedule K, line 20a). Line 4 less line 7		73,870

Schedule M-2 — Analysis of Partners' Capital Accounts

1 Balance at beginning of year	27,550	6 Distributions: a Cash	52,880
2 Capital contributed during year		b Property	
3 Net income per books	48,920	7 Other decreases (itemize):	
4 Other increases (itemize):			
		8 Total of lines 6 and 7	52,880
5 Total of lines 1 through 4	76,470	9 Balance at end of year. Line 5 less line 8	23,590

EXHIBIT 5.1   (Continued)

SCHEDULE K-1 (Form 1065) Department of the Treasury Internal Revenue Service	Partner's Share of Income, Credits, Deductions, Etc. ▶ See separate instructions. For calendar year 1991 or tax year beginning , 1991, and ending , 19	OMB No. 1545-0099 1991

Partner's identifying number ▶ 123-00-6789   Partnership's identifying number ▶ 10-9876543

Partner's name, address, and ZIP code	Partnership's name, address, and ZIP code
Frank W. Able 10 Green Street Anytown, MD 20904	AbleBee Book Store 334 West Main Street Anytown, MD 20904

A Is this partner a general partner? ... ☑ Yes ☐ No

B Partner's share of liabilities (see instructions):
Nonrecourse . . . . . . $ ....
Qualified nonrecourse financing . . $ ....
Other . . . . $ 10,900

C What type of entity is this partner? ▶ Individual

D Is this partner a ☑ domestic or a ☐ foreign partner?

E IRS Center where partnership filed return: Philadelphia

F Enter partner's percentage of: (i) Before change or termination   (ii) End of year
Profit sharing . . . . %   50. %
Loss sharing . . . . %   50. %
Ownership of capital . . . . %   50. %

G(1) Tax shelter registration number . ▶ N/A
(2) Type of tax shelter ▶ ....

H Check here if this partnership is a publicly traded partnership as defined in section 469(k)(2) . . . . . ☐

I Check applicable boxes: (1) ☐ Final K-1 (2) ☐ Amended K-1

J Analysis of partner's capital account:

(a) Capital account at beginning of year	(b) Capital contributed during year	(c) Partner's share of lines 3, 4, and 7, Form 1065, Schedule M-2	(d) Withdrawals and distributions	(e) Capital account at end of year (combine columns (a) through (d))
14,050		24,460	(26,440)	12,070

		(a) Distributive share item		(b) Amount	(c) 1040 filers enter the amount in column (b) on:
Income (Loss)	1	Ordinary income (loss) from trade or business activities . . .	1	24,685	(See Partner's Instructions for Schedule K-1 (Form 1065).)
	2	Net income (loss) from rental real estate activities	2		
	3	Net income (loss) from other rental activities	3		
	4	Portfolio income (loss):			
	a	Interest	4a		Sch. B, Part I, line 1
	b	Dividends	4b	75	Sch. B, Part II, line 5
	c	Royalties	4c		Sch. E, Part I, line 4
	d	Net short-term capital gain (loss)	4d		Sch. D, line 4, col. (f) or (g)
	e	Net long-term capital gain (loss)	4e		Sch. D, line 11, col. (f) or (g)
	f	Other portfolio income (loss) (attach schedule)	4f		(Enter on applicable line of your return.)
	5	Guaranteed payments to partner	5	20,000	(See Partner's Instructions for Schedule K-1 (Form 1065).)
	6	Net gain (loss) under section 1231 (other than due to casualty or theft)	6		
	7	Other income (loss) (attach schedule)	7		(Enter on applicable line of your return.)
Deductions	8	Charitable contributions (see instructions) (attach schedule) .	8	325	Sch. A, line 13 or 14
	9	Section 179 expense deduction	9		(See Partner's Instructions for Schedule K-1 (Form 1065).)
	10	Deductions related to portfolio income (attach schedule) . .	10		
	11	Other deductions (attach schedule)	11		
Investment Interest	12a	Interest expense on investment debts	12a		Form 4952, line 1
	b	(1) Investment income included on lines 4a through 4f above	b(1)	75	(See Partner's Instructions for Schedule K-1 (Form 1065).)
		(2) Investment expenses included on line 10 above	b(2)		
Credits	13a	Credit for income tax withheld	13a		(See Partner's Instructions for Schedule K-1 (Form 1065).)
	b	Low-income housing credit:			
		(1) From section 42(j)(5) partnerships for property placed in service before 1990	b(1)		
		(2) Other than on line 13b(1) for property placed in service before 1990	b(2)		
		(3) From section 42(j)(5) partnerships for property placed in service after 1989	b(3)		Form 8586, line 5
		(4) Other than on line 13b(3) for property placed in service after 1989	b(4)		
	c	Qualified rehabilitation expenditures related to rental real estate activities (see instructions)	13c		
	d	Credits (other than credits shown on lines 13b and 13c) related to rental real estate activities (see instructions)	13d		(See Partner's Instructions for Schedule K-1 (Form 1065).)
	e	Credits related to other rental activities (see instructions) . . .	13e		
	14	Other credits (see instructions)	14		

For Paperwork Reduction Act Notice, see Instructions for Form 1065.   Cat. No. 11394R   Schedule K-1 (Form 1065) 1991

Your Partnership and Taxes

59

EXHIBIT 5.1 (Continued)

Schedule K-1 (Form 1065) 1991 Page **2**

	(a) Distributive share item		(b) Amount	(c) 1040 filers enter the amount in column (b) on:
Self-employment	15a Net earnings (loss) from self-employment	15a	44,685	Sch. SE, Section A or B
	b Gross farming or fishing income.	15b		⎰ See Partner's Instructions for ⎱
	c Gross nonfarm income.	15c		⎱ Schedule K-1 (Form 1065). ⎰
Adjustments and Tax Preference Items	16a Accelerated depreciation of real property placed in service before 1987	16a		
	b Accelerated depreciation of leased personal property placed in service before 1987.	16b		(See Partner's Instructions for Schedule K-1 (Form 1065) and Instructions for Form 6251.)
	c Depreciation adjustment on property placed in service after 1986	16c		
	d Depletion (other than oil and gas)	16d		
	e (1) Gross income from oil, gas, and geothermal properties	e(1)		
	(2) Deductions allocable to oil, gas, and geothermal properties	e(2)		
	f Other adjustments and tax preference items (attach schedule)	16f		
Foreign Taxes	17a Type of income ▶			Form 1116, Check boxes
	b Name of foreign country or U.S. possession ▶			
	c Total gross income from sources outside the U.S. (attach schedule)	17c		Form 1116, Part I
	d Total applicable deductions and losses (attach schedule) . .	17d		
	e Total foreign taxes (check one): ▶ ☐ Paid ☐ Accrued . .	17e		Form 1116, Part II
	f Reduction in taxes available for credit (attach schedule) . .	17f		Form 1116, Part III
	g Other foreign tax information (attach schedule)	17g		See Instructions for Form 1116.
Other	18a Total expenditures to which a section 59(e) election may apply	18a		See Partner's Instructions for Schedule K-1 (Form 1065).
	b Type of expenditures ▶			
	19 Recapture of low-income housing credit:			
	a From section 42(j)(5) partnerships	19a		⎱ Form 8611, line 8
	b Other than on line 19a.	19b		⎰

Supplemental Information

20 Supplemental information required to be reported separately to each partner (attach additional schedules if more space is needed):

.... #25 Tax-exempt Interest — Municipal Bonds ....

....

....

....

....

....

....

....

....

....

....

....

....

....

....

....

EXHIBIT 5.1 (Continued)

SCHEDULE D (Form 1065) Department of the Treasury Internal Revenue Service	**Capital Gains and Losses** ▶ Attach to Form 1065.	OMB No. 1545-0099 19**91**

Name of partnership	Employer identification number

Part I Short-Term Capital Gains and Losses—Assets held one year or less

(a) Description of property (Example, 100 shares 7% preferred of "Z" Co.)	(b) Date acquired (month, day, year)	(c) Date sold (month, day, year)	(d) Sales price (see instructions)	(e) Cost or other basis (see instructions)	(f) Gain (loss) ((d) minus (e))
1					

2 Short-term capital gain from installment sales from Form 6252, line 22 or 30 . . . . | **2** |
3 Partnership's share of net short-term capital gain (loss), including specially allocated short-term capital gains (losses), from other partnerships and from fiduciaries . . . . | **3** |
4 Net short-term capital gain (loss). Combine lines 1 through 3. Enter here and on Form 1065, Schedule K, line 4d or 7 . . . . | **4** |

Part II Long-Term Capital Gains and Losses—Assets held more than one year

5					

6 Long-term capital gain from installment sales from Form 6252, line 22 or 30 . . . . | **6** |
7 Partnership's share of net long-term capital gain (loss), including specially allocated long-term capital gains (losses), from other partnerships and from fiduciaries . . . . | **7** |
8 Capital gain distributions . . . . | **8** |
9 Net long-term capital gain (loss). Combine lines 5 through 8. Enter here and on Form 1065, Schedule K, line 4e or 7 . . . . | **9** |

General Instructions

(Section references are to the Internal Revenue Code.)

Purpose of Schedule

Use Schedule D (Form 1065) to report sales or exchanges of capital assets, except capital gains (losses) that are specially allocated to any partners.

Specially allocated capital gains (losses) received by the partnership as a partner in other partnerships and from fiduciaries are to be entered on Schedule D, line 3 or 7, whichever applies. Capital gains (losses) of the partnership that are specially allocated to partners should be entered directly on line 4d, 4e, or 7 of Schedules K and K-1, whichever applies. Do not include these amounts on Schedule D. See **How Income Is Shared Among Partners** in the General Instructions for Schedules K and K-1 of the Instructions for Form 1065 for more information.

General Information

To report sales or exchanges of property other than capital assets, including the sale or exchange of property used in a trade or business and involuntary conversions (other than casualties and thefts), see **Form 4797,** Sales of Business Property, and related instructions. If property is involuntarily converted because of a casualty or theft, use **Form 4684,** Casualties and Thefts.

For amounts received from an installment sale, the holding period rule in effect in the year of sale will determine the treatment of the amounts received as long-term or short-term capital gain.

Report every sale or exchange of property in detail, even though there is no gain or loss.

For more information, see **Pub. 544,** Sales and Other Dispositions of Assets.

What Are Capital Assets?

Each item of property the partnership held (whether or not connected with its trade or business) is a capital asset **except:**

1. Assets that can be inventoried or property held mainly for sale to customers.

2. Depreciable or real property used in the trade or business.

3. Certain copyrights; literary, musical, or artistic compositions; letters or memorandums; or similar property.

4. Accounts or notes receivable acquired in the ordinary course of trade or business for services rendered or from the sale of property described in 1 above.

5. U.S. Government publications, including the Congressional Record, that the partnership received from the government, other than by purchase at the normal sales price, or that the partnership got from another taxpayer who had received it in a similar way, if the partnership's basis is determined by reference to the previous owner.

Exchange of "Like-Kind" Property

Use **Form 8824,** Like-Kind Exchanges, to report an exchange of like-kind property. Also report the exchange on Schedule D or on Form 4797, whichever applies. Complete and attach a Form 8824 to the partnership's return for each exchange. The partnership must report an exchange of business or investment property for "like-kind" property even if no gain or loss on the property is recognized.

If Schedule D is used to report a like-kind exchange, write **"From Form 8824"** on the appropriate line (line 1 or 5, column (a)). Skip columns (b) through (e) and enter the gain or loss, if any, from Form 8824 in column (f). If an exchange was made with a related party, write **"Related Party Like-Kind Exchange"** in the top margin of Schedule D. See Form 8824 and its instructions for details.

For Paperwork Reduction Act Notice, see page 1 of the instructions for Form 1065.   Cat. No. 11393G   **Schedule D (Form 1065) 1991**

EXHIBIT 5.1 (Continued)

Items for Special Treatment and Special Cases

The following items may require special treatment:

- Transactions by a securities dealer.
- Bonds and other debt instruments.
- Certain real estate subdivided for sale that may be considered a capital asset.
- Gain on the sale of depreciable property to a more than 50%-owned entity, or to a trust in which the partnership is a beneficiary, is treated as ordinary gain.
- Liquidating distributions from a corporation. See **Pub. 550,** Investment Income and Expenses.
- Gain on disposition of stock in an Interest-Charge Domestic International Sales Corporation or a Foreign Sales Corporation.
- Gain or loss on options to buy or sell, including closing transactions.
- Transfer of property to a foreign corporation as paid-in surplus or as a contribution to capital, or to a foreign trust or partnership.
- Transfer of property to a partnership that would be treated as an investment company if the partnership were incorporated.
- Transfer of property to a political organization if the fair market value of the property exceeds the partnership's adjusted basis in such property.
- Any loss on the disposition of converted wetland or highly erodible cropland that is first used for farming after March 1, 1986, is reported as a long-term capital loss on Schedule D, but any gain on such a disposition is reported as ordinary income on Form 4797. See section 1257 for details.
- Conversion of a general partnership interest into a limited partnership interest in the same partnership. See Rev. Rul. 84-52, 1984-1 C.B. 157.
- Transfer of partnership assets and liabilities to a newly formed partnership in exchange for all of its stock. See Rev. Rul. 84-111, 1984-2 C.B. 88.
- Contribution of limited partnership interests in exchange for limited partnership interests in another partnership. See Rev. Rul. 84-115, 1984-2 C.B. 118.
- Disposition of foreign investment in a U.S. real property interest. See section 897.
- Any loss from a sale or exchange of property between the partnership and certain related persons is not allowed, except for distributions in complete liquidation of a corporation. See sections 267 and 707(b) for details.
- Any loss from securities that are capital assets that become worthless during the year is treated as a loss from the sale or exchange of a capital asset on the last day of the tax year.
- Gain from the sale or exchange of stock in a collapsible corporation is not a capital gain. See section 341.

- Any loss from a wash sale of stock or securities (including contracts or options to acquire or sell stock or securities) cannot be deducted unless the partnership is a dealer in stock or securities and the loss was sustained in a transaction made in the ordinary course of the partnership's trade or business. A wash sale occurs if the partnership acquires (by purchase or exchange), or has a contract or option to acquire, substantially identical stock or securities within 30 days before or after the date of the sale or exchange. See section 1091 for more information.
- Gains and losses from section 1256 contracts and straddles are reported on **Form 6781,** Gains and Losses From Section 1256 Contracts and Straddles.

If there are limited partners, see section 1256(e)(4) for the limitation on losses from hedging transactions.

- Gains from the sale of property (other than publicly traded stock or securities) for which any payment is to be received in a tax year after the year of sale must be reported using the installment method on **Form 6252,** Installment Sale Income, unless the partnership elects to report the entire gain in the year of sale. The partnership should also use Form 6252 if it received a payment this year from a sale made in an earlier year on the installment method.

If the partnership wants to elect out of the installment method for installment gain that **is not** specially allocated among the partners, it must do the following on a timely filed return (including extensions):

1. Report the full amount of the gain on Schedule D.

2. If the partnership received a note or other obligation and is reporting it at less than face value (including all contingent obligations), state that fact in the margin, enter the face amount of the note or other obligation, and give the percentage of valuation.

If the partnership wants to elect out of the installment method for installment gain that **is** specially allocated among the partners, it must do the following on a timely filed return (including extensions):

1. For a **short-term capital gain,** report the full amount of the gain on Schedule K, line 4d or 7.

For a **long-term capital gain,** report the full amount of the gain on Schedule K, line 4e or 7.

2. Enter each partner's share of the full amount of the gain on Schedule K-1, line 4d, 4e, or 7, whichever applies.

3. If the partnership received a note or other obligation and is reporting it at less than face value (including all contingent obligations), attach a statement to Form 1065 that states that fact. Also show on the statement the face amount of the note or other obligation and give the percentage of valuation. Label the statement "Specially Allocated Capital Gains from Electing Out of the Installment Method."

If the partnership received more than one note or obligation, list the amounts separately.

Specific Instructions
Column (c)—Date Sold
Be sure to use the trade date, and not the settlement date, as the date sold for year-end stock sales made on an established market.

Column (d)—Sales Price
Enter in this column either the gross sales price or the net sales price from the sale. On sales of stocks and bonds, report the gross amount as reported to the partnership by the partnership's broker on Form 1099-B or similar statement. However, if the broker advised the partnership that gross proceeds (gross sales price) less commissions and option premiums were reported to the IRS, enter that net amount in column (d).

Column (e)—Cost or Other Basis
In general, the cost or other basis is the cost of the property plus purchase commissions and improvements and minus depreciation, amortization, and depletion. If the partnership got the property in a tax-free exchange, involuntary conversion, or wash sale of stock, it may not be able to use the actual cash cost as the basis. If the partnership does not use cash cost, attach an explanation of the basis.

When selling stock, adjust the basis by subtracting all the stock-related nontaxable distributions received before the sale. This includes nontaxable distributions from utility company stock and mutual funds. Also adjust the basis for any stock splits or stock dividends.

If a charitable contribution deduction is passed through to a partner because of a sale of property to a charitable organization, the adjusted basis for determining gain from the sale is an amount that has the same ratio to the adjusted basis as the amount realized has to the fair market value.

See section 852(f) for the treatment of certain load charges incurred in acquiring stock in a mutual fund with a reinvestment right.

If the gross sales price is reported in column (d), increase the cost or other basis by any expense of sale such as broker's fee, commission, or option premium before making an entry in column (e).

For more information, see **Pub. 551,** Basis of Assets.

Lines 3 and 7—Capital Gains and Losses From Other Partnerships and Fiduciaries
See the Schedule K-1 or other information supplied to you by the other partnership or fiduciary.

Line 8—Capital Gain Distributions
On line 8, report as capital gain distributions **(a)** capital gain dividends; and **(b)** the partnership's share of the undistributed capital gain from a regulated investment company. (Also see the instructions for Schedule K-1, line 20, item **(1),** in the Instructions for Form 1065.)

APPENDIX I

THE UNIFORM PARTNERSHIP ACT

The *Uniform Partnership Act* (UPA), 7 U.L.A. 1, approved in 1914, was patterned after the English Partnership Act of 1890. With some local variations, the UPA has been adopted by most of the 50 states, the District of Columbia, and a number of U.S. territories.

CONTENTS

PART I

PRELIMINARY PROVISIONS

U.P.A. § 1. Name of Act

This Act may be cited as Uniform Partnership Act.

U.P.A. § 2. Definition of Terms

In this Act, "Court" includes every court and judge having jurisdiction in the case.
   "Business" includes every trade, occupation, or profession.
   "Person" includes individuals, partnerships, corporations, and other associations.
   "Bankrupt" includes bankrupt under the Federal Bankruptcy Act or insolvent under any state insolvent Act.
   "Conveyance" includes every assignment, lease, mortgage, or encumbrance.
   "Real property" includes land and any interest or estate in land.

U.P.A. § 3. Interpretation of Knowledge and Notice

(1)   A person has "knowledge" of a fact within the meaning of this Act not only when he has actual knowledge thereof, but also when he has knowledge of such other facts as in the circumstances shows bad faith.

(2)   A person has "notice" of a fact within the meaning of this Act when the person who claims the benefit of the notice:

   (a)   States the fact to such person, or

   (b)   Delivers through the mail, or by other means of communication, a written statement of the fact to such person or to a proper person at his place of business or residence.

U.P.A. § 4. Rules of Construction

(1)   The rule that statutes in derogation of the common law are to be strictly construed shall have no application to this Act.

(2)   The law of estoppel shall apply under this Act.

(3)   The law of agency shall apply under this Act.

(4)   This Act shall be so interpreted and construed as to effect its general purpose to make uniform the law of those states which enact it.

(5)   This Act shall not be construed so as to impair the obligations of any contract existing when the Act goes into effect, nor to affect any action or proceedings begun or right accrued before this Act takes effect.

U.P.A. § 5. Rules for Cases Not Provided for in This Act

In any case not provided for in this Act the rules of law and equity, including the law merchant, shall govern.

PART II

NATURE OF PARTNERSHIP

U.P.A. § 6. Partnership Defined

(1)   A partnership is an association of two or more persons to carry on as co-owners a business for profit.

(2)   But any association formed under any other statute of this state, or any statute adopted by authority, other than the authority of this state, is not a partnership under this Act, unless such association would have been a partnership in this state prior to the adoption of this Act; but this Act shall apply to limited partnerships except in so far as the statutes relating to such partnerships are inconsistent herewith.

U.P.A. § 7. Rules for Determining the Existence of a Partnership

In determining whether a partnership exists, these rules shall apply:

(1)   Except as provided in § 16 persons who are not partners as to each other are not partners as to third persons.

(2)   Joint tenancy, tenancy in common, tenancy by the entireties, joint property, common property, or part ownership does not of itself establish a partnership, whether such co-owners do or do not share any profits made by the use of the property.

(3)   The sharing of gross returns does not of itself establish a partnership, whether or not the persons sharing them have a joint or common right or interest in any property from which returns are derived.

(4)   The receipt by a person of a share of the profits of a business is prima facie evidence that he is a partner in the business, but no such inference shall be drawn if such profits were received in payment:

(a)   As a debt by installments or otherwise,

(b)   As wages of an employee or rent to a landlord,

(c)   As an annuity to a widow or representative of a deceased partner,

(d)   As interest on a loan, though the amount of payment vary with the profits of the business,

(e)   As the consideration for the sale of good-will of a business or other property by installments or otherwise.

U.P.A. § 8. Partnership Property

(1)   All property originally brought into the partnership stock or subsequently acquired by purchase or otherwise, on account of the partnership, is partnership property.

(2)   Unless the contrary intention appears, property acquired with partnership funds is partnership property.

(3) Any estate in real property may be acquired in the partnership name. Title so acquired can be conveyed only in the partnership name.

(4) A conveyance to a partnership in the partnership name, though without words of inheritance, passes the entire estate of the grantor unless a contrary intent appears.

PART III

RELATIONS OF PARTNERS TO PERSONS DEALING WITH THE PARTNERSHIP

U.P.A. § 9. Partner Agent of Partnership as to Partnership Business

(1) Every partner is agent of the partnership for the purpose of its business, and the act of every partner, including the execution in the partnership name of any instrument, for apparently carrying on in the usual way the business of the partnership of which he is a member binds the partnership, unless the partner so acting has in fact no authority to act for the partnership in the particular matter, and the person with whom he is dealing has knowledge of the fact that he has no such authority.

(2) An act of a partner which is not apparently for the carrying on of the business of the partnership in the usual way does not bind the partnership unless authorized by the other partners.

(3) Unless authorized by the other partners or unless they have abandoned the business, one or more but less than all the partners have no authority to:

(a) Assign the partnership property in trust for creditors or on the assignee's promise to pay the debts of the partnership,

(b) Dispose of the good-will of the business,

(c) Do any other act which would make it impossible to carry on the ordinary business of a partnership,

(d) Confess a judgment,

(e) Submit a partnership claim or liability in arbitration or reference.

(4) No act of a partner in contravention of a restriction on authority shall bind the partnership to persons having knowledge of the restriction.

U.P.A. § 10. Conveyance of Real Property of the Partnership

(1) Where title to real property is in the partnership name, any partner may convey title to such property by a conveyance executed in the partnership name; but the partnership may recover such property unless the partner's act binds the partnership under the provisions of paragraph (1) of § 9 or unless such property has been conveyed by the grantee or a person claiming through such grantee to a holder for value without knowledge that the partner, in making the conveyance, has exceeded his authority.

(2) Where title to real property is in the name of the partnership, a conveyance executed by a partner, in his own name, passes the equitable interest of the

partnership, provided the act is one within the authority of the partner under the provisions of paragraph (1) of § 9.

(3) Where title to real property is in the name of one or more but not all the partners, and the record does not disclose the right of the partnership, the partners in whose name the title stands may convey title to such property, but the partnership may recover such property if the partners' act does not bind the partnership under the provisions of paragraph (1) of § 9, unless the purchaser or his assignee, is a holder for value, without knowledge.

(4) Where the title to real property is in the name of one or more or all the partners, or in a third person in trust for the partnership, a conveyance executed by a partner in the partnership name, or in his own name, passes the equitable interest of the partnership, provided the act is one within the authority of the partner under the provisions of paragraph (1) of § 9.

(5) Where the title to real property is in the names of all the partners a conveyance executed by all the partners passes all their rights in such property.

U.P.A. § 11. Partnership Bound by Admission of Partner

An admission or representation made by any partner concerning partnership affairs within the scope of his authority as conferred by this Act is evidence against the partnership.

U.P.A. § 12. Partnership Charged with Knowledge of or Notice to Partner

Notice to any partner of any matter relating to partnership affairs, and the knowledge of the partner acting in the particular matter, acquired while a partner or then present to his mind, and the knowledge of any other partner who reasonably could and should have communicated it to the acting partner, operate as notice to or knowledge of the partnership, except in the case of a fraud on the partnership committed by or with the consent of that partner.

U.P.A. § 13. Partnership Bound by Partner's Wrongful Act

Where, by any wrongful act or omission of any partner acting in the ordinary course of the business of the partnership or with the authority of his co-partners, loss or injury is caused to any person, not being a partner in the partnership, or any penalty is incurred, the partnership is liable therefor to the same extent as the partner so acting or omitting to act.

U.P.A. § 14. Partnership Bound by Partner's Breach of Trust

The partnership is bound to make good the loss:

(a) Where one partner acting within the scope of his apparent authority receives money or property of a third person and misapplies it; and

(b) Where the partnership in the course of its business receives money or property of a third person and the money or property so received is misapplied by any partner while it is in the custody of the partnership.

U.P.A. § 15. Nature of Partner's Liability

All partners are liable

(a) Jointly and severally for everything chargeable to the partnership under §§ 13 and 14.

(b) Jointly for all other debts and obligations of the partnership; but any partner may enter into a separate obligation to perform a partnership contract.

U.P.A. § 16. Partner by Estoppel

(1) When a person, by words spoken or written or by conduct, represents himself, or consents to another representing him to any one, as a partner in an existing partnership or with one or more persons not actual partners, he is liable to any such person to whom such representation has been made, who has, on the faith of such representation, given credit to the actual or apparent partnership, and if he has made such representation or consented to its being made in a public manner he is liable to such person, whether the representation has or has not been made or communicated to such person so giving credit by or with the knowledge of the apparent partner making the representation or consenting to its being made.

(a) When a partnership liability results, he is liable as though he were an actual member of the partnership.

(b) When no partnership liability results, he is liable jointly with the other persons, if any, so consenting to the contract or representation as to incur liability, otherwise separately.

(2) When a person has been thus represented to be a partner in an existing partnership, or with one or more persons not actual partners, he is an agent of the persons consenting to such representation to bind them to the same extent and in the same manner as though he were a partner in fact, with respect to persons who rely upon the representation. Where all the members of the existing partnership consent to the representation, a partnership act or obligation results; but in all other cases it is the joint act or obligation of the person acting and the persons consenting to the representation.

U.P.A. § 17. Liability of Incoming Partner

A person admitted as a partner into an existing partnership is liable for all the obligations of the partnership arising before his admission as though he had been a partner when such obligations were incurred, except that this liability shall be satisfied only out of partnership property.

PART IV

RELATIONS OF PARTNERS TO ONE ANOTHER

U.P.A. § 18. Rules Determining Rights and Duties of Partners

The rights and duties of the partners in relation to the partnership shall be determined, subject to any agreement between them, by the following rules:

(a)   Each partner shall be repaid his contributions, whether by way of capital or advances to the partnership property and share equally in the profits and surplus remaining after all liabilities, including those to partners, are satisfied; and must contribute towards the losses, whether of capital or otherwise, sustained by the partnership according to his share in the profits.

(b)   The partnership must indemnify every partner in respect of payments made and personal liabilities reasonably incurred by him in the ordinary and proper conduct of its business, or for the preservation of its business or property.

(c)   A partner, who in aid of the partnership makes any payment or advance beyond the amount of capital which he agreed to contribute, shall be paid interest from the date of the payment or advance.

(d)   A partner shall receive interest on the capital contributed by him only from the date when repayment should be made.

(e)   All partners have equal rights in the management and conduct of the partnership business.

(f)   No partner is entitled to remuneration for acting in the partnership business, except that a surviving partner is entitled to reasonable compensation for his services in winding up the partnership affairs.

(g)   No person can become a member of a partnership without the consent of all the partners.

(h)   Any difference arising as to ordinary matters connected with the partnership business may be decided by a majority of the partners; but no act in contravention of any agreement between the partners may be done rightfully without the consent of all the partners.

U.P.A. § 19. Partnership Books

The partnership books shall be kept, subject to any agreement between the partners, at the principal place of business of the partnership, and every partner shall at all times have access to and may inspect and copy any of them.

U.P.A. § 20. Duty of Partners to Render Information

Partners shall render on demand true and full information of all things affecting the partnership to any partner or the legal representative of any deceased partner or partner under legal disability.

U.P.A. § 21. Partner Accountable as a Fiduciary

(1)   Every partner must account to the partnership for any benefit, and hold as trustee for it any profits derived by him without the consent of the other partners from any transaction connected with the formation, conduct, or liquidation of the partnership or from any use by him of its property.

(2)   This section applies also to the representatives of a deceased partner engaged in the liquidation of the affairs of the partnership as the personal representatives of the last surviving partner.

U.P.A. § 22. Right to an Account

Any partner shall have the right to a formal account as to partnership affairs:

    (a)   If he is wrongfully excluded from the partnership business or possession of its property by his co-partners,

    (b)   If the right exists under the terms of any agreement,

    (c)   As provided by § 21,

    (d)   Whenever other circumstances render it just and reasonable.

U.P.A. § 23. Continuation of Partnership Beyond Fixed Term

    (1)   When a partnership for a fixed term or particular undertaking is continued after the termination of such term or particular undertaking without any express agreement, the rights and duties of the partners remain the same as they were at such termination, so far as is consistent with a partnership at will.

    (2)   A continuation of the business by the partners or such of them as habitually acted therein during the term, without any settlement or liquidation of the partnership affairs, is prima facie evidence of a continuation of the partnership.

PART V

PROPERTY RIGHTS OF A PARTNER

U.P.A. § 24. Extent of Property Rights of a Partner

The property rights of a partner are (1) his rights in specific partnership property, (2) his interest in the partnership, and (3) his right to participate in the management.

U.P.A. § 25. Nature of a Partner's Right in Specific Partnership Property

    (1)   A partner is co-owner with his partners of specific partnership property holding as a tenant in partnership.

    (2)   The incidents of this tenancy are such that:

    (a)   A partner, subject to the provisions of this Act and to any agreement between the partners, has an equal right with his partners to possess specific partnership property for partnership purposes; but he has no right to possess such property for any other purpose without the consent of his partners.

    (b)   A partner's right in specific partnership property is not assignable except in connection with the assignment of rights of all the partners in the same property.

    (c)   A partner's right in specific partnership property is not subject to attachment or execution, except on a claim against the partnership. When partnership property is attached for a partnership debt the partners, or any of them, or the representatives of a deceased partner, cannot claim any right under the homestead or exemption laws.

(d)   On the death of a partner his right in specific partnership property vests in the surviving partner or partners, except where the deceased was the last surviving partner, when his right in such property vests in his legal representative. Such surviving partner or partners, or the legal representative of the last surviving partner, has no right to possess the partnership property for any but a partnership purpose.

(e)   A partner's right in specific partnership property is not subject to dower, curtesy, or allowances to widows, heirs, or next of kin.

U.P.A. § 26. Nature of Partner's Interest in the Partnership

A partner's interest in the partnership is his share of the profits and surplus, and the same is personal property.

U.P.A. § 27. Assignment of Partner's Interest

(1)   A conveyance by a partner of his interest in the partnership does not of itself dissolve the partnership, nor, as against the other partners in the absence of agreement, entitle the assignee, during the continuance of the partnership to interfere in the management or administration of the partnership business or affairs, or to require any information or account of partnership transactions, or to inspect the partnership books; but it merely entitles the assignee to receive in accordance with his contract the profits to which the assigning partner would otherwise be entitled.

(2)   In case of a dissolution of the partnership, the assignee is entitled to receive his assignor's interest and may require an account from the date only of the last account agreed to by all the partners.

U.P.A § 28. Partner's Interest Subject to Charging Order

(1)   On due application to a competent court by any judgment creditor of a partner, the court which entered the judgment, order, or decree, or any other court, may charge the interest of the debtor partner with payment of the unsatisfied amount of such judgment debt with interest thereon; and may then or later appoint a receiver of his share of the profits, and of any other money due or to fall due to him in respect of the partnership, and make all other orders, directions, accounts and inquiries which the debtor partner might have made, or which the circumstances of the case may require.

(2)   The interest charged may be redeemed at any time before foreclosure, or in case of a sale being directed by the court may be purchased without thereby causing a dissolution:

(a)   With separate property, by any one or more of the partners, or

(b)   With partnership property, by any one or more of the partners with the consent of all the partners whose interests are not so charged or sold.

(3)   Nothing in this Act shall be held to deprive a partner of his right, if any, under the exemption laws, as regards his interest in the partnership.

PART VI

DISSOLUTION AND WINDING UP

U.P.A. § 29. Dissolution Defined

The dissolution of a partnership is the change in the relation of the partners caused by any partner ceasing to be associated in the carrying on as distinguished from the winding up of the business.

U.P.A. § 30. Partnership Not Terminated by Dissolution

On dissolution the partnership is not terminated, but continues until the winding up of partnership affairs is completed.

U.P.A. § 31. Causes of Dissolution

Dissolution is caused:

(1) Without violation of the agreement between the partners,

(a) By the termination of the definite term or particular undertaking specified in the agreement,

(b) By the express will of any partner when no definite term or particular undertaking is specified,

(c) By the express will of all the partners who have not assigned their interests or suffered them to be charged for their separate debts, either before or after the termination of any specified term or particular undertaking,

(d) By the expulsion of any partner from the business bona fide in accordance with such a power conferred by the agreement between the partners;

(2) In contravention of the agreement between the partners, where the circumstances do not permit a dissolution under any other provision of this section, by the express will of any partner at any time;

(3) By any event which makes it unlawful for the business of the partnership to be carried on or for the members to carry it on in partnership;

(4) By the death of any partner;

(5) By the bankruptcy of any partner or the partnership;

(6) By decree of court under § 32.

U.P.A. § 32. Dissolution by Decree of Court

(1) On application by or for a partner the court shall decree a dissolution whenever:

(a) A partner has been declared a lunatic in any judicial proceeding or is shown to be of unsound mind,

(b) A partner becomes in any other way incapable of performing his part of the partnership contract,

(c)   A partner has been guilty of such conduct as tends to affect prejudicially the carrying on of the business,

(d)   A partner wilfully or persistently commits a breach of the partnership agreement, or otherwise so conducts himself in matters relating to the partnership business that it is not reasonably practicable to carry on the business in partnership with him,

(e)   The business of the partnership can only be carried on at a loss,

(f)   Other circumstances render a dissolution equitable.

(2)   On the application of the purchaser of a partner's interest under §§ 27 and 28:

(a)   After the termination of the specified term or particular undertaking,

(b)   At any time if the partnership was a partnership at will when the interest was assigned or when the charging order was issued.

U.P.A. § 33. General Effect of Dissolution on Authority of Partner

Except so far as may be necessary to wind up partnership affairs or to complete transactions begun but not then finished, dissolution terminates all authority of any partner to act for the partnership:

(1)   With respect to the partners,

(a)   When the dissolution is not by the act, bankruptcy or death of a partner; or

(b)   When the dissolution is such act, bankruptcy or death of a partner, in cases where § 34 so requires.

(2)   With respect to persons not partners, as declared in § 35.

U.P.A. § 34. Right of Partner to Contribution from Co-Partners after Dissolution

Where the dissolution is caused by the act, death or bankruptcy of a partner, each partner is liable to his co-partners for his share of any liability created by any partner acting for the partnership as if the partnership had not been dissolved unless:

(a)   The dissolution being by act of any partner, the partner acting for the partnership had knowledge of the dissolution, or

(b)   The dissolution being by the death or bankruptcy of a partner, the partner acting for the partnership had knowledge or notice of the death or bankruptcy.

U.P.A. § 35. Power of Partner to Bind Partnership to Third Persons after Dissolution

(1)   After dissolution a partner can bind the partnership except as provided in paragraph (3):

(a)   By any act appropriate for winding up partnership affairs or completing transactions unfinished at dissolution;

(b)   By any transaction which would bind the partnership if dissolution had not taken place, provided the other party to the transaction

---

(I) Had extended credit to the partnership prior to dissolution and had no knowledge or notice of the dissolution; or

(II) Though he had not so extended credit, had nevertheless known of the partnership prior to dissolution, and, having no knowledge or notice of the dissolution, the fact of dissolution had not been advertised in a newspaper of general circulation in the place (or in each place if more than one) at which the partnership business was regularly carried on.

(2) The liability of a partner under paragraph (1b) shall be satisfied out of partnership assets alone when such partner had been prior to dissolution:

(a) Unknown as a partner to the person with whom the contract is made; and

(b) So far unknown and inactive in partnership affairs that the business reputation of the partnership could not be said to have been in any degree due to his connection with it.

(3) The partnership is in no case bound by any act of a partner after dissolution:

(a) Where the partnership is dissolved because it is unlawful to carry on the business, unless the act is appropriate for winding up partnership affairs; or

(b) Where the partner has become bankrupt; or

(c) Where the partner has no authority to wind up partnership affairs; except by a transaction with one who

(I) Had extended credit to the partnership prior to dissolution and had no knowledge or notice of his want of authority; or

(II) Had not extended credit to the partnership prior to dissolution, and, having no knowledge or notice of his want of authority, the fact of his want of authority has not been advertised in the manner provided for advertising the fact of dissolution in Paragraph (1bII).

(4) Nothing in this section shall affect the liability under § 16 of any person who after dissolution represents himself or consents to another representing him as a partner in a partnership engaged in carrying on business.

U.P.A. § 36. Effect of Dissolution on Partner's Existing Liability

(1) The dissolution of the partnership does not of itself discharge the existing liability of any partner.

(2) A partner is discharged from any existing liability upon dissolution of the partnership by an agreement to that effect between himself, the partnership creditor and the person or partnership continuing the business; and such agreement may be inferred from the course of dealing between the creditor having knowledge of the dissolution and the person or partnership continuing the business.

(3) Where a person agrees to assume the existing obligations of a dissolved partnership, the partners whose obligations have been assumed shall be discharged from any liability to any creditor of the partnership who, knowing of the agreement, consents to a material alteration in the nature or time of payment of such obligation.

(4) The individual property of a deceased partner shall be liable for all obligations of the partnership incurred while he was a partner but subject to the prior payment of his separate debts.

U.P.A. § 37. Right to Wind Up

Unless otherwise agreed the partners who have not wrongfully dissolved the partnership or the legal representative of the last surviving partner, not bankrupt, has the right to wind up the partnership affairs; provided, however, that any partner, his legal representative or his assignee, upon cause shown, may obtain winding up by the court.

U.P.A. § 38. Rights of Partners to Application of Partnership Property

(1)   When dissolution is caused in any way, except in contravention of the partnership agreement, each partner as against his co-partners and all persons claiming through them in respect of their interests in the partnership, unless otherwise agreed, may have the partnership property applied to discharge its liabilities, and the surplus applied to pay in cash the net amount owing to the respective partners. But if dissolution is caused by expulsion of a partner, bona fide under the partnership agreement and if the expelled partner is discharged from all partnership liabilities, either by payment or agreement under § 36(2), he shall receive in cash only the net amount due him from the partnership.

(2)   When dissolution is caused in contravention of the partnership agreement the rights of the partners shall be as follows:

(a)   Each partner who has not caused dissolution wrongfully shall have:

(I)   All the rights specified in paragraph (1) of this section, and

(II)   The right, as against each partner who has caused the dissolution wrongfully, to damages for breach of the agreement.

(b)   The partners who have not caused the dissolution wrongfully, if they all desire to continue the business in the same name, either by themselves or jointly with others, may do so, during the agreed term for the partnership and for that purpose may possess the partnership property, provided they secure the payment by bond approved by the court, or pay to any partner who has caused the dissolution wrongfully, the value of his interest in the partnership at the dissolution, less any damages recoverable under clause (2aII) of the section, and in like manner indemnify him against all present or future partnership liabilities.

(c)   A partner who has caused the dissolution wrongfully shall have:

(I)   If the business is not continued under the provisions of paragraph (2b) all the rights of a partner under paragraph (1), subject to clause (2aII), of this section,

(II)   If the business is continued under paragraph (2b) of this section the right as against his co-partners and all claiming through them in respect of their interests in the partnership, to have the value of his interest in the partnership, less any damages caused to his co-partners by the dissolution, ascertained and paid him in cash, or the payment secured by bond approved by the court, and to be released from all existing liabilities of the partnership; but in ascertaining the value of the partner's interest the value of the goodwill of the business shall not be considered.

U.P.A. § 39. Rights Where Partnership Is Dissolved for Fraud or Misrepresentation

Where a partnership contract is rescinded on the ground of the fraud or misrepresentation of one of the parties thereto, the party entitled to rescind is, without prejudice to any other right, entitled:

(a) To a lien on, or a right of retention of, the surplus of the partnership property after satisfying the partnership liabilities to third persons for any sum of money paid by him for the purchase of an interest in the partnership and for any capital or advances contributed by him; and

(b) To stand, after all liabilities to third persons have been satisfied, in the place of the creditors of the partnership for any payments made by him in respect of the partnership liabilities; and

(c) To be indemnified by the person guilty of the fraud or making the representation against all debts and liabilities of the partnership.

U.P.A. § 40. Rules for Distribution

In settling accounts between the partners after dissolution, the following rules shall be observed, subject to any agreement to the contrary:

(a) The assets of the partnership are:

(I) The partnership property,

(II) The contributions of the partners necessary for the payment of all the liabilities specified in clause (b) of this paragraph.

(b) The liabilities of the partnership shall rank in order of payment as follows:

(I) Those owing to creditors other than partners,

(II) Those owing to partners other than for capital and profits,

(III) Those owing to partners in respect of capital,

(IV) Those owing to partners in respect of profits.

(c) The assets shall be applied in the order of their declaration in clause (a) of this paragraph to the satisfaction of the liabilities.

(d) The partners shall contribute, as provided by § 18(a) the amount necessary to satisfy the liabilities; but if any, but not all, of the partners are insolvent, or, not being subject to process, refuse to contribute, the other partners shall contribute their share of the liabilities, and, in the relative proportions in which they share the profits, the additional amount necessary to pay the liabilities.

(e) An assignee for the benefit of creditors or any person appointed by the court shall have the right to enforce the contributions specified in clause (d) of this paragraph.

(f) Any partner or his legal representative shall have the right to enforce the contributions specified in clause (d) of this paragraph, to the extent of the amount which he has paid in excess of his share of the liability.

(g) The individual property of a deceased partner shall be liable for the contributions specified in clause (d) of this paragraph.

(h) When partnership property and the individual properties of the partners are in possession of a court for distribution, partnership creditors shall have priority on partnership property and separate creditors on individual property, saving the rights of lien or secured creditors as heretofore.

(i)   Where a partner has become bankrupt or his estate is insolvent the claims against his separate property shall rank in the following order:

(I)   Those owing to separate creditors,

(II) Those owing to partnership creditors,

(III) Those owing to partners by way of contribution.

U.P.A. § 41. Liability of Persons Continuing the Business in Certain Cases

(1)   When any new partner is admitted into an existing partnership or when any partner retires and assigns (or the representative of the deceased partner assigns) his rights in partnership property to two or more of the partners, or to one or more of the partners and one or more third persons, if the business is continued without liquidation of the partnership affairs, creditors of the first or dissolved partnership are also creditors of the partnership so continuing the business.

(2)   When all but one partner retire and assign (or the representative of a deceased partner assigns) their rights in partnership property to the remaining partner, who continues the business without liquidation of partnership affairs, either alone or with others, creditors of the dissolved partnership are also creditors of the person or partnership so continuing the business.

(3)   When any partner retires or dies and the business of the dissolved partnership is continued as set forth in paragraphs (1) and (2) of this section, with the consent of the retired partners or the representative of the deceased partner, but without any assignment of his right in partnership property, rights of creditors of the dissolved partnership and of the creditors of the person or partnership continuing the business shall be as if such assignment had been made.

(4)   When all the partners or their representatives assign their rights in partnership property to one or more third persons who promise to pay the debts and who continue the business of the dissolved partnership, creditors of the dissolved partnership are also creditors of the person or partnership continuing the business.

(5)   When any partner wrongfully causes a dissolution and the remaining partners continue the business under the provisions of § 38(2b), either alone or with others, and without liquidation of the partnership affairs, creditors of the dissolved partnership are also creditors of the person or partnership continuing the business.

(6)   When a partner is expelled and the remaining partners continue the business either alone or with others, without liquidation of the partnership affairs, creditors of the dissolved partnership are also creditors of the person or partnership continuing the business.

(7)   The liability of a third person becoming a partner in the partnership continuing the business, under this section, to the creditors of the dissolved partnership shall be satisfied out of partnership property only.

(8)   When the business of a partnership after dissolution is continued under any conditions set forth in this section the creditors of the dissolved partnership, as against the separate creditors of the retiring or deceased partner or the representative of the deceased partner, have a prior right to any claim of the retired partner or the

representative of the deceased partner against the person or partnership continuing the business, on account of the retired or deceased partner's interest in the dissolved partnership or on account of any consideration promised for such interest or for his right in partnership property.

(9) Nothing in this section shall be held to modify any right of creditors to set aside any assignment on the ground of fraud.

(10) The use by the person or partnership continuing the business of the partnership name, or the name of a deceased partner as part thereof, shall not of itself make the individual property of the deceased partner liable for any debts contracted by such person or partnership.

U.P.A. § 42. Rights of Retiring or Estate of Deceased Partner When the Business Is Continued

When any partner retires or dies, and the business is continued under any of the conditions set forth in § 41(1,2,3,5,6), or § 38(2b), without any settlement of accounts as between him or his estate and the person or partnership continuing the business, unless otherwise agreed, he or his legal representative as against such persons or partnership may have the value of his interest at the date of dissolution ascertained, and shall receive as an ordinary creditor an amount equal to the value of his interest in the dissolved partnership with interest, or, at his option or at the option of his legal representative, in lieu of interest, the profits attributable to the use of his right in the property of the dissolved partnership; provided that the creditors of the dissolved partnership as against the separate creditors, or the representative of the retired or deceased partner, shall have priority on any claim arising under this section, as provided by § 41(8) of this Act.

U.P.A. § 43. Accrual of Actions

The right to an account of his interest shall accrue to any partner or his legal representative, as against the winding up partners or the surviving partners or the person or partnership continuing the business, at the date of dissolution, in the absence of any agreement to the contrary.

PART VII

MISCELLANEOUS PROVISIONS

U.P.A. § 44. When Act Takes Effect

This Act shall take effect on the . . . day of . . . one thousand nine hundred and . . .

U.P.A. § 45. Legislation Repealed

All Acts or parts of Acts inconsistent with this Act are hereby repealed.

APPENDIX II

THE UNIFORM LIMITED PARTNERSHIP ACT

The *Uniform Limited Partnership Act* (ULPA), 8 U.L.A. 1, was approved in 1916 and adopted by New York in 1822. With some local variations, it has been adopted as law by most of the 50 states, the District of Columbia, and a number of U.S. territories. The following version is dated 1976, with 1985 amendments.

In interpreting the ULPA, the courts usually assume two fundamental principles:

First: That a limited (also called "special") partner is a partner in all respects like any other partner, except that to obtain the privilege of a limitation in liability, the limited partner has conformed to the statutory requirements in respect to filing a certificate and refraining from participation in the conduct of the business.

Second: The limited partner, on any failure to follow the requirements in regard to the certificate or any participation in the conduct of partnership business, loses his privileges of limited liability and becomes, as far as those dealing with the business are concerned, in all respects a partner.

LIMITED PARTNERSHIP AGREEMENTS

There are several important concepts to keep in mind when drafting a limited partnership agreement:

1. If you will be making a sweeping offer, you may find that you will need special registration to meet financial market regulations. Check first with your attorney.
2. If you intend to make a multi-state campaign for limited partner investments, you will need to consider registering your limited partnership campaign not only in your own state, but in the other states where you will be soliciting limited partner investments.
3. For partnership aspects not covered by the Uniform Limited Partnership Act, § 1105 states "In any case not provided for in this Act the provisions of the Uniform Partnership Act govern."
4. The "limited liability" of the limited partner is not absolute under all circumstances. For example:

- A general partner who is also a limited partner (which is allowed) can be liable for actions as a general partner (see § 303), or
- A limited partner who participates in the control of the business may be liable to persons who believe that the limited partner is a general partner (also in § 303), or
- A person believing themselves to be a limited partner, but who make the types of contributions to the limited partnership usually attributed to a general partner, may become liable as a general partner when making partnership transactions with third parties (see § 304).

5. And, most importantly of all, most states adopting the Uniform Limited Partnership Act have made modifications to adapt the ULPA to their own statutory situations. Those who have made no or few changes may not have adopted the most current version of the ULPA. And, since the ULPA itself refers to the UPA, as noted in note (3) above, here is another area of difference, depending on how a particular state has made modifications before adoption of the UPA.

Simply stated, the establishment of a limited partnership for the purposes of raising capital for the partnership business activities is complicated, and fraught with numerous legal and regulatory pitfalls. The help of an attorney with experience in the laws and regulations of limited partnerships is essential.

CONTENTS

ARTICLE 1: General Provisions

ARTICLE 2: Formation; Certificate of Limited Partnership

ARTICLE 3: Limited Partners

ARTICLE 4: General Partners

ARTICLE 5: Finance

ARTICLE 6: Distributions and Withdrawal

ARTICLE 7: Assignment of Partnership Interests

ARTICLE 8: Dissolution

ARTICLE 1

GENERAL PROVISIONS

§ 101. Definitions

As used in this Act, unless the context otherwise requires:

(1) "Certificate of limited partnership" means the certificate referred to in § 201, and the certificate as amended or restated.

(2) "Contribution" means any cash, property, services rendered, or a promissory note or other binding obligation to contribute cash or property or to perform services, which a partner contributes to a limited partnership in his capacity as a partner.

(3) "Event of withdrawal of a general partner" means an event that causes a person to cease to be a general partner as provided in § 402.

(4) "Foreign limited partnership" means a partnership formed under the laws of any state other than this State and having as partners one or more general partners and one or more limited partners.

(5) "General partner" means a person who has been admitted to a limited partnership as a general partner in accordance with the partnership agreement and named in the certificate of limited partnership as a general partner.

(6) "Limited partner" means a person who has been admitted to a limited partnership as a limited partner in accordance with the partnership agreement.

(7) "Limited partnership" and "domestic limited partnership" mean a partnership formed by two or more persons under the laws of this State and having one or more general partners and one or more limited partners.

(8) "Partner" means a limited or general partner.

(9) "Partnership agreement" means any valid agreement, written or oral, of the partners as to the affairs of a limited partnership and the conduct of its business.

(10) "Partnership interest" means a partner's share of the profits and losses of a limited partnership and the right to receive distributions of partnership assets.

(11) "Person" means a natural person, partnership, limited partnership (domestic or foreign), trust, estate, association, or corporation.

(12) "State" means a state, territory, or possession of the United States, the District of Columbia, or the Commonwealth of Puerto Rico.

§ 102. Name

The name of each limited partnership as set forth in its certificate of limited partnership:

(1) shall contain without abbreviation the words "limited partnership;"

(2) may not contain the name of a limited partner unless

(i) it is also the name of a general partner or the corporate name of a corporate general partner, or

(ii) the business of the limited partnership had been carried on under that name before the admission of that limited partner;

(3) may not be the same as, or deceptively similar to, the name of any corporation or limited partnership organized under the laws of this State or licensed or registered as a foreign corporation or limited partnership in this State; and

(4) may not contain the following words [here insert prohibited words].

§ 103. Reservation of Name

(a) The exclusive right to the use of a name may be reserved by:

(1) any person intending to organize a limited partnership under this Act and to adopt that name;

(2) any domestic limited partnership or any foreign limited partnership registered in this State which, in either case, intends to adopt that name;

(3) any foreign limited partnership intending to register in this State and adopt that name; and

(4) any person intending to organize a foreign limited partnership and intending to have it registered in this State and adopt that name.

(b)   The reservation shall be made by filing with the Secretary of State an application, executed by the applicant, to reserve a specified name. If the Secretary of State finds that the name is available for use by a domestic or foreign limited partnership, he [or she] shall reserve the name for the exclusive use of the applicant for a period of 120 days. Once having so reserved a name, the same applicant may not again reserve the same name until more than 60 days after the expiration of the last 120-day period for which that applicant reserved that name. The right to the exclusive use of a reserved name may be transferred to any other person by filing in the office of the Secretary of State a notice of the transfer, executed by the applicant for whom the name was reserved and specifying the name and address of the transferee.

§ 104. Specified Office and Agent

Each limited partnership shall continuously maintain in this State:

(1)   an office, which may but need not be a place of its business in this State, at which shall be kept the records required by § 105 to be maintained; and

(2)   an agent for service of process on the limited partnership, which agent must be an individual resident of this State, a domestic corporation, or a foreign corporation authorized to do business in this State.

§ 105. Records to Be Kept

(a)   Each limited partnership shall keep at the office referred to in § 104(1) the following:

(1)   a current list of the full name and last known business address of each partner, separately identifying the general partners (in alphabetical order) and the limited partners (in alphabetical order);

(2)   a copy of the certificate of limited partnership and all certificates of amendment thereto, together with executed copies of any powers of attorney pursuant to which any certificate has been executed;

(3)   copies of the limited partnership's federal, state, and local income tax returns and reports, if any, for the three most recent years;

(4)   copies of any then effective written partnership agreements and of any financial statements of the limited partnership for the three most recent years; and

(5)   unless contained in a written partnership agreement, a writing setting out:

(i)   the amount of cash and a description and statement of the agreed value of the other property or services contributed by each partner and which each partner has agreed to contribute;

(ii)   the times at which or events on the happening of which any additional contributions agreed to be made by each partner are to be made;

(iii)   any right of a partner to receive, or of a general partner to make, distributions to a partner which include a return of all or any part of the partner's contribution; and

(iv)   any events upon the happening of which the limited partnership is to be dissolved and its affairs wound up.

(b)   Records kept under this section are subject to inspection and copying at the reasonable request and at the expense of any partner during ordinary business hours.

§ 106. Nature of Business

A limited partnership may carry on any business that a partnership without limited partners may carry on except [here designate prohibited activities].

§ 107. Business Transactions of Partner with Partnership

Except as provided in the partnership agreement, a partner may lend money to and transact other business with the limited partnership and, subject to other applicable law, has the same rights and obligations with respect thereto as a person who is not a partner.

ARTICLE 2

FORMATION; CERTIFICATE OF LIMITED PARTNERSHIP

§ 201. Certificate of Limited Partnership

(a)   In order to form a limited partnership, a certificate of limited partnership must be executed and filed in the office of the Secretary of State. The certificate shall set forth:

(1)   the name of the limited partnership;

(2)   the address of the office and the name and address of the agent for service of process required to be maintained by § 104;

(3)   the name and the business address of each general partner;

(4)   the latest date upon which the limited partnership is to dissolve; and

(5)   any other matters the general partners determine to include therein.

(b)   A limited partnership is formed at the time of filing of the certificate of limited partnership in the office of the Secretary of State or at any later time specified in the certificate of limited partnership if, in either case, there has been substantial compliance with the requirements of this section.

§ 202. Amendment to Certificate

(a)   A certificate of limited partnership is amended by filing a certificate of amendment thereto in the office of the Secretary of State. The certificate shall set forth:

(1)   the name of the limited partnership;

(2)   the date of filing the certificate; and

(3)   the amendment to the certificate.

(b)   Within 30 days after the happening of any of the following events, an amendment to a certificate of limited partnership reflecting the occurrence of the event or events shall be filed:

(1)   the admission of a new general partner;

(2)   the withdrawal of a general partner; or

(3)   the continuation of the business under § 801 after an event of withdrawal of a general partner.

(c)   A general partner who becomes aware that any statement in a certificate of limited partnership was false when made or that any arrangements or other facts described have changed, making the certificate inaccurate in any respect, shall promptly amend the certificate.

(d)   A certificate of limited partnership may be amended at any time for any other proper purpose the general partners determine.

(e)   No person has any liability because an amendment to a certificate of limited partnership has not been filed to reflect the occurrence of any event refereed to in subsection (b) of this section if the amendment is filed within the 30-day period specified in subsection (b).

(f)   A restated certificate of limited partnership may be executed and filed in the same manner as a certificate of amendment.

§ 203. Cancellation of Certificate

A certificate of limited partnership shall be canceled upon the dissolution and the commencement of winding up of the partnership or at any other time there are no limited partners. A certificate of cancellation shall be filed in the office of the Secretary of State and set forth:

(1)   the name of the limited partnership;

(2)   the date of filing of its certificate of limited partnership;

(3)   the reason for filing the certificate of cancellation;

(4)   the effective date (which shall be a date certain) of cancellation if it is not to be effective upon the filing of the certificate; and

(5)   any other information the general partners filing the certificate determine.

§ 204. Execution of Certificates

(a)   Each certificate required by this Article to be filed in the office of the Secretary of State shall be executed in the following manner:

(1)   an original certificate of limited partnership must be signed by all general partners;

(2)   a certificate of amendment must be signed by at least one general partner and by each other general partner designated in the certificate as a new general partner; and

(3)   a certificate of cancellation must be signed by all general partners.

(b)   Any person may sign a certificate by an attorney-in-fact, but a power of attorney to sign a certificate relating to the admission of a general partner must specifically describe the admission.

(c)   The execution of a certificate by a general partner constitutes an affirmation under the penalties of perjury that the facts stated therein are true.

§ 205. Execution by Judicial Act

If a person required by § 204 to execute any certificate fails or refuses to do so, any other person who is adversely affected by the failure or refusal, may petition the [designate the appropriate court] to direct the execution of the certificate. If the court finds that it is proper for the certificate to be executed and that any person so designated has failed or refused to execute the certificate, it shall order the Secretary of State to record an appropriate certificate.

§ 206. Filing in Office of Secretary of State

(a)   Two signed copies of the certificate of limited partnership and of any certificates of amendment or cancellation (or of any judicial decree of amendment or cancellation) shall be delivered to the Secretary of State. A person who executes a certificate as an agent or fiduciary need not exhibit evidence of his [or her] authority as a prerequisite to filing. Unless the Secretary of State finds that any certificate does not conform to law, upon receipt of all filing fees required by law he [or she] shall:

(1)   endorse on each duplicate original the word "Filed" and the day, month, and year of the filing thereof;

(2)   file one duplicate original in his [or her] office; and

(3)   return the other duplicate original to the person who filed it or his [or her] representative.

(b)   Upon the filing of a certificate of amendment (or judicial decree of amendment) in the office of the Secretary of State, the certificate of limited partnership shall be amended as set forth therein, and upon the effective date of a certificate of cancellation (or a judicial decree thereof), the certificate of limited partnership is canceled.

§ 207. Liability for False Statement in Certificate

If any certificate of limited partnership or certificate of amendment or cancellation contains a false statement, one who suffers loss by reliance on the statement may recover damages for the loss from:

(1)   any person who executes the certificate, or causes another to execute it on his behalf, and knew, and any general partner who knew or should have known, the statement to be false at the time the certificate was executed; and

(2)   any general partner who thereafter knows or should have known that any arrangement or other fact described in the certificate has changed, making the statement inaccurate in any respect within a sufficient time before the statement was relied upon reasonably to have enabled that general partner to cancel or amend the certificate, or to file a petition for its cancellation or amendment under § 205.

§ 208. Scope of Notice

The fact that a certificate of limited partnership is on file in the office of the Secretary of State is notice that the partnership is a limited partnership and the persons designated therein as general partners are general partners, but it is not notice of any other fact.

§ 209. Delivery of Certificates to Limited Partners

Upon the return by the Secretary of State pursuant to § 206 of a certificate marked "Filed," the general partners shall promptly deliver or mail a copy of the certificate of limited partnership and each certificate of amendment or cancellation to each limited partner unless the partnership agreement provides otherwise.

ARTICLE 3

LIMITED PARTNERS

§ 301. Admission of Limited Partners

(a)   A person becomes a limited partner:

(1)   at the time the limited partnership is formed; or

(2)   at any later time specified in the records of the limited partnership for becoming a limited partner.

(b)   After the filing of a limited partnership's original certificate of limited partnership, a person may be admitted as an additional limited partner:

(1)   in the case of a person acquiring a partnership interest directly from the limited partnership, upon compliance with the partnership agreement or, if the partnership agreement does not so provide, upon the written consent of all partners; and

(2)   in the case of an assignee of a partnership interest of a partner who has the power, as provided in § 704, to grant the assignee the right to become a limited partner, upon the exercise of that power and compliance with any conditions limiting the grant or exercise of the power.

§ 302. Voting

Subject to § 303, the partnership agreement may grant to all or a specified group of the limited partners the right to vote (on a per capita or other basis) upon any matter.

§ 303. Liability to Third Parties

(a)   Except as provided in subsection (d), a limited partner is not liable for the obligation of a limited partnership unless he [or she] is also a general partner or, in addition to the exercise of his [or her] rights and powers as a limited partner, he [or she] participates in the control of the business. However, if the limited partner participates in the control of the business, he [or she] is liable only to persons who transact business with the limited partnership reasonably believing, based upon the limited partner's conduct, that the limited partner is a general partner.

(b)   A limited partner does not participate in the control of the business within the meaning of subsection (a) solely by doing one or more of the following:

(1)   being a contractor for or an agent or employee of the limited partnership or of a general partner or being an officer, director, or shareholder of a general partner that is a corporation;

(2)   consulting with and advising a general partner with respect to the business of the limited partnership;

(3)   acting as surety for the limited partnership or guaranteeing or assuming one or more specific obligations of the limited partnership;

(4)   taking any action required or permitted by law to bring or pursue a derivative action in the right of the limited partnership;

(5)   requesting or attending a meeting of the partners;

(6)   proposing, approving, or disapproving, by voting or otherwise, one or more of the following matters:

(i)   the dissolution and winding up of the limited partnership;

(ii)   the sale, exchange, lease, mortgage, pledge, or other transfer of all or substantially all of the assets of the limited partnership;

(iii)   the incurrence of indebtedness by the limited partnership other than in the ordinary course of its business;

(iv)   a change in the nature of the business;

(v)   the admission or removal of a general partner;

(vi)   the admission or removal of a limited partner;

(vii)   a transaction involving an actual or potential conflict of interest between a general partner and the limited partnership or the limited partners;

(viii)   an amendment to the partnership agreement or certificate of limited partnership; or

(ix)   matters related to the business of the limited partnership not otherwise enumerated in this subsection (b), which the partnership agreement states in writing may be subject to the approval or disapproval of limited partners;

(7)   winding up the limited partnership pursuant to § 803; or

(8)   exercising any right or power permitted to limited partners under this Act and not specifically enumerated in this subsection (b).

(c)   The enumeration in subsection (b) does not mean that the possession or exercise of any other powers by a limited partner constitutes participation by him [or her] in the business of the limited partnership.

(d)   A limited partner who knowingly permits his [or her] name to be used in the name of the limited partnership, except under circumstances permitted by § 102(2), is liable to creditors who extend credit to the limited partnership without actual knowledge that the limited partner is not a general partner.

§ 304. Person Erroneously Believing Himself [or Herself] Limited Partner

(a)   Except as provided in subsection (b), a person who makes a contribution to a business enterprise and erroneously but in good faith believes that he [or she] has become a limited partner in the enterprise is not a general partner in the enterprise and is not bound by its obligations by reason of making the contribution, receiving distributions from the enterprise, or exercising any rights of a limited partner, if, on ascertaining the mistake, he [or she]:

(1)   causes an appropriate certificate of limited partnership or a certificate of amendment to be executed and filed; or

(2) withdraws from future equity participation in the enterprise by executing and filing in the office of the Secretary of State a certificate declaring withdrawal under this section.

(b) A person who makes a contribution of the kind described in subsection (a) is liable as a general partner to any third party who transacts business with the enterprise

(i) before the person withdraws and an appropriate certificate is filed to show withdrawal, or

(ii) before an appropriate certificate is filed to show that he [or she] is not a general partner, but in either case only if the third party actually believed in good faith that the person was a general partner at the time of the transaction.

§ 305. Information

Each limited partner has the right to:

(1) inspect and copy any of the partnership records required to be maintained by § 105; and

(2) obtain from the general partners from time to time upon reasonable demand

(i) true and full information regarding the state of the business and financial condition of the limited partnership,

(ii) promptly after becoming available, a copy of the limited partnership's federal, state, and local income tax returns for each year, and

(iii) other information regarding the affairs of the limited partnership as is just and reasonable.

ARTICLE 4

GENERAL PARTNERS

§ 401. Admission of Additional General Partners

After the filing of a limited partnership's original certificate of limited partnership, additional general partners may be admitted as provided in writing in the partnership agreement or, if the partnership agreement does not provide in writing for the admission of additional general partners, with the written consent of all partners.

§ 402. Events of Withdrawal

Except as approved by the specific written consent of all partners at the time, a person ceases to be a general partner of a limited partnership upon the happening of any of the following events:

(1) the general partner withdraws from the limited partnership as provided in § 602;

(2) the general partner ceases to be a member of the limited partnership as provided in § 702;

(3)   the general partner is removed as a general partner in accordance with the partnership agreement;

(4)   unless otherwise provided in writing in the partnership agreement, the general partner:

    (i)   makes an assignment for the benefit of creditors;

    (ii)   files a voluntary petition in bankruptcy;

    (iii)   is adjudicated a bankrupt or insolvent;

    (iv)   files a petition or answer seeking for himself [or herself] any reorganization, arrangement, composition, readjustment, liquidation, dissolution, or similar relief under any statute, law, or regulation;

    (v)   files an answer or other pleading admitting or failing to contest the material allegations of a petition against him [or her] in any proceeding of this nature; or

    (vi)   seeks, consents to, or acquiesces in the appointment of a trustee, receiver, or liquidator of the general partner or of all or any substantial part of his [or her] properties;

(5)   unless otherwise provided in writing in the partnership agreement, 120 days after the commencement of any proceeding against the general partner seeking reorganization, arrangement, composition, readjustment, liquidation, dissolution, or similar relief under any statute, law, or regulation, the proceeding has not been dismissed, or if within 90 days after the appointment without his [or her] consent or acquiescence of a trustee, receiver, or liquidator of the general partner or all or any substantial part of his [or her] properties, the appointment is not vacated or stayed or within 90 days after the expiration of any such stay, the appointment is not vacated;

(6)   in the case of a general partner who is a natural person:

    (i)   his [or her] death; or

    (ii)   the entry of an order by a court of competent jurisdiction adjudicating him [or her] incompetent to manage his [or her] person or his [or her] estate;

(7)   in the case of a general partner who is acting as a general partner by virtue of being a trustee of a trust, the termination of the trust (but not merely the substitution of a new trustee);

(8)   in the case of a general partner that is a separate partnership, the dissolution and commencement of winding up of the separate partnership;

(9)   in the case of a general partner that is a corporation, the filing of a certificate of dissolution, or its equivalent, for the corporation or the revocation of its charter; or

(10)   in the case of an estate, the distribution by the fiduciary of the estate's entire interest in the partnership.

§ 403. General Powers and Liabilities

(a)   Except as provided in this Act, or in the partnership agreement, a general partner of a limited partnership has the rights and powers and is subject to the restrictions of a partner in a partnership without limited partners.

(b)   Except as provided in this Act, a general partner of a limited partnership has the liabilities of a partner in a partnership without limited partners to persons other than the partnership and the other partners. Except as provided in this Act or in the partnership agreement, a general partner of a limited partnership has the liabilities of a partner in a partnership without limited partners to the partnership and to the other partners.

§ 404. Contributions by General Partner

A general partner of a limited partnership may make contributions to the partnership and share in the profits and losses of, and in distributions from, the limited partnership as a general partner. A general partner also may make contributions to and share in profits, losses, and distributions as a limited partner. A person who is both a general partner and a limited partner has the rights and powers, and is subject to the restrictions and liabilities, of a general partner and, except as provided in the partnership agreement, also has the powers, and is subject to the restrictions, of a limited partner to the extent of his [or her] participation in the partnership as a limited partner.

§ 405. Voting

The partnership agreement may grant to all or certain identified general partners the right to vote (on a per capita or any other basis), separately or with all or any class of the limited partners, on any matter.

ARTICLE 5

FINANCE

§ 501. Form of Contribution

The contribution of a partner may be in cash, property, or services rendered, or a promissory note or other obligation to contribute cash or property or to perform services.

§ 502. Liability for Contribution

(a) A promise by a limited partner to contribute to the limited partnership is not enforceable unless set out in a writing signed by the limited partner.

(b) Except as provided in the partnership agreement, a partner is obligated to the limited partnership to perform any enforceable promise to contribute cash or property or to perform services, even if he [or she] is unable to perform because of death, disability, or any other reason. If a partner does not make the required contribution of property or services, he [or she] is obligated at the option of the limited partnership to contribute cash equal to that portion of the value, as stated in the partnership records required to be kept pursuant to § 105, of the stated contribution which has not been made.

(c) Unless otherwise provided in the partnership agreement, the obligation of a partner to make a contribution or return money or other property paid or distributed in violation of this Act may be compromised only by consent of all partners. Notwithstanding the compromise, a creditor of a limited partnership who extends credit, or otherwise acts in reliance on that obligation after the partner signs a writing which reflects the obligation, and before the amendment or cancellation thereof to reflect the compromise, may enforce the original obligation.

§ 503. Sharing of Profits and Losses

The profits and losses of a limited partnership shall be allocated among the partners, and among classes of partners, in the manner provided in writing in the partnership agreement. If the partnership agreement does not so provide in writing, profits and losses shall be allocated on the basis of the value, as stated in the partnership records required to be kept pursuant to § 105, of the contributions made by each partner to the extent they have been received by the partnership and have not been returned.

§ 504. Sharing of Distributions

Distributions of cash or other assets of a limited partnership shall be allocated among the partners and among classes of partners in the manner provided in writing in the partnership agreement. If the partnership agreement does not so provide in writing, distributions shall be made on the basis of the value, as stated in the partnership records required to be kept pursuant to § 105, of the contributions made by each partner to the extent they have been received by the partnership and have not been returned.

ARTICLE 6

DISTRIBUTIONS AND WITHDRAWAL

§ 601. Interim Distributions

Except as provided in this Article, a partner is entitled to receive distributions from a limited partnership before his [or her] withdrawal from the limited partnership and before the dissolution and winding up thereof to the extent and at the times or upon the happening of the events specified in the partnership agreement.

§ 602. Withdrawal of General Partner

A general partner may withdraw from a limited partnership at any time by giving written notice to the other partners, but if the withdrawal violates the partnership agreement, the limited partnership may recover from the withdrawing general partner damages for breach of the partnership agreement and offset the damages against the amount otherwise distributable to him [or her].

§ 603. Withdrawal of Limited Partner

A limited partner may withdraw from a limited partnership at the time or upon the happening of events specified in writing in the partnership agreement. If the agreement does not specify in writing the time or the events upon the happening of which a limited partner may withdraw or a definite time for the dissolution and winding up of the limited partnership, a limited partner may withdraw upon not less than six months' prior written notice to each general partner at his [other] address on the books of the limited partnership at its office in this State.

§ 604. Distribution upon Withdrawal

Except as provided in this Article, upon withdrawal any withdrawing partner is entitled to receive any distribution to which he [or she] is entitled under the partnership agreement and, if not otherwise provided in the agreement, he [or she] is entitled to receive, within a reasonable time after witdrawal, the fair value of his [or her] interest in the limited partnership as of the date of withdrawal based upon his [or her] right to share in distributions from the limited partnership.

§ 605. Distribution in Kind

Except as provided in writing in the partnership agreement, a partner, regardless of the nature of his [or her] contribution, has no right to demand and receive any distribution from a limited partnership in any form other than cash. Except as provided in writing in the partnership agreement, a partner may not be compelled to accept a distribution of any asset in kind from a limited partnership to the extent that the percentage of the asset distributed to him [or her] exceeds a percentage of that asset which is equal to the percentage in which he [or she] shares in distributions from the limited partnership.

§ 606. Right to Distribution

At the time a partner becomes entitled to receive a distribution, he [or she] has the status of, and is entitled to all remedies available to, a creditor of the limited partnership with respect to the distribution.

§ 607. Limitations on Distribution

A partner may not receive a distribution from a limited partnership to the extent that, after giving effect to the distribution, all liabilities of the limited partnership, other than liabilities to partners on account of their partnership interests, exceed the fair value of the partnership assets.

§ 608. Liability upon Return of Contribution

(a) If a partner has received the return of any part of his [or her] contribution without violation of the partnership agreement or this Act, he [or she] is liable to the limited partnership for a period of one year thereafter for the amount of the returned contribution, but only to the extent necessary to discharge the limited partnership's liabilities to creditors who extended credit to the limited partnership during the period the contribution was held by the partnership.

(b) If a partner has received the return of any part of his [or her] contribution in violation of the partnership agreement or this Act, he [or she] is liable to the limited partnership for a period of six years thereafter for the amount of the contribution wrongfully returned.

(c) A partner receives a return of his [or her] contribution to the extent that a distribution to him [or her] reduces his [or her] share of the fair value of the net assets of the limited partnership below the value, as set forth in the partnership records required to be kept pursuant to § 105, of his contribution which has not been distributed to him [or her].

ARTICLE 7

ASSIGNMENT OF PARTNERSHIP INTERESTS

§ 701. Nature of Partnership Interest

A partnership interest is personal property.

§ 702. Assignment of Partnership Interest

Except as provided in the partnership agreement, a partnership interest is assignable in whole or in part. An assignment of a partnership interest does not dissolve a limited partnership or entitle the assignee to become or to exercise any rights of a partner. An assignment entitles the assignee to receive, to the extent assigned, only the distribution to which the assignor would be entitled. Except as provided in the partnership agreement, a partner ceases to be a partner upon assignment of all his [or her] partnership interest.

§ 703. Rights of Creditor

On application to a court of competent jurisdiction by any judgment creditor of a partner, the court may charge the partnership interest of the partner with payment of the unsatisfied amount of the judgment with interest. To the extent so charged, the judgment creditor has only the rights of an assignee of the partnership interest. This Act does not deprive any partner of the benefit of any exemption laws applicable to his [or her] partnership interest.

§ 704. Right of Assignee to Become Limited Partner

(a)   An assignee of a partnership interest, including an assignee of a general partner, may become a limited partner if and to the extent that:

(i)   the assignor gives the assignee that right in accordance with authority described in the partnership agreement; or

(ii)   all other partners consent.

(b)   An assignee who has become a limited partner has, to the extent assigned, the rights and powers, and is subject to the restrictions and liabilities, of a limited partner under the partnership agreement and this Act. An assignee who becomes a limited partner also is liable for the obligations of his [or her] assignor to make and return contributions as provided in Articles 5 and 6. However, the assignee is not obligated for liabilities unknown to the assignee at the time he [or she] became a limited partner.

(c)   If an assignee of a partnership interest becomes a limited partner, the assignor is not released from his [or her] liability to the limited partnership under §§ 207 and 502.

§ 705. Power of Estate of Deceased or Incompetent Partner

If a partner who is an individual dies or a court of competent jurisdiction adjudges him [or her] to be incompetent to manage his [or her] person or his [or her] property, the partner's executor, administrator, guardian, conservator, or other legal representative may exercise all of the partner's rights for the purpose of settling his [or her] estate or administering his [or her] property, including any power the partner had to give an assignee the right to become a limited partner. If a partner is a corporation, trust, or other entity and is dissolved or terminated, the powers of that partner may be exercised by its legal representative or successor.

ARTICLE 8

DISSOLUTION

§ 801. Nonjudicial Dissolution

A limited partnership is dissolved and its affairs shall be wound up upon the happening of the first to occur of the following:

(1) at the time specified in the certificate of limited partnership;

(2) upon the happening of events specified in writing in the partnership agreement;

(3) written consent of all partners;

(4) an event of withdrawal of a general partner unless at the time there is at least one other general partner and the written provisions of the partnership agreement permit the business of the limited partnership to be carried on by the remaining general partner and that partner does so, but the limited partnership is not dissolved and is not required to be wound up by reason of any event of withdrawal, if, within 90 days after withdrawal, all partners agree in writing to continue the business of the limited partnership and to the appointment of one or more additional general partners if necessary or desired; or

(5) entry of a decree of judicial dissolution under § 802.

§ 802. Judicial Dissolution

On application by or for a partner the [designate the appropriate court] court may decree dissolution of a limited partnership whenever it is not reasonably practicable to carry on the business in conformity with the partnership agreement.

§ 803. Winding Up

Except as provided in the partnership agreement, the general partners who have not wrongfully dissolved a limited partnership or, if none, the limited partners, may wind up the limited partnership's affairs; but the [designate the appropriate court] court may wind up the limited partnership's affairs upon application of any partner, his [or her] legal representative, or assignee.

§ 804. Distribution of Assets

Upon the winding up of a limited partnership, the assets shall be distributed as follows:

(1) to creditors, including partners who are creditors, to the extent permitted by law, in satisfaction of liabilities of the limited partnership other than liabilities for distributions to partners under § 601 or § 604;

(2) except as provided in the partnership agreement, to partners and former partners in satisfaction of liabilities for distributions under § 601 or § 604; and

(3) except as provided in the partnership agreement, to partners first for the return of their contributions and secondly respecting their partnership interests, in the proportions in which the partners share in distributions.

ARTICLE 9

FOREIGN LIMITED PARTNERSHIPS

§ 901. Law Governing

Subject to the Constitution of this State:

(i) the laws of the state under which a foreign limited partnership is organized govern its organization and internal affairs and the liability of its partners; and

(ii) a foreign limited partnership may not be denied registration by reason of any difference between those laws and the laws of this State.

§ 902. Registration

Before transacting business in this State, a foreign limited partnership shall register with the Secretary of State. In order to register, a foreign limited partnership shall submit to the Secretary of state, in duplicate, an application for registration as a foreign limited partnership, signed and sworn to by a general partner and setting forth:

(1) the name of the foreign limited partnership and, if different, the name under which it proposes to register and transact business in this State;

(2) the state and date of its formation;

(3) the name and address of any agent for service of process on the foreign limited partnership whom the foreign limited partnership elects to appoint; the agent must be an individual resident of this State, a domestic corporation, or a foreign corporation having a place of business in, and authorized to do business in, this State;

(4) a statement that the Secretary of State is appointed the agent of the foreign limited partnership for service of process if no agent has been appointed under paragraph (3) or, if appointed, the agent's authority has been revoked or if the agent cannot be found or served with the exercise of reasonable diligence;

(5) the address of the office required to be maintained in the state of its organization by the laws of that state or, if not so required, of the principal office of the foreign limited partnership;

(6)   the name and business address of each general partner; and

(7)   the address of the office at which is kept a list of the names and addresses of the limited partners and their capital contributions, together with an undertaking by the foreign limited partnership to keep those records until the foreign limited partnership's registration in this State is canceled or withdrawn.

§ 903. Issuance of Registration

(a)   If the Secretary of State finds that an application for registration conforms to law and all requisite fees have been paid, he [or she] shall:

(1)   endorse on the application the word "Filed," and the month, day, and year of the filing thereof;

(2)   file in his [or her] office a duplicate original of the application; and

(3)   issue a certificate of registration to transact business in this State.

(b)   The certificate of registration, together with a duplicate original of the application, shall be returned to the person who filed the application or his [or her] representative.

§ 904. Name

A foreign limited partnership may register with the Secretary of State under any name, whether or not it is the name under which it is registered in its state of organization, that includes without abbreviation the words "limited partnership" and that could be registered by a domestic limited partnership.

§ 905. Changes and Amendments

If any statement in the application for registration of a foreign limited partnership was false when made or any arrangements or other facts described have changed, making the application inaccurate in any respect, the foreign limited partnership shall promptly file in the office of the Secretary of State a certificate, signed and sworn to by a general partner, correcting such statement.

§ 906. Cancellation of Registration

A foreign limited partnership may cancel its registration by filing with the Secretary of State a certificate of cancellation signed and sworn to by a general partner. A cancellation does not terminate the authority of the Secretary of State to accept service of process on the foreign limited partnership with respect to [claims for relief] [causes of action] arising out of the transactions of business in this State.

§ 907. Transaction of Business Without Registration

(a)   A foreign limited partnership transacting business in this State may not maintain any action, suit, or proceeding in any court of this State until it has registered in this State.

(b)   The failure of a foreign limited partnership to register in this State does not impair the validity of any contract or act of the foreign limited partnership or prevent the foreign limited partnership from defending any action, suit, or proceeding in any court of this State.

(c)   A limited partner of a foreign partnership is not liable as a general partner of the foreign limited partnership solely by reason of having transacted business in this State without registration.

(d)   A foreign limited partnership, by transacting business in this State without registration, appoints the Secretary of state as its agent for service of process with respect to [claims for relief] [causes of action] arising out of the transaction of business in this State.

§ 908. Action by [Appropriate Official]

The [designate the appropriate official] may bring an action to restrain a foreign limited partnership from transacting business in this State in violation of this Article.

ARTICLE 10

DERIVATIVE ACTIONS

§ 1001. Right of Action

A limited partner may bring an action in the right of a limited partnership to recover a judgment in its favor if general partners with authority to do so have refused to bring the action or if an effort to cause those general partners to bring the action is not likely to succeed.

§ 1002. Proper Plaintiff

In a derivative action, the plaintiff must be a partner at the time of bringing the action, and

(i)   must have been a partner at the time of the transaction of which he [or she] complains or

(ii)   his [or her] status as a partner must have devolved upon him [or her] by operation of law or pursuant to the terms of the partnership agreement from a person who was a partner at the time of the transaction.

§ 1003. Pleading

In a derivative action, the complaint shall set forth with particularity the effort of the plaintiff to secure initiation of the action by a general partner or the reasons for not making the effort.

§ 1004. Expenses

If a derivative action is successful, in whole or in part, or if anything is received by the plaintiff as a result of a judgment, compromise, or settlement of an action or claim, the court may award the plaintiff reasonable expenses, including reasonable attorney's fees, and shall direct him [or her] to remit to the limited partnership the remainder of those proceeds received by him [or her].

ARTICLE 11

MISCELLANEOUS

§ 1101. Construction and Application

This Act shall be so applied and construed to effectuate its general purpose to make uniform the law with respect to the subject of this Act among states enacting it.

§ 1102. Short Title

This Act may be cited as the Uniform Limited Partnership Act.

§ 1103. Severability

If any provision of this Act or its application to any person or circumstance is held invalid, the invalidity does not affect other provisions or applications of the Act which can be given effect without the invalid provision or application, and to this end the provisions of this Act are severable.

§ 1104. Effective Date, Extended Effective Date and Repeal

Except as set forth below, the effective date of this Act is _____ and the following acts [list existing limited partnership acts] are hereby repealed:

(1) The existing provisions for execution and filing of certificates of limited partnerships and amendments thereunder and cancellations thereof continue in effect until [specify time required to create central filing system], the extended effective date, and §§ 102, 103, 104, 105, 201, 202, 203, 204 and 206 are not effective until the extended effective date.

(2) § 402, specifying the conditions under which a general partner ceases to be a member of a limited partnership, is not effective until the extended effective date, and the applicable provisions of existing law continue to govern until the extended effective date.

(3) §§ 501, 502 and 608 apply only to contributions and distributions made after the effective date of this Act.

(4) § 704 applies only to assignments made after the effective date of this Act.

(5) Article 9, dealing with registration of foreign limited partnerships, is not effective until the extended effective date.

(6) Unless otherwise agreed by the partners, the applicable provisions of existing law governing allocation of profits and losses (rather than the provisions of § 503), distributions to a withdrawing partner (rather than the provisions of § 604), and distributions of assets upon the winding up of a limited partnership (rather than the provisions of § 804) govern limited partnerships formed before the effective date of this Act.

§ 1105. Rules for Cases Not Provided for in This Act

In any case not provided for in this Act the provisions of the Uniform Partnership Act govern.

§ 1106. Savings Clause

The repeal of any statutory provision by this Act does not impair, or otherwise affect, the organization or the continued existence of a limited partnership existing at the effective date of this Act, nor does the repeal of any existing statutory provision by this Act impair any contract or affect any right accrued before the effective date of this Act.

APPENDIX III

COMPARISON OF GENERAL AND LIMITED PARTNERSHIPS

Following are the primary differences between a regular partnership with at least two general partners and a limited partnership with one or more general partners and at least one limited partner. For details and further comparisons, refer to the complete text of the Uniform Partnership Act in Appendix I and the Uniform Limited Partnership Act in Appendix II.

1. **Partner Requirements**

   General: At least two partners; all general.

   Limited: At least one general partner and one limited partner.

2. **Liability Risks**

   General: Personal liability unlimited for each general partner.

   Limited: Liability for each limited partner limited to the agreed-on contribution to the partnership.

3. **Partner Surname in Partnership Name**

   General: No restriction.

   Limited: Limited partner surname not allowed unless also the surname of a general partner, or was part of the name of the business before the limited partner joined.

4. **Control of Partnership Business**

   General: Control by each general partner.

   Limited: No participation in control by limited partner.

5. **Allowable Types of Contribution to Partnership**

   General: General partners may contribute money, other property, or services.

   Limited: Limited partners may contribute money or other property, but not services.

6. **Basis for Dissolution**

   General: Partnership dissolution caused by any partner ceasing to be associated in carrying out partnership business; dissolution also caused by death, bankruptcy, or withdrawal of a general partner from the partnership.

   Limited: Partnership dissolution not the result of a limited partner ceasing to be associated in carrying out partnership business; the death, bankruptcy, or withdrawal of a limited partner does not cause dissolution of the partnership.

7. **Parties for Actions by or against Partnership**

   General: Can be general partner.

   Limited: Cannot be limited partner, except to enforce limited partner's right against or liability to partnership; also when action by limited partner is for the right of the limited partnership to obtain a judgment in its favor.

8. **Transferrable Partnership Interests**

   General: Only a general partner's own interest in the partnership can be transferred without the consent of the other partners in the partnership.

   Limited: A limited partner can transfer interests (but not full rights) without consent of other partners or limited partners.

9. **Priorities upon Partnership Dissolution**

   General: a. outside creditors
   b. general partners-creditors
   c. general partners re capital
   d. general partners re profits

   Limited: Each limited partner has priority over the general partners according to the following:
   a. outside creditors and limited partners-creditors
   b. limited partners re profits
   c. limited partners re capital
   d. general partners-creditors
   e. general partners re profits
   f. general partners re capital

APPENDIX IV

HELPFUL IRS PUBLICATIONS

The Internal Revenue Service makes available a number of publications covering specific areas of tax law. These publications can be quite helpful in the management of both general and limited partnerships. Addresses for obtaining these publications can be found on p. 105.

Addresses for obtaining these publications can be found on p. 105.

1: Your Rights as a Taxpayer
15: Employer's Tax Guide
463: Travel, Entertainment, and Gift Expenses
505: Tax Withholding and Estimated Tax
509: Tax Calendars
510: Excise Taxes
533: Self-Employment Tax
534: Depreciation
535: Business Expenses
536: Net Operating Losses
537: Installment Sales
538: Accounting Periods and Methods
539: Employment Taxes
541: Tax Information for Partnerships
544: Sales and Other Dispositions of Assets
545: Interest Expense
548: Deductions for Bad Debts
549: Condemnations and Business Casualties and Thefts
550: Investment Income and Expenses
551: Basis of Assets
556: Examination of Returns, Appeal Rights, and Claims for Refund
560: Retirement Plans for the Self-Employed
583: Taxpayers Starting a Business
587: Business Use of Your Home
590: Individual Retirement Arrangements (IRAs)
910: Guide to Free Tax Services
911: Tax Information for Direct Sellers
916: Information Returns
917: Business Use of a Car
925: Passive Activity and At-Risk Rules
937: Business Reporting

How to Get IRS Forms and Publications

You can order tax forms and publications from the IRS Forms Distribution Center for your state at the address below. Or, if you prefer, you can photocopy tax forms from reproducible copies kept at participating public libraries. In addition, many of these libraries have reference sets of IRS publications that you can read or copy.

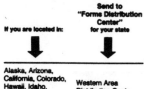

If you are located in:

Alaska, Arizona, California, Colorado, Hawaii, Idaho, Montana, Nevada, New Mexico, Oregon, Utah, Washington, Wyoming

Send to "Forms Distribution Center" for your state

Western Area Distribution Center Rancho Cordova, CA 95743-0001

Alabama, Arkansas, Illinois, Indiana, Iowa, Kansas, Kentucky, Louisiana, Michigan, Minnesota, Mississippi, Missouri, Nebraska, North Dakota, Ohio, Oklahoma, South Dakota, Tennessee, Texas, Wisconsin

Central Area Distribution Center P.O. Box 9903 Bloomington, IL 61799

Connecticut, Delaware, District of Columbia, Florida, Georgia, Maine, Maryland, Massachusetts, New Hampshire, New Jersey, New York, North Carolina, Pennsylvania, Rhode Island, South Carolina, Vermont, Virginia, West Virginia

Eastern Area Distribution Center P.O. Box 85074 Richmond, VA 23261-5074

Foreign Addresses—Taxpayers with mailing addresses in foreign countries should send their requests for forms and publications to: Forms Distribution Center, P.O. Box 25866, Richmond, VA 23289; or Forms Distribution Center, Rancho Cordova, CA 95743-0001, whichever is closer.

Puerto Rico—Forms Distribution Center, P.O. Box 25866, Richmond, VA 23289

Virgin Islands—V.I. Bureau of Internal Revenue, Lockharts Garden, No. 1A, Charlotte Amalie, St. Thomas, VI 00802

☆ U.S. Government Printing Office: 1991-285-595

GENERAL PARTNERSHIP FORMS

107—Article of Co-Partnership.   W   JULIUS BLUMBERG. INC., LAW BLANK PUBLISHERS

Articles of Agreement,

Made the   *day of*   *one thousand nine hundred and*

BETWEEN

   WITNESSETH: *The said parties above named have agreed to become co-partners and by these presents form a partnership under the trade name and style of*

for the purpose of buying, selling, vending and manufacturing

and all other goods, wares and merchandise belonging to the said business and to occupy the following premises:

their co-partnership to commence on the   *day of*   19
and to continue

and to that end and purpose the said

to be used and employed in common between them for the support and management of the said business, to their mutual benefit and advantage. AND it is agreed by and between the parties to these presents, that at all times during the continuance of their co-partnership, they and each of them will give their attendance, and do their and each of their best endeavors, and to the utmost of their skill and power, exert themselves for their joint interest, profit, benefit and advantage, and truly employ, buy, sell and merchandise with their joint stock, and the increase thereof, in the business aforesaid. AND ALSO, that they shall and will at all times during the said co-partnership, bear, pay and discharge equally between them, all rents and other expenses that may be required for the support and management of the said business; and that all gains, profit and increase, that shall come, grow or arise from or by means of their said business shall be divided between them, as follows:

and all loss that shall happen to their said joint business by ill-commodities, bad debts or otherwise shall be borne and paid between them, as follows:

AND *it is agreed by and between the said parties, that there shall be had and kept at all times during the continuance of their co-partnership, perfect, just, and true books of account, wherein each of the said co-partners shall enter and set down, as well all money by them or either of them received, paid, laid out and expended in and about the said business, as also all goods, wares, commodities and merchandise, by them or either of them, bought or sold, by reason or on account of the said business, and all other matters and things whatsoever, to the said business and the management thereof in anywise belonging; which said book shall be used in common between the said co-partners, so that either of them may have access thereto, without any interruption or hindrance of the other. AND ALSO, the said co-partners, once in*

or oftener if necessary, shall make, yield and render, each to the other, a true, just and perfect inventory and account of all profits and increase by them or either of them, made, and of all losses by them or either of them, sustained; and also all payments, receipts, disbursements and all other things by them made, received, disbursed, acted, done, or suffered in this said co-partnership and business; and the same account so made, shall and will clear, adjust, pay and deliver, each to the other, at the time, their just share of the profits so made as aforesaid.

AND *the said parties hereby mutually covenant and agree to and with each other, that during the continuance of the said co-partnership,   of them shall nor will endorse any note, or otherwise become surety for any person or persons whomsoever, nor will sell, assign, transfer, mortgage or otherwise dispose of the business of the co-partnership, nor each of   share, title and interest therein without the written consent of the parties hereto. And at the end or other sooner termination of their co-partnership the said co-partners each to the other, shall and will make a true, just and final account of all things relating to their said business, and in all things truly adjust the same; and all and every the stock and stocks as well as the gains and increase thereof, which shall appear to be remaining, either in money, goods, wares, fixtures, debts or otherwise, shall be divided between them as follows:*

after the payment of the co-partnership liabilities; and should said co-partners be unable to ascertain the value of any of the assets belonging to the co-partnership at the termination of their co-partnership, the said assets shall then be sold either at private or public sale to be agreed upon by the parties hereto and a division of the proceeds of said sale shall be made as herein provided.

IT IS FURTHER AGREED *that during the continuance of the co-partnership herein, all notes, drafts or money received for and in behalf of the said co-partnership by the parties hereto shall be deposited in a bank to be agreed upon by the parties hereto and the moneys credited to said co-partnership shall only be withdrawn by check signed by*

who shall also receive said notes, drafts or moneys or other orders for payment of moneys of the said co-partnership for the purpose of making said deposits.

IT IS FURTHER AGREED *that during the continuance of said co-partnership the parties hereto shall mutually agree in writing, upon a weekly allowance, to be paid to each of the parties hereto for services to be rendered, and said allowance shall be charged as an item of expense of the co-partnership busi-*

ness, or if otherwise agreed upon in writing may be charged against their personal interest in said business.

IN THE EVENT of the death of a party hereto, the surviving co-partner   shall within a period of
            weeks, make and give, to the legal representative of the deceased co-partner, a true, just and final account of all things relating to the co-partnership business, and within a period of
            months, in all things truly adjust the same with the legal representative of the deceased co-partner. The surviving co-partner   shall have the privilege of purchasing the interest of the deceased co-partner from his legal representative, upon a true and proper valuation of the interest of the deceased co-partner; and until the purchase of said interest by the surviving co-partner , or a division as herein agreed upon, the legal representative of the deceased co-partner during reasonable business hours shall have access to the books of the co-partnership and examine same personally or with the aid of other persons and make copies thereof or any portion thereof without any interruption or hindrance, and the said legal representative of said deceased co-partner shall have equal and joint control of the said co-partnership with the surviving partner or partners.

This instrument may not be changed orally.

IN WITNESS WHEREOF, the parties hereto have hereunto set their hands and seals the day and year first above mentioned.

In presence of:

STATE OF

            of   ) ss.:
County of   )

            On the   day of   in the year
one thousand nine hundred and   before me personally came

to me known, and known to me to be the individual   described in, and who executed the foregoing instrument, and   acknowledged to me that   he   executed the same.

X 74—Certificate of Conducting Business as Partners
Individual   Corporation. 12-88

© 1973 BY JULIUS BLUMBERG, INC.,
PUBLISHER, NYC 10013

Business Certificate for Partners

The undersigned do hereby certify that they are conducting or transacting business as members of a partnership under the name or designation of

at

in the County of   , State of New York, and do further certify that the full names of all the persons conducting or transacting such partnership including the full names of all the partners with the residence address of each such person, and the age of any who may be infants, are as follows:

NAME *Specify which are infants and state ages.*   **RESIDENCE**

....

....

....

....

....

....

WE DO FURTHER CERTIFY that we are the successors in interest to

the person or persons heretofore using such name or names to carry on or conduct or transact business.

In Witness Whereof, *We have this   day of   19   made and signed this certificate.*

....

....

....

....

....

....

State of New York, County of   **ss.:**   **INDIVIDUAL ACKNOWLEDGMENT**

On this   day of   19   , before me personally appeared

to me known and known to me to be the individual   described in, and who executed the foregoing certificate, and   he   thereupon   duly acknowledged to me that   he   executed the same.

_____

𝕾tate of 𝔑ew 𝔜ork, 𝕮ounty of   ss.:   **CORPORATE ACKNOWLEDGMENT**

On this   *day of*   19   *, before me personally appeared*

to me known, who being by me duly sworn, did depose and say, that   *he resides in*

that   *he is the*   *of*

the corporation described in and which executed the foregoing certificate; that   *he knows the seal of said corporation; that the seal affixed to said certificate is such corporate seal; that it was so affixed by order of the Board of*   *of said corporation, and that*   *he signed h*   *name thereto by like order.*

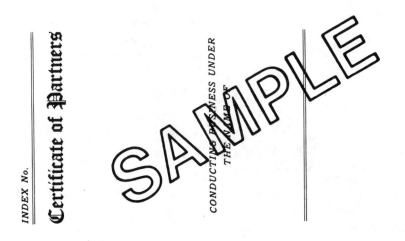

𝕾tate of 𝔑ew 𝔜ork, 𝕮ounty of   ss.:   **INDIVIDUAL ACKNOWLEDGMENT**

On this   *day of*   19   *, before me personally appeared*

to me known and known to me to be the individual   *described in, and who executed the foregoing certificate, and*   *he*   *thereupon*   *duly acknowledged to me that*   *he*   *executed the same.*

T 224—Amended Business Certificate
For Individual or Partners, 10-88

JULIUS BLUMBERG, INC.,
PUBLISHER, NYC 10013

Amended Business Certificate

The undersigned hereby certify that a certificate of doing business under the assumed name

for the conduct of business at

was filed in the office of the County Clerk   County, State of New York, on the
day of   19   under index number   ; that the
last amended certificate was filed on the   day of   19   in the
office of the said County Clerk under index number
    It is hereby further certified that this amended certificate is made for the purpose of more accu-
rately setting forth the facts recited in the original certificate or the last amended certificate and to set
forth the following changes in such facts;*

In Witness Whereof, *the undersigned have this   day of   19*
made and signed this certificate.

_____

_____

_____

_____

State of New York, County of   **ss.:**
    On this   day of   19   , before me personally appeared

to me known and known to me to be the individual   described in and who executed the foregoing
certificate, and   he   thereupon   duly acknowledged to me that   he   executed the same.

....

* Set forth the residence address of each new partner, if any.

State of New York, County of   **ss.:**

    On this   day of   , 19   , before me personally appeared

to me known and known to me to be the individual   described in, and who executed the foregoing
certificate, and   he   thereupon   duly acknowledged to me that   he   executed the same.

DISSOLUTION OF CO-PARTNERSHIP

177.—Dissolution of Co-partnership.   W   JULIUS BLUMBERG, INC., LAW BLANK PUBLISHERS

This Indenture *made the*   *day of*

nineteen hundred and   *between*

WITNESSETH: WHEREAS *the parties hereto have heretofore formed a co-partnership for the purpose of*

under the firm name of

and have maintained and continued said partnership up to the present time, and WHEREAS *the parties hereto have agreed that the partnership existing between them should be terminated and dissolved, and* WHEREAS *an accounting of the assets and liabilities of the said firm has been duly had by the parties hereto, for the purpose of ascertaining the share due to each of the parties hereto, and on said accounting the following was found to be and is a true statement of the condition and of the affairs of such co-partnership to wit:—*

ASSETS:

Cash on hand -   -   -   -   -   -   -   -   -   -   - $

Outstanding accounts as enumerated in the schedule hereto annexed -   -   -

Stock on hand -   -   -   -   -   -   -   -   -   -   -   -   -   -

Fixtures -   -   -   -   -   -   -   -   -   -   -   -   -   -

Total Assets $

LIABILITIES:

For merchandise as enumerated in the schedule hereto annexed $

other liabilities as enumerated in the schedule hereto annexed $

Total Liabilities $

Balance $

AND WHEREAS *the parties hereto have agreed to distribute said assets in the following manner:*

NOW IN CONSIDERATION *of the sum of One Dollar each to the other in hand paid, and in consideration of the premises, the parties hereto have and hereby do terminate and dissolve said co-partnership and each of the parties hereto hereby releases the other of and from any and all obligations growing out of the said partnership.*

Forms may be purchased from Julius Blumberg, Inc., NYC 10013, or any of its dealers. Reproduction prohibited.

AND IT IS FURTHER AGREED, *that the part   of the   part in consideration of the sum of   dollars paid to   by the part   of the
                        part   the receipt whereof is hereby acknowledged,   transferred,
assigned and set over and by these presents   assign, transfer and set over unto said part   of the
                        part   all   right, title, interest and share of, in and into
the assets and property of every kind of said co-partnership together with the good will of the business
thereof to have and to hold the same unto the said part   of the   part   ,
                        executors, administrators and assigns, to   own use, benefit and behoof forever.*

AND EACH OF THE PARTIES HERETO HEREBY AGREES, *that   has not signed
or endorsed the firm name to any commercial paper, or other evidence of debt, and has not incurred any obligation or liability, contingent or actual, in behalf of said co-partnership, except as mentioned or included
in the accounting herein set forth.*

AND IT IS FURTHER AGREED *by the parties hereto that the part   of the
        part   shall and will pay and discharge all the firm obligations and liabilities referred to and
mentioned in the accounting herein before set forth, without contribution by the part   of the
        part   thereto, and that the said part   of the   part   do
hereby agree to save, indemnify and keep harmless the said part   of the
        part   of and from such firm obligations and liabilities and of and from all damage, cost and ex-
pense occurring through the default or failure of the part   of the
        part   to promptly and fully pay and discharge the same.*

SAMPLE

*STATE OF
COUNTY OF*   } *ss.:*

*On the   day of   nineteen hundred and
before me came*

*to me known and known to me to be the individual   described in, and who executed the foregoing instrument,
and   acknowledged to me that   he   executed the same.*

T 176—Certificate of Discontinuance of Business as Partners

JULIUS BLUMBERG, INC.,
PUBLISHER, NYC 10013

Certificate of Discontinuance of Business as Partners

The undersigned do hereby certify that they have conducted or transacted business as partners under the name or designation of

at

County of   , State of New York, and that a certificate of conducting business as partners was filed in the office of the County Clerk, County of   , State of New York, on the   day of   19   under index number and that the last amended certificate was filed on the   day of   19 in the office of the said County Clerk under index number   and we hereby further certify that the filing of a certificate in said county is no longer required for the reason that the said business was discontinued on the   day of   19   or the conditions under which the business is conducted have changed so that the filing of a certificate in said County is no longer required for the reason that

The full names of all the persons named in the original certificate or the amended certificate last previously filed as persons conducting or transacting the business or as partners are as follows:

NAME Write "Deceased" after names of those not living.   **RESIDENCE**

....

....

....

....

....

We therefore desire to file this certificate of discontinuance.

In Witness Whereof, We have this   day of   19   , made and signed this certificate.

....

....

....

....

....

....

State of New York, County of   **ss.:**

On this   day of   , 19   , before me personally appeared

to me known and known to me to be the individual   described in, and who executed the foregoing certificate, and   he   thereupon   duly acknowledged to me that   he   executed the same.

....

State of New York, County of   **ss.:**

On this   day of   , 19   , before me personally appeared

to me known and known to me to be the individual   described in, and who executed the foregoing certificate, and   he   thereupon   duly acknowledged to me that   he   executed the same.

TAX FORMS

Form **SS-4** (Rev. April 1991) Department of the Treasury Internal Revenue Service	**Application for Employer Identification Number** (For use by employers and others. Please read the attached instructions before completing this form.)	EIN OMB No. 1545-0003 Expires 4-30-94

Please type or print clearly.

1 Name of applicant (True legal name) (See instructions.)

2 Trade name of business, if different from name in line 1	**3** Executor, trustee, "care of" name

4a Mailing address (street address) (room, apt., or suite no.)	**5a** Address of business (See instructions.)

4b City, state, and ZIP code	**5b** City, state, and ZIP code

6 County and state where principal business is located

7 Name of principal officer, grantor, or general partner (See instructions.) ▶

8a Type of entity (Check only one box.) (See instructions.)
- ☐ Individual SSN _____
- ☐ REMIC
- ☐ State/local government
- ☐ Other nonprofit organization (specify) _____
- ☐ Other (specify) ▶ _____
- ☐ Personal service corp.
- ☐ National guard
- ☐ Estate
- ☐ Plan administrator SSN _____
- ☐ Other corporation (specify) _____
- ☐ Federal government/military
- ☐ Trust
- ☐ Partnership
- ☐ Farmers' cooperative
- ☐ Church or church controlled organization
- If nonprofit organization enter GEN (if applicable) _____

8b If a corporation, give name of foreign country (if applicable) or state in the U.S. where incorporated ▶	Foreign country	State

9 Reason for applying (Check only one box.)
- ☐ Started new business
- ☐ Hired employees
- ☐ Created a pension plan (specify type) ▶ _____
- ☐ Banking purpose (specify) ▶
- ☐ Changed type of organization (specify) ▶ _____
- ☐ Purchased going business
- ☐ Created a trust (specify) ▶ _____
- ☐ Other (specify) ▶

10 Date business started or acquired (Mo., day, year) (See instructions.)	**11** Enter closing month of accounting year. (See instructions.)

12 First date wages or annuities were paid or will be paid (Mo., day, year). **Note:** *If applicant is a withholding agent, enter date income will first be paid to nonresident alien. (Mo., day, year)* . . . . ▶

13 Enter highest number of employees expected in the next 12 months. **Note:** *If the applicant does not expect to have any employees during the period, enter "0."* . . . . ▶	Nonagricultural	Agricultural	Household

14 Principal activity (See instructions.) ▶

15 Is the principal business activity manufacturing? . . . . ☐ Yes ☐ No
If "Yes," principal product and raw material used ▶

16 To whom are most of the products or services sold? Please check the appropriate box. ☐ Business (wholesale)
☐ Public (retail) ☐ Other (specify) ▶ ☐ N/A

17a Has the applicant ever applied for an identification number for this or any other business? . . . . ☐ Yes ☐ No
Note: *If "Yes," please complete lines 17b and 17c.*

17b If you checked the "Yes" box in line 17a, give applicant's true name and trade name, if different than name shown on prior application.

True name ▶ Trade name ▶

17c Enter approximate date, city, and state where the application was filed and the previous employer identification number if known.

Approximate date when filed (Mo., day, year)	City and state where filed	Previous EIN

Under penalties of perjury, I declare that I have examined this application, and to the best of my knowledge and belief, it is true, correct, and complete	Telephone number (include area code)

Name and title (Please type or print clearly.) ▶

Signature ▶ Date ▶

Note: *Do not write below this line.* *For official use only.*

Please leave blank ▶	Geo.	Ind.	Class	Size	Reason for applying

For Paperwork Reduction Act Notice, see attached instructions. Cat. No. 16055N Form **SS-4** (Rev. 4-91)

Form SS-4 (Rev. 4-91)

General Instructions

(Section references are to the Internal Revenue Code unless otherwise noted.)

Paperwork Reduction Act Notice.—We ask for the information on this form to carry out the Internal Revenue laws of the United States. You are required to give us this information. We need it to ensure that you are complying with these laws and to allow us to figure and collect the right amount of tax.

The time needed to complete and file this form will vary depending on individual circumstances. The estimated average time is:

Recordkeeping	7 min.
Learning about the law or the form	21 min.
Preparing the form	42 min.
Copying, assembling, and sending the form to IRS	20 min.

If you have comments concerning the accuracy of these time estimates or suggestions for making this form more simple, we would be happy to hear from you. You can write to both the **Internal Revenue Service,** Washington, DC 20224, Attention: IRS Reports Clearance Officer, T:FP; and the **Office of Management and Budget,** Paperwork Reduction Project (1545-0003), Washington, DC 20503. **DO NOT** send the tax form to either of these offices. Instead, see **Where To Apply.**

Purpose.—Use Form SS-4 to apply for an employer identification number (EIN). The information you provide on this form will establish your filing requirements.

Who Must File.—You must file this form if you have not obtained an EIN before and
• You pay wages to one or more employees.
• You are required to have an EIN to use on any return, statement, or other document, even if you are not an employer.
• You are required to withhold taxes on income, other than wages, paid to a nonresident alien (individual, corporation, partnership, etc.). For example, individuals who file **Form 1042,** Annual Withholding Tax Return for U.S. Source Income of Foreign Persons, to report alimony paid to nonresident aliens must have EINs.

Individuals who file **Schedule C,** Profit or Loss From Business, or **Schedule F,** Profit or Loss From Farming, of **Form 1040,** U.S. Individual Income Tax Return, must use EINs if they have a Keogh plan or are required to file excise, employment, or alcohol, tobacco, or firearms returns.

The following must use EINs even if they do not have any employees:
• Trusts, except an IRA trust, unless the IRA trust is required to file **Form 990-T,** Exempt Organization Business Income Tax Return, to report unrelated business taxable income or is filing Form 990-T to obtain a refund of the credit from a regulated investment company.
• Estates
• Partnerships
• REMICS (real estate mortgage investment conduits)
• Corporations
• Nonprofit organizations (churches, clubs, etc.)
• Farmers' cooperatives
• Plan administrators

New Business.—If you become the new owner of an existing business, **DO NOT** use the EIN of the former owner. If you already have an EIN, use that number. If you do not have an EIN, apply for one on this form. If you become the "owner" of a corporation by acquiring its stock, use the corporation's EIN.

If you already have an EIN, you may need to get a new one if either the organization or ownership of your business changes. If you incorporate a sole proprietorship or form a partnership, you must get a new EIN. However, **DO NOT** apply for a new EIN if you change only the name of your business.

File Only One Form SS-4.—File only one Form SS-4, regardless of the number of businesses operated or trade names under which a business operates. However, each corporation in an affiliated group must file a separate application.

If you do not have an EIN by the time a return is due, write "Applied for" and the date you applied in the space shown for the number. **DO NOT** show your social security number as an EIN on returns.

If you do not have an EIN by the time a tax deposit is due, send your payment to the Internal Revenue service center for your filing area. (See **Where To Apply** below.) Make your check or money order payable to Internal Revenue Service and show your name (as shown on Form SS-4), address, kind of tax, period covered, and date you applied for an EIN.

For more information about EINs, see **Pub. 583,** Taxpayers Starting a Business.

How To Apply.—You can apply for an EIN either by mail or by telephone. You can get an EIN immediately by calling the Tele-TIN phone number for the service center for your state, or you can send the completed Form SS-4 directly to the service center to receive your EIN in the mail.

Application by Tele-TIN.—The Tele-TIN program is designed to assign EINs by telephone. Under this program, you can receive your EIN over the telephone and use it immediately to file a return or make a payment.

To receive an EIN by phone, complete Form SS-4, then call the Tele-TIN phone number listed for your state under **Where To Apply.** The person making the call must be authorized to sign the form (see **Signature block** on page 3).

An IRS representative will use the information from the Form SS-4 to establish your account and assign you an EIN. Write the number you are given on the upper right-hand corner of the form, sign and date it, and promptly mail it to the Tele-TIN Unit at the service center address for your state.

Application by mail.—Complete Form SS-4 at least 4 to 5 weeks before you will need an EIN. Sign and date the application and mail it to the service center address for your state. You will receive your EIN in the mail in approximately 4 weeks.

Note: *The Tele-TIN phone numbers listed below will involve a long-distance charge to callers outside of the local calling area, and should only be used to apply for an EIN. Use 1-800-829-1040 to ask about an application by mail.*

Where To Apply.—

If your principal business, office or agency, or legal residence in the case of an individual, is located in:	Call the Tele-TIN phone number shown or file with the Internal Revenue service center at:
Florida, Georgia, South Carolina	Atlanta, GA 39901 (404) 455-2360
New Jersey, New York City and counties of Nassau, Rockland, Suffolk, and Westchester	Holtsville, NY 00501 (516) 447-4955
New York (all other counties), Connecticut, Maine, Massachusetts, New Hampshire, Rhode Island, Vermont	Andover, MA 05501 (508) 474-9717
Illinois, Iowa, Minnesota, Missouri, Wisconsin	Kansas City, MO 64999 (816) 926-5999
Delaware, District of Columbia, Maryland, Pennsylvania, Virginia	Philadelphia, PA 19255 (215) 961-3980
Indiana, Kentucky, Michigan, Ohio, West Virginia	Cincinnati, OH 45999 (606) 292-5467
Kansas, New Mexico, Oklahoma, Texas	Austin, TX 73301 (512) 462-7845
Alaska, Arizona, California (counties of Alpine, Amador, Butte, Calaveras, Colusa, Contra Costa, Del Norte, El Dorado, Glenn, Humboldt, Lake, Lassen, Marin, Mendocino, Modoc, Napa, Nevada, Placer, Plumas, Sacramento, San Joaquin, Shasta, Sierra, Siskiyou, Solano, Sonoma, Sutter, Tehama, Trinity, Yolo, and Yuba), Colorado, Idaho, Montana, Nebraska, Nevada, North Dakota, Oregon, South Dakota, Utah, Washington, Wyoming	Ogden, UT 84201 (801) 625-7645
California (all other counties), Hawaii	Fresno, CA 93888 (209) 456-5900
Alabama, Arkansas, Louisiana, Mississippi, North Carolina, Tennessee	Memphis, TN 37501 (901) 365-5970

If you have no legal residence, principal place of business, or principal office or agency in any Internal Revenue District, file your form with the Internal Revenue Service Center, Philadelphia, PA 19255 or call (215) 961-3980.

Specific Instructions

The instructions that follow are for those items that are not self-explanatory. Enter N/A (nonapplicable) on the lines that do not apply.

Line 1.—Enter the legal name of the entity applying for the EIN.

Individuals.—Enter the first name, middle initial, and last name.

Trusts.—Enter the name of the trust.

Estate of a decedent.—Enter the name of the estate.

Partnerships.—Enter the legal name of the partnership as it appears in the partnership agreement.

Corporations.—Enter the corporate name as set forth in the corporation charter or other legal document creating it.

Plan administrators.—Enter the name of the plan administrator. A plan administrator who already has an EIN should use that number.

Line 2.—Enter the trade name of the business if different from the legal name.

Note: *Use the full legal name entered on line 1 on all tax returns to be filed for the entity. However, if a trade name is entered on line 2, use only the name on line 1 or the name on line 2 consistently when filing tax returns.*

Line 3.—Trusts enter the name of the trustee. Estates enter the name of the executor, administrator, or other fiduciary. If the entity applying has a designated person to receive tax information, enter that person's name as the "care of" person. Print or type the first name, middle initial, and last name.

Lines 5a and 5b.—If the physical location of the business is different from the mailing address (lines 4a and 4b), enter the address of the physical location on lines 5a and 5b.

Line 7.—Enter the first name, middle initial, and last name of a principal officer if the business is a corporation; of a general partner if a partnership; and of a grantor if a trust.

Line 8a.—Check the box that best describes the type of entity that is applying for the EIN. If not specifically mentioned, check the "other" box and enter the type of entity. Do not enter N/A.

Individual.—Check this box if the individual files Schedule C or F (Form 1040) and has a Keogh plan or is required to file excise, employment, or alcohol, tobacco, or firearms returns. If this box is checked, enter the individual's SSN (social security number) in the space provided.

Plan administrator.—The term plan administrator means the person or group of persons specified as the administrator by the instrument under which the plan is operated. If the plan administrator is an individual, enter the plan administrator's SSN in the space provided.

New withholding agent.—If you are a new withholding agent required to file Form 1042, check the "other" box and enter in the space provided "new withholding agent."

REMICs.—Check this box if the entity is a real estate mortgage investment conduit (REMIC). A REMIC is any entity

1. To which an election to be treated as a REMIC applies for the tax year and all prior tax years,

2. In which all of the interests are regular interests or residual interests,

3. Which has one class of residual interests (and all distributions, if any, with respect to such interests are pro rata),

4. In which as of the close of the 3rd month beginning after the startup date and at all times thereafter, substantially all of its assets consist of qualified mortgages and permitted investments,

5. Which has a tax year that is a calendar year, and

6. With respect to which there are reasonable arrangements designed to ensure that: (a) residual interests are not held by disqualified organizations (as defined in section 860E(e)(5)), and (b) information necessary for the application of section 860E(e) will be made available.

For more information about REMICs see the Instructions for **Form 1066**, U. S. Real Estate Mortgage Investment Conduit Income Tax Return.

Personal service corporations.—Check this box if the entity is a personal service corporation. An entity is a personal service corporation for a tax year only if

1. The entity is a C corporation for the tax year.

2. The principal activity of the entity during the testing period (as defined in Temporary Regulations section 1.441-4T(f)) for the tax year is the performance of personal service.

3. During the testing period for the tax year, such services are substantially performed by employee-owners.

4. The employee-owners own 10 percent of the fair market value of the outstanding stock in the entity on the last day of the testing period for the tax year.

For more information about personal service corporations, see the instructions for **Form 1120**, U.S. Corporation Income Tax Return, and Temporary Regulations section 1.441-4T.

Other corporations.—This box is for any corporation other than a personal service corporation. If you check this box, enter the type of corporation (such as insurance company) in the space provided.

Other nonprofit organizations.—Check this box if the nonprofit organization is other than a church or church-controlled organization and specify the type of nonprofit organization (for example, an educational organization.)

Group exemption number (GEN).—If the applicant is a nonprofit organization that is a subordinate organization to be included in a group exemption letter under Revenue Procedure 80-27, 1980-1 C.B. 677, enter the GEN in the space provided. If you do not know the GEN, contact the parent organization for it. GEN is a four-digit number. Do not confuse it with the nine-digit EIN.

Line 9.—Check only one box. Do not enter N/A.

Started new business.—Check this box if you are starting a new business that requires an EIN. If you check this box, enter the type of business being started. **DO NOT** apply if you already nave an EIN and are only adding another place of business.

Changed type of organization.—Check this box if the business is changing its type of organization, for example, if the business was a sole proprietorship and has been incorporated or has become a partnership. If you check this box, specify in the space provided the type of change made, for example, "from sole proprietorship to partnership."

Purchased going business.—Check this box if you acquired a business through purchase. Do not use the former owner's EIN. If you already have an EIN, use that number.

Hired employees.—Check this box if the existing business is requesting an EIN because it has hired or is hiring employees and is therefore required to file employment tax return for which an EIN is required. **DO NOT** apply if you already have an EIN and are only hiring employees.

Created a trust.—Check this box if you created a trust, and enter the type of trust created.

Created a pension plan.—Check this box if you have created a pension plan and need this number for reporting purposes. Also, enter the type of plan created.

Banking purpose.—Check this box if you are requesting an EIN for banking purpose only and enter the banking purpose (for example, checking, loan, etc.).

Other (specify).—Check this box if you are requesting an EIN for any reason other than those for which there are checkboxes and enter the reason.

Line 10.—If you are starting a new business, enter the starting date of the business. If the business you acquired is already operating, enter the date you acquired the business. Trusts should enter the date the trust was legally created. Estates should enter the date of death of the decedent whose name appears on line 1.

Line 11.—Enter the last month of your accounting year or tax year. An accounting year or tax year is usually 12 consecutive months. It may be a calendar year or a fiscal year (including a period of 52 or 53 weeks). A calendar year is 12 consecutive months ending on December 31. A fiscal year is either 12 consecutive months ending on the last day of any month other than December or a 52-53 week year. For more information

on accounting periods, see **Pub. 538,** Accounting Periods and Methods.

Individuals.—Your tax year generally will be a calendar year.

Partnerships.—Partnerships generally should conform to the tax year of either (1) its majority partners; (2) its principal partners; (3) the tax year that results in the least aggregate deferral of income (see Temporary Regulations section 1.706-1T); or (4) some other tax year, if (a) a business purpose is established for the fiscal year, or (b) the fiscal year is a "grandfather" year, or (c) an election is made under section 444 to have a fiscal year. (See the Instructions for **Form 1065,** U.S. Partnership Return of Income, for more information.)

REMICs.—Remics must have a calendar year as their tax year.

Personal service corporations.—A personal service corporation generally must adopt a calendar year unless:

1. It can establish to the satisfaction of the Commissioner that there is a business purpose for having a different tax year, or

2. It elects under section 444 to have a tax year other than a calendar year.

Line 12.—If the business has or will have employees, enter on this line the date on which the business began or will begin to pay wages to the employees. If the business does not have any plans to have employees, enter N/A on this line.

New withholding agent.—Enter the date you began or will begin to pay income to a nonresident alien. This also applies to individuals who are required to file Form 1042 to report alimony paid to a nonresident alien.

Line 14.—Generally, enter the exact type of business being operated (for example, advertising agency, farm, labor union, real estate agency, steam laundry, rental of coin-operated vending machine, investment club, etc.).

Governmental.—Enter the type of organization (state, county, school district, or municipality, etc.)

Nonprofit organization (other than governmental).—Enter whether organized for religious, educational, or humane purposes, and the principal activity (for example, religious organization—hospital, charitable).

Mining and quarrying.—Specify the process and the principal product (for example, mining bituminous coal, contract drilling for oil, quarrying dimension stone, etc.).

Contract construction.—Specify whether general contracting or special trade contracting. Also, show the type of work normally performed (for example, general contractor for residential buildings, electrical subcontractor, etc.).

Trade.—Specify the type of sales and the principal line of goods sold (for example, wholesale dairy products, manufacturer's representative for mining machinery, retail hardware, etc.).

Manufacturing.—Specify the type of establishment operated (for example, sawmill, vegetable cannery, etc.).

Signature block.—The application must be signed by: (1) the individual, if the person is an individual, (2) the president, vice president, or other principal officer, if the person is a corporation, (3) a responsible and duly authorized member or officer having knowledge of its affairs, if the person is a partnership or other unincorporated organization, or (4) the fiduciary, if the person is a trust or estate.

Form **940**	**Employer's Annual Federal Unemployment (FUTA) Tax Return**	OMB No. 1545-0028

Department of the Treasury
Internal Revenue Service

▶ **For Paperwork Reduction Act Notice, see separate instructions.**

1991

		T	
	Name (as distinguished from trade name) Calendar year	FF	
If incorrect, make any necessary change. ▶		FD	
	Trade name, if any	FP	
		I	
	Address and ZIP code Employer identification number	T	

A Did you pay all required contributions to state unemployment funds by the due date of Form 940? (If a 0% experience rate is granted, check "Yes" and see instructions.) . . . . ☐ **Yes** ☐ **No**
  If you checked the "Yes" box, enter the amount of contributions paid to state unemployment funds . ▶ $ ....

B Are you required to pay contributions to only one state? . . . . ☐ **Yes** ☐ **No**
  If you checked the "Yes" box: (1) Enter the name of the state where you have to pay contributions ▶ ....
  (2) Enter your state reporting number(s) as shown on state unemployment tax return. ▶ ....
  If you checked the "No" box, be sure to complete Part III and see the instructions.

C If any part of wages taxable for FUTA tax is exempt from state unemployment tax, check the box. (See the instructions.). . . . . ☐

If you will not have to file returns in the future, check here, complete, and sign the return . . . . ▶ ☐
If this is an Amended Return, check here . . . . ▶ ☐

Part I **Computation of Taxable Wages** *(to be completed by all taxpayers)*

1	Total payments (including exempt payments) during the calendar year for services of employees.	**1**	
2	Exempt payments. (Explain each exemption shown, attach additional sheets if necessary.) ▶	Amount paid **2**	
3	Payments of more than $7,000 for services. Enter only the amounts over the first $7,000 paid to each employee. Do not include payments from line 2. Do not use the state wage limitation	**3**	
4	Total exempt payments (add lines 2 and 3)	**4**	
5	**Total taxable wages** (subtract line 4 from line 1) . . . . ▶	**5**	
6	Additional tax resulting from credit reduction for unpaid advances to the state of Michigan. Enter the wages included on line 5 above for that state and multiply by the rate shown. (See the instructions.) Enter the credit reduction amount here and in Part II, line 2, or Part III, line 5: Michigan wages _____ × .008 = ... ▶	**6**	

Cat. No. 11234O   Form **940** (1991)

Form 940 (1991)   Page **2**

Part II   Tax Due or Refund *(Complete if you checked the "Yes" boxes in both questions A and B and did not check the box in C.)*

1	**FUTA tax.** Multiply the wages in Part I, line 5, by .008 and enter here.	**1**	
2	Enter amount from Part I, line 6	**2**	
3	**Total FUTA tax** (add lines 1 and 2) . . . . ▶	**3**	
4	Total FUTA tax deposited for the year, including any overpayment applied from a prior year . .	**4**	
5	**Balance due** (subtract line 4 from line 3). This should be $100 or less. Pay to the Internal Revenue Service. . . . . ▶	**5**	
6	**Overpayment** (subtract line 3 from line 4). Check if it is to be: ☐ **Applied to next return,** or ☐ **Refunded** . . . . ▶	**6**	

Part III   Tax Due or Refund *(Complete if you checked the "No" box in either question A or B or you checked the box in C.)*

1	Gross FUTA tax. Multiply the wages in Part I, line 5, by .062	**1**	
2	Maximum credit. Multiply the wages in Part I, line 5, by .054 . . .	**2**	
3	Computation of tentative credit		

(a) Name of state	(b) State reporting number(s) as shown on employer's state contribution returns	(c) Taxable payroll (as defined in state act)	(d) State experience rate		(e) State experience rate	(f) Contributions if rate had been 5.4% (col. (c) x .054)	(g) Contributions payable at experience rate (col. (c) x col. (e))	(h) Additional credit (col. (f) minus col.(g)). If 0 or less, enter 0.	(i) Contributions actually paid to the state
			From	To					

3a	Totals . . . ▶		
3b	**Total tentative credit** (add line 3a, columns (h) and (i) only—see instructions for limitations on late payments) ▶		
4	**Credit:** Enter the smaller of the amount in Part III, line 2, or line 3b **4**		
5	Enter the amount from Part I, line 6	**5**	
6	**Credit allowable** (subtract line 5 from line 4). (If zero or less, enter 0.)	**6**	
7	**Total FUTA tax** (subtract line 6 from line 1)	**7**	
8	Total FUTA tax deposited for the year, including any overpayment applied from a prior year . .	**8**	
9	**Balance due** (subtract line 8 from line 7). This should be $100 or less. Pay to the Internal Revenue Service. . . . . ▶	**9**	
10	**Overpayment** (subtract line 7 from line 8). Check if it is to be: ☐ **Applied to next return,** or ☐ **Refunded** . . . . ▶	**10**	

Part IV   Record of Quarterly Federal Tax Liability for Unemployment Tax *(Do not include state liability)*

Quarter	First	Second	Third	Fourth	Total for year
Liability for quarter					

Under penalties of perjury. I declare that I have examined this return, including accompanying schedules and statements, and to the best of my knowledge and belief, it is true, correct, and complete, and that no part of any payment made to a state unemployment fund claimed as a credit was or is to be deducted from the payments to employees.

Signature ▶ _____   Title (Owner, etc.) ▶ _____   Date ▶ _____

19**91**   Department of the Treasury
Internal Revenue Service

Instructions for Form 940

Employer's Annual Federal Unemployment (FUTA) Tax Return

(Section references are to the Internal Revenue Code unless otherwise noted.)

Paperwork Reduction Act Notice.—We ask for the information on this form to carry out the Internal Revenue laws of the United States. You are required to give us the information. We need it to ensure that you are complying with these laws and to allow us to figure and collect the right amount of tax.

The time needed to complete and file this form will vary depending on individual circumstances. The estimated average time is:

Recordkeeping . . . 14 hr., 21 min.

Learning about the law or the form . . . . . 12 min.

Preparing and sending the form to the IRS . . . 26 min.

If you have comments concerning the accuracy of these time estimates or suggestions for making this form more simple, we would be happy to hear from you. You can write to both the **Internal Revenue Service,** Washington, DC 20224, Attention: IRS Reports Clearance Officer, T:FP; and the **Office of Management and Budget,** Paperwork Reduction Project (1545-0028), Washington, DC 20503. Do not send the tax form to either of these offices. Instead, see the instructions for Where To File on page 2.

Items You Should Note

Credit Reduction State.—For 1991, Michigan is a credit reduction state. If you pay any wages that are subject to the unemployment compensation laws of the state of Michigan, you must file Form 940, instead of Form 940-EZ, described next.

Form 940-EZ.—You may be able to use Form 940-EZ. It is a simplified version of Form 940. Generally, employers who pay all unemployment contributions to only one state in a timely manner and do not have taxable FUTA wages that are exempt from state

unemployment tax, can use Form 940-EZ. For more details, get Form 940-EZ. Do not file Form 940 if you have already filed Form 940-EZ for 1991.

FUTA Tax Rate.—The FUTA tax rate is scheduled to remain at 6.2% for years 1991 through 1995.

Revised Part III.—The Computation of Tentative Credit, previously Part V, was combined with Part III and is labeled line 3.

Final and Amended Returns.—Checkboxes have been added for you to mark if this is your final return or an amended return.

General Instructions

Purpose of Form.—The Federal Unemployment Tax Act (FUTA), together with state unemployment systems, provides for payments of unemployment compensation to workers who have lost their jobs. Most employers pay both a Federal and state unemployment tax. Use this form for your annual FUTA tax report. **Only the employer pays this tax.**

Who Must File

In General.—You must file this form if you were not a household or agricultural employer during 1990 or 1991, and you: (a) paid wages of $1,500 or more in any calendar quarter or (b) had one or more employees for some part of a day in any 20 different weeks. Count all regular, temporary, and part-time employees. A partnership should not count its partners. If there is a change in ownership or other transfer of business during the year, each employer who meets test (a) or (b) must file. Neither should report wages paid by the other. Organizations described in section 501(c)(3) of the Internal Revenue Code do not have to file.

Household Employers.—You do not have to file this form unless you paid

cash wages of $1,000 or more in any calendar quarter in 1990 or 1991 for household work in a private home, local college club, or a local chapter of a college fraternity or sorority. **Note:** *See Pub. 926, Employment Taxes for Household Employers, for more information.*

Agricultural Employers.—You must file Form 940 if either of the following applies to you:

1. You paid cash wages of $20,000 or more to farmworkers during any calendar quarter in 1990 or 1991.

2. You employed 10 or more farmworkers during some part of a day (whether or not at the same time) for at least one day during any 20 different weeks in 1990 or 1991.

Count aliens admitted to the United States on a temporary basis to perform farmwork to determine if you meet either of the tests. However, wages paid to these aliens are not subject to FUTA tax before 1993.

Completing Form 940

Employers Who Are Not Required To Deposit FUTA Tax.—If your total FUTA tax for the year is $100 or less, you do not have to deposit the tax. Make your FUTA tax payment when you file Form 940. If you do not have to deposit FUTA tax and you:

(a) made all required payments to state unemployment funds by the due date of Form 940,

(b) are required to make payments to the unemployment fund of only one state, and

(c) paid wages subject to Federal unemployment tax that are also subject to state unemployment tax, complete Parts I and II. Otherwise, complete Parts I and III.

Employers Who Are Required To Deposit FUTA Tax.—If you meet tests (a), (b), and (c) above, complete Parts I, II, and IV.

Cat. No. 13660I

Otherwise, complete Parts I, III, and IV.

Not Liable for FUTA Tax.—If you receive Form 940 and are not liable for FUTA tax for 1991, write "Not Liable" across the front, sign the return, and return it to the IRS. If you will not have to file returns in the future, check the box above Part I indicating that you will not have to file Form 940 in the future. Then complete and sign the return.

Due Date.—Form 940 for 1991 is due by January 31, 1992. However, if you deposited all tax due on time, you have 10 more days to file.

Where To File.—

If your principal business, office or agency is located in:	File with the Internal Revenue Service Center at:
Florida. Georgia. South Carolina	Atlanta. GA 39901
New Jersey. New York (New York City and counties of Nassau. Rockland. Suffolk. and Westchester)	Holtsville. NY 00501
New York (all other counties). Connecticut. Maine, Massachusetts. New Hampshire. Rhode Island. Vermont	Andover. MA 05501
Illinois. Iowa. Minnesota. Missouri. Wisconsin	Kansas City. MO 64999
Delaware. District of Columbia. Maryland. Pennsylvania, Puerto Rico. Virginia. Virgin Islands	Philadelphia. PA 19255
Indiana. Kentucky. Michigan. Ohio. West Virginia	Cincinnati. OH 45999
Kansas. New Mexico. Oklahoma. Texas	Austin. TX 73301
Alaska. Arizona. California (counties of Alpine. Amador. Butte. Calaveras. Colusa. Contra Costa. Del Norte. El Dorado. Glenn. Humboldt. Lake. Lassen. Marin. Mendocino. Modoc. Napa. Nevada. Placer. Plumas. Sacramento. San Joaquin. Shasta. Sierra. Siskiyou. Solano. Sonoma. Sutter. Tehama. Trinity. Yolo. and Yuba). Colorado. Idaho. Montana. Nebraska. Nevada. North Dakota. Oregon. South Dakota. Utah. Washington. Wyoming	Ogden. UT 84201
California (all other counties). Hawaii	Fresno. CA 93888
Alabama. Arkansas. Louisiana. Mississippi. North Carolina. Tennessee	Memphis. TN 37501

If you have no legal residence or principal place of business in any IRS district, file with the Internal Revenue Service Center, Philadelphia, PA 19255.

Employer's Name, Address, and Identification Number.—Use the

Page 2

preaddressed Form 940 mailed to you. If you must use a form that is not preaddressed, type or print your name, trade name, address, and employer identification number on it.

See **Pub. 583,** Taxpayers Starting a Business, for details on how to make tax deposits, file a return, etc., if these are due before you receive your employer identification number.

Identifying Your Payments.—On balance due payments of $100 or less made to the IRS (Part II, line 5, and Part III, line 9) and Federal tax deposit payments, write your employer identification number, "Form 940," and the tax period to which the payment applies on your check or money order. This will help ensure proper crediting of your account.

Penalties and Interest.—Avoid penalties and interest by making tax deposits when due, filing a correct return, and paying the proper amount of tax when due. The law provides penalties for late deposits and late filing unless you show reasonable cause for the delay. If you file late, attach an explanation to the return. See **Circular E,** Employer's Tax Guide, for information on penalties.

There are also penalties for willful failure to pay tax, keep records, make returns, and filing false or fraudulent returns.

Credit for Contributions Paid Into State Funds.—You can claim credit for amounts you pay into a certified state (including Puerto Rico and the Virgin Islands) unemployment fund by the due date of Form 940. Your FUTA tax will be higher if you do not pay the state contributions timely.

Note: Be sure to enter your state reporting number where required on Form 940. This number is needed for the IRS to verify your state contributions.

"Contributions" are payments that state law requires you to make to an unemployment fund because you are an employer. These payments are "contributions" only to the extent that they are not deducted or deductible from the employees' pay.

Do not take credit for penalties, interest, or special administrative taxes which are not included in the contribution rate the state assigned to you. Also, do not take credit for voluntary contributions paid to obtain a lower assigned rate.

If you have been assigned an experience rate lower than 5.4% (.054) by a state for the whole or part of the year, you are entitled to an additional credit. This **additional** credit is equal to the difference between actual payments and the amount you would have been required to pay at 5.4%.

The total credit allowable may not be more than 5.4% of the total taxable FUTA wages eligible for credit.

Special Credit for Successor Employers.—If you are claiming special credit as a successor employer, see section 3302(e) or Circular E, for the conditions you must meet.

Amended Returns.—If you are amending a previously filed return, complete a new Form 940, using the amounts that should have been used on the original return, and sign the return. Attach a statement explaining why you are filing an amended return. Be sure to use a Form 940 for the year you are amending. If you are correcting a 1990 or prior year form, write "Amended Return" at the top of the form. To amend a 1991 Form 940, check the amended return box above Part I. File the amended return with the Internal Revenue Service Center where you filed the original return.

Specific Instructions

You must answer questions A and B (check the box in C only if it applies), complete Part I and the other Parts that apply, and sign the return.

Note: *If you have been assigned a 0% experience rate by your state so that there are no required contributions to the state unemployment fund, check the "Yes" box in question A and write "0% rate" on the dollar amount line.*

Use Part II only if you checked the "Yes" boxes in questions A and B and did not check the box in C. Otherwise, skip Part II and complete Part III.

Complete Part IV if your total tax for the year is more than $100.

Box C.—Check this box **ONLY** if you pay any wages that are taxable for FUTA tax but are exempt from your state's unemployment tax.

Part I.—Computation of Taxable Wages

Line 1—Total payments.—Enter the total payments you made to employees during the calendar year, even if they are not taxable. Include salaries, wages, commissions, fees, bonuses, vacation allowances, amounts paid to temporary or part-time employees, and the value of goods, lodging, food, clothing, and noncash fringe benefits. Include the amount of tips reported to you in writing by your employees. Also, include contributions to a 401(k) pension plan. Enter the amount before any deductions.

How the payments are made is not important in determining if they are wages. Thus, you may pay wages for piecework or as a percentage of profits, and you may pay wages hourly, daily, weekly, monthly, or yearly. You may pay wages in cash or some other way, such as goods, lodging, food, or clothing. For items other than cash, use the fair market value at the time of payment.

Line 2—Exempt payments.—"Wages" and "employment" as defined for FUTA purposes do not include every payment and every kind of service an employee may perform. In general, payments excluded from wages and payments for services excepted from employment are not subject to tax. You may deduct these exempt payments from total payments only if you explain them on line 2.

Enter payments for the following items:

(1) Agricultural labor, if you did not meet either of the tests in **Agricultural Employers** on page 1.

(2) Benefit payments for sickness or injury under a worker's compensation law.

(3) Household service if you did not pay cash wages of $1,000 or more in any calendar quarter in 1990 or 1991.

(4) Certain family employment.

(5) Certain fishing activities.

(6) Noncash payments for farmwork or household services in a private home that are included on line 1. Only cash wages to these workers are taxable.

(7) Value of certain meals and lodging.

(8) Cost of group-term life insurance.

(9) Payments attributable to the employee's contributions to a sick pay plan.

(10) Any other exempt service or pay.

For more information, see Circular E.

Line 3.—Enter the total amounts over $7,000 you paid each employee. For example, if you have 10 employees to whom you paid $8,000 each during the year, enter $80,000 on line 1 and $10,000 on line 3. Only the first $7,000 paid to your employee is subject to FUTA tax. Do not use the state wage limitation for this entry.

Line 5—Total taxable wages.—If any part of these wages is exempt from state unemployment taxes, you must fill out Part III. For example, if you pay wages to corporate officers in a state that exempts these wages from its unemployment taxes (these wages are taxable for FUTA tax), you would check the box in C on page 1 and complete Part III.

Line 6—Computation of credit reduction.—Enter the amount of wages included on line 5 subject to the unemployment compensation laws of the state of Michigan. The wages shown on line 6 cannot exceed the total taxable wages shown on line 5. If no wages are subject to these laws, enter "none" on line 6. Multiply the wages by the rate shown.

The amount of this adjustment increases the FUTA tax by reducing the credit otherwise allowable against the FUTA tax for contributions made to state unemployment funds. However, the increase cannot be more than the credit otherwise allowable.

Part II.—Tax Due or Refund

Use this part only if you checked "Yes" for both questions A and B on Form 940, and did not check the box in C. The tax rate of .008 gives you credit for your payments to your state's unemployment fund.

The amount on line 2 is the additional tax resulting from credit reduction attributable to wages paid that are subject to the unemployment tax laws of the state of Michigan.

Part III.—Tax Due or Refund

Use this part if you do not qualify for Part II. Failure to provide this information could increase your tax.

Line 3.—Complete this schedule if you checked the "No" box in either question A or B on Form 940, or if you checked the box in C. If you have been assigned an experience rate by your state of 0% or more, but less than 5.4% for all or part of the year, use columns (a) through (i). If you have not been assigned any experience rate by your state, use columns (a), (b), (c), and (i) only. If you have been assigned a rate of 5.4% or higher, use columns (a), (b), (c), (d), (e) and (i) only. If you were assigned an experience rate for only part of the year or the rate was changed during the year, complete a separate line for each rate period.

If you need additional lines, attach a separate statement with a similar format.

Column (a).—Enter the name of the state(s) that you were required to pay contributions to (including Puerto Rico and the Virgin Islands).

Column (b).—Enter the state reporting number that was assigned to you when you registered as an employer with each state.

Column (c).—Enter the taxable payroll on which you must pay taxes to the unemployment fund of each state in column (a). If your experience rate is 0%, enter the amount of wages that you would have had to pay on if the rate had not been granted.

Columns (d) and (e).—Your "state experience rate" is the rate at which the state taxes your payroll for state unemployment purposes. This rate may be adjusted from time to time based on your "experience" with the state tax fund, that is, unemployment compensation paid to your former employees and other factors. If you do not know your rate, contact your state unemployment insurance service. The state experience rate can be stated as a percent or a decimal.

Column (h).—Subtract column (g) from column (f). If zero or less, enter "0."

Column (i).—Enter the contributions actually paid into the state fund by the due date of Form 940. Do not include any special assessments, surtaxes, surcharges, etc., used by the state to pay interest on unpaid advances from the Federal Government.

Line 3a.—Enter the totals of columns (c), (h), and (i) on this line. The total of all amounts reported in column (i) should equal the amount entered under question A at the top of Form 940.

Line 3b.—Add line 3a, columns (h) and (i) only. If you file Form 940 after its due date and any contributions in column (i) were made after the due date, your credit for late contributions is limited to **90%** of their amount. For example, if $1,500 of state contributions was paid on time, and $1,000 was paid after the due date for filing Form 940, the total tentative credit on line 3b would be $2,400 ($1,500 + $900 (90% of $1,000)). This is assuming there is no additional credit in column (h).

Note: *If you are receiving additional credit (column (h)) because your state experience rate is less than 5.4%, the additional credit is not subject to the 90% limitation.*

Line 4.—Enter the smaller of Part III, line 3b, or Part III, line 2. This is the credit allowable for your payments to state unemployment funds. If you do not have to make payments to the state, enter "0" on this line.

Lines 5 and 6.—Enter the amount from Part I, line 6 on line 5. Subtract this amount from line 4. The result on line 6 is your allowable credit for payments to the state.

Part IV.—Record of Federal Tax Liability

Complete this part if your total tax (Part II, line 3, or Part III, line 7) is over $100. To figure your FUTA tax liability **for each of the first 3 quarters of 1991,** multiply by .008 that part of the first $7,000 of each employee's annual wages you paid during the quarter. Enter this amount under that quarter.

Your liability for the 4th quarter is the total tax (Part II, line 3 or Part III, line 7) minus your liability for the first 3 quarters of the year. The total liability must equal your total tax. Otherwise, you may be charged a failure to deposit penalty figured on your average liability.

Depositing FUTA tax.—Generally, FUTA taxes are deposited on a quarterly basis. If your liability for any of the first 3 quarters of 1991 (plus any undeposited amount of $100 or less from any earlier quarter) is over $100, deposit it by the last day of the first month following the close of the quarter. If it is $100 or less, you may carry it to the next quarter; a deposit is not required. If your liability for the 4th quarter (plus any undeposited amount from any earlier quarter) is over $100, deposit the entire amount by January 31, 1992. If it is $100 or less, you can either make a deposit or pay it with your Form 940 by January 31, 1992.

Note: *The total amount of all deposits must be shown in Part II, line 4 or Part III, line 8.*

If you deposited the correct amounts, following these rules, the balance due with Form 940 will never be more than $100.

Deposit FUTA tax in an authorized financial institution or the Federal Reserve bank for your area. To avoid a possible penalty, do not mail deposits directly to the IRS. Records of your deposits will be sent to the IRS for crediting to your business accounts. See **Identifying Your Payments** on page 2.

You must use **Form 8109,** Federal Tax Deposit Coupon, when making each tax deposit. The IRS will send you a book of deposit coupons when you apply for an employer identification number. Follow the instructions in the coupon book. If you do not have coupons, see Circular E.

★U.S.GPO:1991-0-285-489

Form **940-EZ**	**Employer's Annual Federal Unemployment (FUTA) Tax Return**	OMB No. 1545-1110
Department of the Treasury Internal Revenue Service		19**91**

	Name (as distinguished from trade name)	
If incorrect, make any necessary changes. ▶	Trade name, if any	EMPLOYER'S COPY
	Address and ZIP code	
		Employer identification number

Follow the chart under "Who Can Use Form 940-EZ" on page 2. If you cannot use Form 940-EZ, you must use Form 940 instead.

A Enter the amount of contributions paid to your state unemployment fund. (See instructions for line A on page 4.) ▶ $ ....

B (1) Enter the name of the state where you have to pay contributions . . . . ▶ ....

  (2) Enter your state reporting number(s) as shown on state unemployment tax return. ▶ ....

If you will not have to file returns in the future, check here (see *Who Must File a Return* on page 2) **complete, and sign the return** . . . ▶ ☐

If this is an Amended Return check here . . . . ▶ ☐

Part I   Taxable Wages and FUTA Tax

1	Total payments (including payments shown on lines 2 and 3) during the calendar year for services of employees		**1**		
			Amount paid		
2	Exempt payments. (Explain all exempt payments. attaching additional sheets if necessary.) ▶	**2**			
3	Payments for services of more than $7.000. Enter only amounts over the first $7.000 paid to each employee. Do not include any exempt payments from line 2 . . .	**3**			
4	Total exempt payments (add lines 2 and 3) . . . . ▶		**4**		
5	**Total taxable wages** (subtract line 4 from line 1) . . . . ▶		**5**		
6	**FUTA tax.** Multiply the wages on line 5 by .008 and enter here. (If the result is over $100. also complete Part II.) .		**6**		
7	Total FUTA tax deposited for the year. including any overpayment applied from a prior year (from your records)		**7**		
8	**Amount you owe** (subtract line 7 from line 6). This should be $100 or less. Pay to "Internal Revenue Service". ▶		**8**		
9	**Overpayment** (subtract line 6 from line 7). Check if it is to be: ☐ Applied to next return, or ☐ Refunded ▶		**9**		

Part II   Record of Quarterly Federal Unemployment Tax Liability (Do not include state liability.) Complete only if line 6 is over $100.

Quarter	First (Jan. 1 – Mar. 31)	Second (Apr. 1 – June 30)	Third (July 1 – Sept. 30)	Fourth (Oct. 1 – Dec. 31)	Total for Year
Liability for quarter					

Under penalties of perjury. I declare that I have examined this return. including accompanying schedules and statements. and. to the best of my knowledge and belief. it is true. correct. and complete. and that no part of any payment made to a state unemployment fund claimed as a credit was. or is to be. deducted from the payments to employees.

Signature ▶   Title (Owner, etc.) ▶   Date ▶

If You Are Not Liable for FUTA Tax.—If you receive Form 940-EZ and are not liable for FUTA tax for 1991, write "Not Liable" across the front of the form. sign the return, and return it to the IRS. **Note:** *If you will not have to file returns in the future, check the box on the line below B(2), complete and sign the return.*

Due Date.—Form 940-EZ for 1991 is due by January 31, 1992. However. if you deposited all tax due on time. you have 10 more days to file.

Employer's Name, Address, and Identification Number.—If you are not using a preaddressed Form 940-EZ. type or print your name, trade name. address. and employer identification number (EIN) on Form 940-EZ.

See **Pub. 583,** Taxpayers Starting a Business. for details on how to make tax deposits. file a return. etc., if these are due before you get your EIN.

Identifying Your Payments.—When you pay any amount you owe to the IRS (line 8) or make Federal tax deposits, write on your check or money order: Your EIN. "Form 940-EZ." and the tax period to which the payment applies. This helps make sure we credit your account properly.

Paperwork Reduction Act Notice.—We ask for the information on this form to carry out the Internal Revenue laws of the United States. You are required to give us the information. We need it to ensure that you are complying with these laws and to allow us to figure and collect the correct tax.

The time needed to complete and file this form will vary depending on individual circumstances. The estimated average time is:

Recordkeeping . . . . . .5 hr., 20 min.

**Learning about the
law or the form** . . . . 7 min.

**Preparing and sending
the form to IRS** . . . . . . 26 min.

If you have comments concerning the accuracy of these time estimates or suggestions for making this form more simple, we would be happy to hear from you. You can write to both the **Internal Revenue Service**, Washington, DC 20224. Attention: IRS Reports Clearance Officer. T:FP; and the **Office of Management and Budget**, Paperwork Reduction Project (1545-1110), Washington, DC 20503. **DO NOT** send the form to either of these offices. Instead, see **Where To File.**

Who May Not Use Form 940-EZ.—

If you pay any wages that are subject to the unemployment compensation laws of the state of Michigan, you must file **Form 940**, instead of Form 940-EZ.

Who May Use Form 940-EZ.—You may use Form 940-EZ if:

(1) You paid unemployment taxes ("contributions") to only one state;

(2) You paid these taxes by the due date of Form 940-EZ; and

(3) All wages that were taxable for FUTA tax were also taxable for your state's unemployment tax. Otherwise, use Form 940. For example, if you paid wages to corporate officers (these wages are taxable for FUTA tax) in a state that exempts these wages from its unemployment taxes, you cannot use Form 940-EZ.

The following chart will lead you to the right form to use.

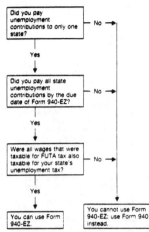

Note: *Do not file Form 940-EZ if you have already filed Form 940 for 1991.*

General Instructions

Purpose of Form.—The Federal Unemployment Tax Act (FUTA), together with state unemployment systems, provides for payments of unemployment compensation to workers who have lost their jobs. Most employers pay both Federal and state unemployment taxes. Use this form for your annual FUTA tax report. **Only the employer pays this tax.**

Who Must File

General Rule (household and agricultural employers see next column).—File a FUTA tax return if either of the following applies:

(1) You paid wages of $1,500 or more in any calendar quarter in 1990 or 1991; or

(2) You had at least one employee for some part of a day in any 20 different weeks in 1990 or 1991.

Count all regular, temporary, and part-time employees. A partnership should not count its partners. If a business changes hands during the year, each employer meeting test (1) or (2) above must file. Neither should report wages paid by the other.

Household Employers.—File a FUTA tax return **ONLY** if you paid cash wages of $1,000 or more in any calendar quarter in 1990 or 1991 for household work in a private home, local college club, or a local chapter of a college fraternity or sorority.

Note: *See Pub. 926, Employment Taxes for Household Employers, for more information.*

Agricultural Employers.—File a FUTA tax return if either of the following applies:

(1) You paid cash wages of $20,000 or more to farmworkers during any calendar quarter in 1990 or 1991; or

(2) You employed 10 or more farmworkers during some part of a day (whether or not at the same time) for at least 1 day during any 20 different weeks in 1990 or 1991.

Count aliens admitted to the United States temporarily to do farmwork to see if you met either of the above tests. However, wages paid to these aliens are not subject to FUTA tax before 1993.

Nonprofit Organizations.—Religious. educational, charitable, etc., organizations described in section 501(c)(3) of the Internal Revenue Code and exempt from tax under section 501(a) are not subject to FUTA tax and are not required to file.

Completing Form 940-EZ.—If your FUTA tax for 1991 (line 6) is $100 or less. complete only Part I of the form. If your FUTA tax is over $100. complete Parts I and II. See the instructions for Part II for information on FUTA tax deposits.

Filing Hint.—You can help avoid IRS contacts for missing information and delays in processing your return by making sure you fill in all the lines that apply to you. And, if you are not using a preaddressed Form 940-EZ. be sure you fill in the name lines exactly as they were shown on your **Form SS-4,** Application for Employer Identification Number.

(Instructions continued on next page.)

Form 940-EZ (1991)   **Page 4**

Where To File

If your principal business, office, or agency is located in:	File with the Internal Revenue Service Center at:
Florida, Georgia, South Carolina	Atlanta, GA 39901
New Jersey, New York (New York City and counties of Nassau, Rockland, Suffolk, and Westchester)	Holtsville, NY 00501
New York (all other counties), Connecticut, Maine, Massachusetts, New Hampshire, Rhode Island, Vermont	Andover, MA 05501
Illinois, Iowa, Minnesota, Missouri, Wisconsin	Kansas City, MO 64999
Delaware, District of Columbia, Maryland, Pennsylvania, Puerto Rico, Virginia, Virgin Islands	Philadelphia, PA 19255
Indiana, Kentucky, Michigan, Ohio, West Virginia	Cincinnati, OH 45999
Kansas, New Mexico, Oklahoma, Texas	Austin, TX 73301
Alaska, Arizona, California (counties of Alpine, Amador, Butte, Calaveras, Colusa, Contra Costa, Del Norte, El Dorado, Glenn, Humboldt, Lake, Lassen, Marin, Mendocino, Modoc, Napa, Nevada, Placer, Plumas, Sacramento, San Joaquin, Shasta, Sierra, Siskiyou, Solano, Sonoma, Sutter, Tehama, Trinity, Yolo, and Yuba), Colorado, Idaho, Montana, Nebraska, Nevada, North Dakota, Oregon, South Dakota, Utah, Washington, Wyoming	Ogden, UT 84201
California (all other counties), Hawaii	Fresno, CA 93888
Alabama, Arkansas, Louisiana, Mississippi, North Carolina, Tennessee	Memphis, TN 37501

If you have no legal residence or principal place of business in any IRS district, file with the Internal Revenue Service Center, Philadelphia, PA 19255.

Penalties and Interest.—Avoid penalties and interest by making tax deposits when due, filing a correct return, and paying all taxes when due. There are penalties for late deposits and late filing unless you can show reasonable cause. If you file late, attach an explanation to the return.

There are also penalties for willful failure to pay tax, keep records, make returns, and for filing false or fraudulent returns.

Credit for Contributions Paid Into State Funds.—You get a credit for amounts you pay to a state (including Puerto Rico and the Virgin Islands) unemployment fund by the due date of Form 940-EZ. This credit is reflected in the tax rate (.008) shown on line 6.

"Contributions" are payments that a state requires you, as an employer, to make to its unemployment fund for the payment of unemployment benefits. However, contributions do not include:

● Any payments you deducted or are deductible from your employees' pay.

● Penalties, interest, or special administrative taxes which are not included in the contribution rate the state assigned to you.

● Voluntary contributions you paid to get a lower assigned rate.

Note: *Be sure to enter your state reporting number(s) on line B(2) at the top of the form. We need this to verify your state contributions.*

Special Credit for Successor Employers.—If you are claiming special credit as a successor employer, you must use Form 940.

Amended Returns.—Use a new Form 940-EZ to amend a previously filed Form 940-EZ. Check the Amended Return box above Part I, enter the amounts that should have been on the original return, and sign the amended return. Explain why you are amending Form 940-EZ.

If you were required to file Form 940 but filed Form 940-EZ instead, file the amended return on Form 940. See Form 940 and the instructions for information.

Specific Instructions

You must complete lines A and B and Part I. If your FUTA tax (line 6) is over $100, you must also complete Part II. Please remember to sign the return.

Line A.—Enter the dollar amount of state unemployment contributions. However, if your state has given you a 0% experience rate, so that there are no required contributions, write "0% rate" in the space.

Part I. Taxable Wages and FUTA Tax

Line 1—Total payments.—Enter the total payments you made to employees during the calendar year, even if they are not taxable. Include salaries, wages, commissions, fees, bonuses, vacation allowances, amounts paid to temporary or part-time employees, and the value of goods, lodging, food, clothing, and noncash fringe benefits. Also include the amount of tips reported to you in writing by your employees. Enter the amount before any deductions.

How the payments are made is not important to determine if they are wages. Thus, you may pay wages for piecework or as a percentage of profits. You may pay wages hourly, daily, weekly, monthly, or yearly. You may pay wages in cash or some other way, such as goods, lodging, food, or clothing. For items other than cash, use the fair market value when paid.

Line 2—Exempt payments.—"Wages" and "employment" for FUTA purposes do not include every payment and every kind of service an employee may perform. In general, payments that are not wages and payments for services that are not employment are not subject to tax. You may deduct these payments from total payments only if you explain them on line 2.

Enter such items as the following:

(1) Agricultural labor, if you did not meet either of the tests in **Agricultural Employers** on page 2.

(2) Benefit payments for sickness or injury under a worker's compensation law.

(3) Household service if you did not pay cash wages of $1,000 or more in any calendar quarter in 1990 and 1991.

(4) Certain family employment.

(5) Certain fishing activities.

(6) Noncash payments for farmwork or household services in a private home that are included on line 1. Only cash wages to these workers are taxable.

(7) Value of certain meals and lodging.

(8) Cost of group-term life insurance.

(9) Payments attributable to the employee's contributions to a sick pay plan.

(10) Any other exempt service or pay.

For more information, see **Circular E,** Employer's Tax Guide.

Line 3—Enter the total amounts over $7,000 you paid each employee. For example, if you have 10 employees to whom you paid $8,000 each during the year, enter $80,000 on line 1 and $10,000 on line 3. Do not include any exempt payments from line 2 in figuring the $7,000.

Part II. Record of Quarterly Federal Unemployment Tax Liability

Complete this part only if your FUTA tax on line 6 is over $100. To figure your FUTA tax liability, multiply by .008 that part of the first $7,000 of each employee's annual wages you paid during the quarter. Enter the result in the space for that quarter.

Your total liability must equal your total tax. If not, you may be charged a failure to deposit penalty figured on your average liability.

Record your liability based on when you pay the wages, not on when you deposit the tax. For example, assume that you pay wages on March 29 and your FUTA tax liability on those wages is $200. You deposit the $200 by April 30. You would include that $200 in the first quarter, not the second.

Depositing FUTA Tax.—Generally, FUTA taxes are deposited quarterly. If your liability for any of the first 3 quarters of 1991 (plus any undeposited amount of $100 or less from any earlier quarter) is over $100, deposit it by the last day of the month after the end of the quarter. If it is $100 or less, carry it to the next quarter; a deposit is not required. If your liability for the 4th quarter (plus any undeposited amount from any earlier quarter) is over $100, deposit the entire amount by January 31, 1992. If it is $100 or less, you can either make a deposit or pay it with your Form 940-EZ by January 31.

Note: *The total amount of all deposits must be shown on line 7.*

If you deposited the right amounts, following these rules, the amount you owe with Form 940-EZ will never be over $100.

Deposit FUTA tax in an authorized financial institution or the Federal Reserve bank for your area. To avoid a possible penalty, do not mail deposits directly to the IRS. Records of your deposits will be sent to the IRS for crediting to your business accounts. See **Identifying Your Payments.**

You must use **Form 8109,** Federal Tax Deposit Coupon, when making tax deposits. IRS will send you a book of deposit coupons when you apply for an EIN. Follow the instructions in the coupon book. If you do not have coupons, see Circular E.

Form **940-EZ**	**Employer's Annual Federal Unemployment (FUTA) Tax Return**	OMB No. 1545-1110

Department of the Treasury
Internal Revenue Service

1991

T	
FF	
FD	
FP	
I	
T	

If incorrect, make any necessary changes. ▶

DD 10-1234567   9112   S28   B
Peter Cone
362 Main Street
Anytown   VA   23000

Calendar year

IRS or identification number

Follow the chart under "Who Can Use Form 940-EZ" on page 2. If you cannot use Form 940-EZ, you must use Form 940 instead.

A Enter the amount of contributions paid to your state unemployment fund. (See instructions for line A on page 4.) ▶ $ *630.00*

B (1) Enter the name of the state where you have to pay contributions .... ▶ *Virginia* ....

   (2) Enter your state reporting number(s) as shown on state unemployment tax return. ▶ *98765432* ....

If you will not have to file returns in the future, check here (see Who Must File a Return on page 2) complete, and sign the return . . . ▶ ☐

If this is an Amended Return check here . . . . ▶ ☐

Part I   Taxable Wages and FUTA Tax

1	Total payments (including payments shown on lines 2 and 3) during the calendar year for services of employees	**1**	*78,000.00*	
2	Exempt payments. (Explain all exempt payments, attaching additional sheets if necessary.) ▶		Amount paid	
		2		
3	Payments for services of more than $7,000. Enter only amounts over the first $7,000 paid to each employee. Do not include any exempt payments from line 2 . . .	**3**	*57,000.00*	
4	Total exempt payments (add lines 2 and 3)		**4**	*57,000.00*
5	Total taxable wages (subtract line 4 from line 1) . . . . ▶		**5**	*21,000.00*
6	FUTA tax. Multiply the wages on line 5 by .008 and enter here. (If the result is over $100, also complete Part II.) .		**6**	*168.00*
7	Total FUTA tax deposited for the year, including any overpayment applied from a prior year (from your records)		**7**	*142.40*
8	Amount you owe (subtract line 7 from line 6). This should be $100 or less. Pay to "Internal Revenue Service". ▶		**8**	*25.60*
9	Overpayment (subtract line 6 from line 7). Check if it is to be: ☐ Applied to next return, or ☐ Refunded ▶	$	**9**	

Part II   Record of Quarterly Federal Unemployment Tax Liability (Do not include state liability.) Complete only if line 6 is over $100.

Quarter	First (Jan. 1 – Mar. 31)	Second (Apr. 1 – June 30)	Third (July 1 – Sept. 30)	Fourth (Oct. 1 – Dec. 31)	Total for Year
Liability for quarter	*142.40*	*25.60*			*168.00*

Under penalties of perjury, I declare that I have examined this return, including accompanying schedules and statements, and, to the best of my knowledge and belief, it is true, correct, and complete, and that no part of any payment made to a state unemployment fund claimed as a credit was, or is to be, deducted from the payments to employees.

Signature ▶ *Peter Cone*   Title (Owner, etc.) ▶ *Owner*   Date ▶ *1-24-92*

☐ CORRECTED (if checked)

PAYER'S name, street address, city, state, and ZIP code		1 Rents $	OMB No. 1545-0115	**Miscellaneous Income**
		2 Royalties $	19**91**	
		3 Prizes, awards, etc. $		
PAYER'S Federal identification number	RECIPIENT'S identification number	4 Federal income tax withheld $	5 Fishing boat proceeds $	**Copy B For Recipient**
RECIPIENT'S name		6 Medical and health care payments $	7 Nonemployee compensation $	This is important tax information and is being furnished to the Internal Revenue Service. If you are required to file a return, a negligence penalty or other sanction may be imposed on you if this income is taxable and the IRS determines that it has not been reported.
Street address (including apt. no.)		8 Substitute payments in lieu of dividends or interest $	9 Payer made direct sales of $5,000 or more of consumer products to a buyer (recipient) for resale ▶ ☐	
City, state, and ZIP code		10 Crop insurance proceeds $	11 State income tax withheld $	
Account number (optional)		12 State/Payer's state number		

Form **1099-MISC**   Department of the Treasury - Internal Revenue Service

☐ CORRECTED (if checked)

PAYER'S name, street address, city, state, and ZIP code		1 Rents $	OMB No. 1545-0115	**Miscellaneous Income**
		2 Royalties $	19**91**	
		3 Prizes, awards, etc. $		
PAYER'S Federal identification number	RECIPIENT'S identification number	4 Federal income tax withheld $	5 Fishing boat proceeds $	**Copy B For Recipient**
RECIPIENT'S name		6 Medical and health care payments $	7 Nonemployee compensation $	This is important tax information and is being furnished to the Internal Revenue Service. If you are required to file a return, a negligence penalty or other sanction may be imposed on you if this income is taxable and the IRS determines that it has not been reported.
Street address (including apt. no.)		8 Substitute payments in lieu of dividends or interest $	9 Payer made direct sales of $5,000 or more of consumer products to a buyer (recipient) for resale ▶ ☐	
City, state, and ZIP code		10 Crop insurance proceeds $	11 State income tax withheld $	
Account number (optional)		12 State/Payer's state number		

Form **1099-MISC**   Department of the Treasury - Internal Revenue Service

☐ CORRECTED (if checked)

PAYER'S name, street address, city, state, and ZIP code		1 Rents $	OMB No. 1545-0115	**Miscellaneous Income**
		2 Royalties $	19**91**	
		3 Prizes, awards, etc. $		
PAYER'S Federal identification number	RECIPIENT'S identification number	4 Federal income tax withheld $	5 Fishing boat proceeds $	**Copy B For Recipient**
RECIPIENT'S name		6 Medical and health care payments $	7 Nonemployee compensation $	This is important tax information and is being furnished to the Internal Revenue Service. If you are required to file a return, a negligence penalty or other sanction may be imposed on you if this income is taxable and the IRS determines that it has not been reported.
Street address (including apt. no.)		8 Substitute payments in lieu of dividends or interest $	9 Payer made direct sales of $5,000 or more of consumer products to a buyer (recipient) for resale ▶ ☐	
City, state, and ZIP code		10 Crop insurance proceeds $	11 State income tax withheld $	
Account number (optional)		12 State/Payer's state number		

Form **1099-MISC**   Department of the Treasury - Internal Revenue Service

1099-MISC
(FRONT SIDE)

Instructions for Recipient

If you are an individual, report the taxable amounts shown on this form on your tax return, as explained below. (Other taxpayers, such as fiduciaries or partnerships, report the amounts on the corresponding lines of your tax return.)

Boxes 1 and 2.—Report on Schedule E (Form 1040); or Schedule C (Form 1040) if you provided services that were primarily for your customer's convenience, such as regular cleaning, changing linen, or maid service. But for royalties on timber, coal, and iron ore, see **Pub. 544,** Sales and Other Dispositions of Assets.

Box 3.—Report on the line for "Other income" on Form 1040 and identify the payment. If it is trade or business income, report this amount on Schedule C or F (Form 1040).

Box 4.—Shows backup withholding. For example, persons not furnishing their taxpayer identification number to the payer become subject to backup withholding at a 20% rate on certain payments. See **Form W-9,** Request for Taxpayer Identification Number and Certification, for information on backup withholding. **Include this on your income tax return as tax withheld.**

Box 5.—An amount in this box means the fishing boat operator considers you self-employed. Report this amount on Schedule C (Form 1040). See **Publication 595,** Tax Guide for Commercial Fishermen.

Box 6.—Report on Schedule C (Form 1040).

Box 7.—Generally, this amount is considered income from self-employment. Report it as part of your trade or business income on Schedule C or F (Form 1040). If you are not self-employed, amounts paid

to you for services rendered are generally reported on Form 1040 on the line for "Wages, salaries, tips, etc."

If there are two amounts shown in this box, one may be labeled "EPP." This represents excess golden parachute payments. You must pay a 20% excise tax on this amount. See your Form 1040 instructions under "Other Taxes." The unlabeled amount is your total compensation.

Box 8.—Report as "Other income" on your tax return. The amount shown is substitute payments in lieu of dividends or tax-exempt interest received by your broker on your behalf after transfer of your securities for use in a short sale.

Box 9.—An entry in the checkbox means sales to you of consumer products on a buy-sell, deposit-commission, or any other basis for resale have amounted to $5,000 or more. The person filing this return does not have to show a dollar amount in this box. Any income from your sale of these products should generally be reported on Schedule C (Form 1040).

Box 10.—Report on the line for "Crop insurance proceeds" on Schedule F (Form 1040).

Certain amounts shown on this form may be subject to self-employment (social security) tax computed on **Schedule SE (Form 1040).** See **Publication 533,** Self-Employment Tax, for more information on amounts considered self-employment income. Since no income or social security taxes are withheld by the payer, you may have to make estimated tax payments if you are still receiving these payments. See **Form 1040-ES,** Estimated Tax for Individuals.

Instructions for Recipient

If you are an individual, report the taxable amounts shown on this form on your tax return, as explained below. (Other taxpayers, such as fiduciaries or partnerships, report the amounts on the corresponding lines of your tax return.)

Boxes 1 and 2.—Report on Schedule E (Form 1040); or Schedule C (Form 1040) if you provided services that were primarily for your customer's convenience, such as regular cleaning, changing linen, or maid service. But for royalties on timber, coal, and iron ore, see **Pub. 544,** Sales and Other Dispositions of Assets.

Box 3.—Report on the line for "Other income" on Form 1040 and identify the payment. If it is trade or business income, report this amount on Schedule C or F (Form 1040).

Box 4.—Shows backup withholding. For example, persons not furnishing their taxpayer identification number to the payer become subject to backup withholding at a 20% rate on certain payments. See **Form W-9,** Request for Taxpayer Identification Number and Certification, for information on backup withholding. **Include this on your income tax return as tax withheld.**

Box 5.—An amount in this box means the fishing boat operator considers you self-employed. Report this amount on Schedule C (Form 1040). See **Publication 595,** Tax Guide for Commercial Fishermen.

Box 6.—Report on Schedule C (Form 1040).

Box 7.—Generally, this amount is considered income from self-employment. Report it as part of your trade or business income on Schedule C or F (Form 1040). If you are not self-employed, amounts paid

to you for services rendered are generally reported on Form 1040 on the line for "Wages, salaries, tips, etc."

If there are two amounts shown in this box, one may be labeled "EPP." This represents excess golden parachute payments. You must pay a 20% excise tax on this amount. See your Form 1040 instructions under "Other Taxes." The unlabeled amount is your total compensation.

Box 8.—Report as "Other income" on your tax return. The amount shown is substitute payments in lieu of dividends or tax-exempt interest received by your broker on your behalf after transfer of your securities for use in a short sale.

Box 9.—An entry in the checkbox means sales to you of consumer products on a buy-sell, deposit-commission, or any other basis for resale have amounted to $5,000 or more. The person filing this return does not have to show a dollar amount in this box. Any income from your sale of these products should generally be reported on Schedule C (Form 1040).

Box 10.—Report on the line for "Crop insurance proceeds" on Schedule F (Form 1040).

Certain amounts shown on this form may be subject to self-employment (social security) tax computed on **Schedule SE (Form 1040).** See **Publication 533,** Self-Employment Tax, for more information on amounts considered self-employment income. Since no income or social security taxes are withheld by the payer, you may have to make estimated tax payments if you are still receiving these payments. See **Form 1040-ES,** Estimated Tax for Individuals.

Instructions for Recipient

If you are an individual, report the taxable amounts shown on this form on your tax return, as explained below. (Other taxpayers, such as fiduciaries or partnerships, report the amounts on the corresponding lines of your tax return.)

Boxes 1 and 2.—Report on Schedule E (Form 1040); or Schedule C (Form 1040) if you provided services that were primarily for your customer's convenience, such as regular cleaning, changing linen, or maid service. But for royalties on timber, coal, and iron ore, see **Pub. 544,** Sales and Other Dispositions of Assets.

Box 3.—Report on the line for "Other income" on Form 1040 and identify the payment. If it is trade or business income, report this amount on Schedule C or F (Form 1040).

Box 4.—Shows backup withholding. For example, persons not furnishing their taxpayer identification number to the payer become subject to backup withholding at a 20% rate on certain payments. See **Form W-9,** Request for Taxpayer Identification Number and Certification, for information on backup withholding. **Include this on your income tax return as tax withheld.**

Box 5.—An amount in this box means the fishing boat operator considers you self-employed. Report this amount on Schedule C (Form 1040). See **Publication 595,** Tax Guide for Commercial Fishermen.

Box 6.—Report on Schedule C (Form 1040).

Box 7.—Generally, this amount is considered income from self-employment. Report it as part of your trade or business income on Schedule C or F (Form 1040). If you are not self-employed, amounts paid

to you for services rendered are generally reported on Form 1040 on the line for "Wages, salaries, tips, etc."

If there are two amounts shown in this box, one may be labeled "EPP." This represents excess golden parachute payments. You must pay a 20% excise tax on this amount. See your Form 1040 instructions under "Other Taxes." The unlabeled amount is your total compensation.

Box 8.—Report as "Other income" on your tax return. The amount shown is substitute payments in lieu of dividends or tax-exempt interest received by your broker on your behalf after transfer of your securities for use in a short sale.

Box 9.—An entry in the checkbox means sales to you of consumer products on a buy-sell, deposit-commission, or any other basis for resale have amounted to $5,000 or more. The person filing this return does not have to show a dollar amount in this box. Any income from your sale of these products should generally be reported on Schedule C (Form 1040).

Box 10.—Report on the line for "Crop insurance proceeds" on Schedule F (Form 1040).

Certain amounts shown on this form may be subject to self-employment (social security) tax computed on **Schedule SE (Form 1040).** See **Publication 533,** Self-Employment Tax, for more information on amounts considered self-employment income. Since no income or social security taxes are withheld by the payer, you may have to make estimated tax payments if you are still receiving these payments. See **Form 1040-ES,** Estimated Tax for Individuals.

1099-MISC
(REVERSE SIDE)

Form **1128**

(Rev. June 1991)
Department of the Treasury
Internal Revenue Service

Application to Adopt, Change, or Retain a Tax Year

▶ For Paperwork Reduction Act Notice, see page 1 of Separate Instructions.

OMB No. 1545-0134
Expires 8-31-93

Before completing Form 1128, see Sections B and C of the General Instructions to determine if this form must be filed.

Form 1128 consists of three parts:

- **Part I** must be completed by all applicants.
- **Part II** must be completed only by applicants requesting approval on a change or retention of a tax year under an expeditious approval rule. See the "Expeditious Approval Rules" in the Specific Instructions to determine who qualifies.
- **Part III,** Section A must be completed by all applicants requesting a ruling from the IRS National Office on a change, adoption, or retention of their tax year. For this type of application, a user fee must be attached. In addition to completing Section A, corporations, S corporations, partnerships, controlled foreign corporations, tax-exempt organizations, estates, and passive foreign investment companies must also complete the specific section in Part III that applies to the particular entity.

Each applicant must check one of the boxes below:

- ☐ Individual
- ☐ Partnership
- ☐ Estate
- ☐ Corporation
- ☐ S Corporation
- ☐ Personal Service Corporation
- ☐ Cooperative (Sec. 1381(a))
- ☐ Tax-Exempt Organization
- ☐ Controlled Foreign Corporation (Sec. 957)
- ☐ Passive Foreign Investment Company (Sec. 1296)
- ☐ Foreign Personal Holding Company (Sec. 552)
- ☐ Other Foreign Corporation
- ☐ Other _____
  (Specify entity and applicable Code section)

Part I   **All Applicants (See page 4 for required signature(s)).**

Please Type or Print	
Name of applicant (if joint return is filed, also show your spouse's name)	Identifying number (See Specific Instructions.)
Number, street, and room or suite no. (If a P.O. box, see specific Instructions.)	Service Center where tax return will be filed
City or town, state, and ZIP code	Applicant's telephone number ( )
Name of person to contact (See Specific Instructions.)	Telephone number of contact person ( )

1a Approval is requested to (check one):

☐ Adopt a tax year ending ▶ ....
  (If filing to adopt a tax year, go to Part III after completing Part I.)

☐ Change to a tax year ending ▶ ....

☐ Retain a tax year ending ▶ ....

b If changing a tax year, indicate the date the present tax year ends ▶ ....

c If adopting or changing a tax year, indicate the short period return that will be required to be filed for the tax year
  beginning ▶ _____ , 19 ____ , and ending ▶ _____ , 19 ____ .

2 Nature of business or principal source of income:

3 Indicate the applicant's overall method of accounting:

☐ Cash receipts and disbursements

☐ Accrual

☐ Other (explain) ▶

Form **1128** (Rev. 6-91)

Form 1128 (Rev. 6-91)   Page **2**

		Yes	No

Part II **Expeditious Approval Rules**
(If Part II applies, file Form 1128 with the IRS Service Center where the applicant's tax return is filed.)

		Yes	No
1	Is this a corporation described in section 3 of Rev. Proc. 84-34, 1984-1 C.B. 508 that is requesting a change in a tax year under Rev. Proc. 84-34? . . . . ▶		
2a	Is this a partnership, an S corporation, or a personal service corporation that is requesting a tax year under the expeditious approval rules in section 4 of Rev. Proc. 87-32, 1987-2 C.B. 396, **and** that is not precluded from using the expeditious approval rules under section 3 of that revenue procedure? . . . . ▶		
b	Is this a partnership, an S corporation, or a personal service corporation that is retaining or changing to a tax year that coincides with its natural business year as defined in section 4.01(1) of Rev. Proc. 87-32, **and** such tax year results in no greater deferral of income to the partners or shareholders than the present tax year? ▶		
c	Is this an S corporation whose shareholders hold more than half of the shares of stock (as of the first day of the tax year to which the request relates) of the corporation **and** have the same tax year that the corporation is retaining or changing to? . . . . ▶		
d	Is this an S corporation whose shareholders hold more than half of the shares of stock (as of the first day of the tax year to which the request relates) of the corporation **and** have requested approval to concurrently change to the tax year that the corporation is retaining or changing to? . . . . ▶		
3	Are you an individual requesting a change from a fiscal year to a calendar year under Rev. Proc. 66-50, 1966-2 C.B. 1260? . . . . ▶		
4	Is this a tax-exempt organization requesting a change under Rev. Proc. 85-58, 1985-2 C.B. 740, or Rev. Proc. 76-10, 1976-1 C.B. 548? . . . . ▶		

If the answer to any of the above questions is "Yes," see the Instructions for the "Expeditious Approval Rules" and file this form with the Internal Revenue Service Center where the income tax return of the applicant is filed. **Do not** file Form 1128 with the National Office and do not include a user fee. See the Instructions for "Where To File" under Part II.

Form 1128 (Rev. 6-91)   Page **3**

| Part III | Ruling Provisions (If Part III applies, file Form 1128 with the National Office and attach a user fee. See Specific Instructions.) |

SECTION A.—General Information

		Yes	No
1	In the last 6 years have you changed or requested approval to change your tax year? (See Part III in the Specific Instructions.) . . . . ▶		
a	If "Yes" and there was a ruling letter issued granting approval to make the change, attach a copy. If a copy of the ruling letter is not available, explain and give the date approval was granted. If a ruling letter was not issued, explain the facts and give the date the change was implemented.		
b	If a change in tax year was granted within the last 6 years, explain in detail why another change in tax year is necessary.		
2	Do you have pending any accounting method, tax year, ruling, or technical advice request in the National Office? ▶		
	If "Yes," attach a statement explaining the type of request (method, tax year, etc.) and the specific issues involved in each request.		
3	Enter the taxable income * or (loss) for the 3 tax years immediately before the short period and for the short period. If necessary, estimate the amount for the short period.		

First preceding year $ ....   Second preceding year $ ....
Third preceding year $ ....   Short period $ ....

Individuals enter adjusted gross income. Partnerships and S corporations enter ordinary income. Section 501(c) organizations enter unrelated business taxable income. Corporations enter taxable income before net operating loss deduction and special deductions. Estates enter adjusted total income.

		Yes	No
4	Are you a U.S. shareholder in a controlled foreign corporation (CFC)? . . . . ▶		
	If "Yes," attach a statement for each CFC stating the name, address, identifying number, tax year, your percentage of total combined voting power, and the amount of income included in your gross income under section 951 for the 3 tax years immediately before the short period and for the short period.		
5a	Are you a U.S. shareholder in a passive foreign investment company as defined in section 1296 of the Code? . ▶		
	If "Yes," attach a statement showing the name, address, identifying number and tax year of the passive foreign investment company, your percentage of interest owned, and the amount of ordinary earnings and net capital gain from the passive foreign investment company included in your income.		
b	Did you elect under section 1295 to treat the passive foreign investment company as a qualified electing fund? . ▶		
6	Are you a member of a partnership, a beneficiary of a trust or estate, a shareholder of an S corporation, a shareholder of an Interest Charge Domestic International Sales Corporation (IC-DISC) or a shareholder in a Foreign Sales Corporation (FSC)? . . . . ▶		
	If "Yes," attach a statement showing the name, address, identifying number, tax year, percentage of interest in capital and profits, or percentage of interest of each IC-DISC and the amount of income received from each partnership, trust, estate, S corporation, IC-DISC, or FSC for the first preceding year and for the short period. Also indicate the percentage of your gross income represented by each amount.		
7	State the reasons for requesting the change. (Attach a separate sheet if you need more space.) This is required by Regulations section 1.442-1(b)(1). If this information is not provided, the application will be denied.		

....
....

SECTION B.—Corporations (other than S corporations and controlled foreign corporations)

		Yes	No
1	Date of incorporation ▶		
2	Is the corporation a member of an affiliated group filing a consolidated return? . . . . ▶		
	If "Yes," attach a statement showing: (a) the name, address, identifying number used on the consolidated return, the tax year, and the Internal Revenue Service Center where the taxpayer files the return; (b) the name, address, and identifying number of each member of the affiliated group; (c) the taxable income (loss) of each member for the 3 years immediately before the short period and for the short period; and (d) the name of the parent corporation.		
3	Did the corporation make any distributions to its shareholders during the short period? . . . . . ▶		
	If "Yes," furnish the following information:		
a	Taxable dividends . . . . $		
b	Nondividend distributions (explain how determined) . . . . $		
4	If this is a personal service corporation, attach a statement showing each shareholder's name, type of entity (e.g., individual, partnership, corporation, etc.), address, identifying number, tax year, and percentage of ownership.		

Form 1128 (Rev. 6-91)   Page **4**

SECTION C.—S Corporations

		Yes	No
1	Date of election ▶		
2	Is any shareholder applying for a corresponding change in tax year? . . . . ▶		
3	Attach a statement showing each shareholder's name, type of entity (e.g., individual, estate, trust, or qualified Subchapter S Trust as defined in section 1361(d)(3)), address, identifying number, tax year, and percentage of ownership.		

SECTION D.—Partnerships

		Yes	No
1	Date business began (See Specific Instructions.) ▶		
2	Is any partner applying for a corresponding change in tax year? . . . . ▶		
3	Attach a statement showing each partner's name, type of partner (e.g., individual, partnership, estate, trust, corporation, S corporation, IC-DISC, etc.), address, identifying number, tax year, and the percentage of interest in capital and profits.		
4	Is any partner of this partnership a shareholder of a personal service corporation as defined in Temporary Regulations section 1.441-4T(d)(1)? . . . . ▶		
	If "Yes," attach a separate sheet providing the name, address, identifying number, tax year, percentage of interest in capital and profits, and the amount of income received from each personal service corporation for the first preceding year and the short period.		

SECTION E.—Controlled Foreign Corporations

Attach a statement for each U.S. shareholder (as defined in section 951(b)) stating the name, address, identifying number, tax year, percentage of total combined voting power, and the amount of income included in gross income under section 951 for the 3 tax years immediately before the short period and for the short period.

SECTION F.—Tax-Exempt Organizations

		Yes	No
1	Form of organization: ☐ Corporation ☐ Trust ☐ Other (specify) ▶		
2	Date of organization ▶		
3	Code section under which the organization is exempt ▶		
4	Is the organization required to file an annual return on Form 990, 990-C, 990-PF, 990-T, 1120-H, or 1120-POL? . . . . ▶		
5	Date exemption was granted ▶................................ Attach a copy of the ruling letter granting exemption. If a copy of the letter is not available, attach explanation.		
6	If a private foundation, is the foundation terminating its status under section 507? . . . . ▶		

SECTION G.—Estates

1 Date estate established ▶

2 Attach a statement showing:
  a Name, identifying number, address, and tax year of each beneficiary and each person who is an owner or treated as an owner of any portion of the estate.
  b Based on the taxable income of the estate entered in Part III, Section A, line 3, show the distribution deduction and the taxable amounts distributed to each beneficiary for the 2 tax years immediately before the short period and for the short period.

SECTION H.—Passive Foreign Investment Company

Attach a statement showing each U.S. shareholder's name, address, identifying number, and the percentage of interest owned.

Signature—All Filers (See Specific Instructions.)

Under penalties of perjury, I declare that I have examined this application, including accompanying schedules and statements, and to the best of my knowledge and belief it is true, correct, and complete. Declaration of preparer (other than applicant) is based on all information of which preparer has any knowledge.

Applicant's name	**Date**
Signature (officer of parent corporation, if applicable)	**Title**
Signing official's name (print or type)	**Date**
Signature of individual or firm (other than applicant) preparing the application	**Date**
Firm or preparer's name	

● Has the authorized representative attached a power of attorney? (For information on a power of attorney, see "Preparer Other Than Applicant" in the Specific Instructions.) . . . . ▶ ☐ **Yes** ☐ **No**

*U.S. Government Printing Office: 1991 — 282-002/40043

1991

**Department of the Treasury
Internal Revenue Service**

Instructions for Form 4562

Depreciation and Amortization

(Section references are to the Internal Revenue Code, unless otherwise noted.)

General Instructions

Paperwork Reduction Act Notice

We ask for the information on this form to carry out the Internal Revenue laws of the United States. You are required to give us the information. We need it to ensure that taxpayers are complying with these laws and to allow us to figure and collect the right amount of tax.

The time needed to complete and file this form will vary depending on individual circumstances. The estimated average time is:

Recordkeeping	35 hrs., 17 min.
Learning about the law or the form	.3 hrs., 35 min.
Preparing and sending the form to the IRS . . .	.4 hrs., 35 min.

If you have comments concerning the accuracy of these time estimates or suggestions for making this form more simple, we would be happy to hear from you. You can write to both the IRS and the Office of Management and Budget at the addresses listed in the instructions for the tax return with which this form is filed.

Purpose of Form

Use Form 4562 to claim your deduction for depreciation and amortization; to make the election to expense certain tangible property (section 179); and to provide information on the business/investment use of automobiles and other listed property.

Who Must File

You must complete and file Form 4562 if you are claiming:

● Depreciation for property placed in service during the 1991 tax year;

● A section 179 expense deduction (which may include a carryover from a previous year);

● Depreciation on any listed property (regardless of when it was placed in service);

● The standard mileage rate (unless **Form 2106**, Employee Business Expenses, is used for this purpose—see the Part V instructions); or

● Amortization of costs that begins during the 1991 tax year.

All corporations (other than S corporations) must also file Form 4562 for any depreciation claimed on assets acquired in previous tax years.

You should prepare and submit a separate Form 4562 for each business or activity on your return. If more space is needed, attach additional sheets. However, complete only one Part I in its entirety when computing your allowable section 179 expense deduction.

Definitions

Depreciation.—Depreciation is the annual deduction allowed to recover the cost or other basis of business or income-producing property with a determinable useful life of more than 1 year. However, land and goodwill are not depreciable.

Depreciation starts when you first use the property in your business or for the production of income. It ends when you take the property out of service, deduct all your depreciable cost or other basis, or no longer use the property in your business or for the production of income. For additional information, see **Pub. 534**, Depreciation, **Pub. 946**, How To Begin Depreciating Your Property, and **Pub. 917**, Business Use of a Car.

Amortization.—Amortization is similar to the straight line method of depreciation in that an annual deduction is allowed to recover certain costs over a fixed period of time. You can amortize such items as the costs of starting a business, reforestation, and pollution control facilities. For additional information, see **Pub. 535**, Business Expenses.

"Listed Property".—For a definition of "listed property" see the Part V instructions.

Recordkeeping

Except for Part V, relating to listed property, the IRS does not require you to submit detailed information with your return regarding the depreciation of assets placed in service in previous tax years. However, the information needed to compute your depreciation deduction (basis, method, etc.) must be part of your permanent records.

Because Form 4562 does not provide for permanent recordkeeping, you may use the depreciation worksheet on page 8 to assist you in maintaining depreciation records. However, the worksheet is designed only for Federal income tax purposes. You may need to keep additional records for accounting and state income tax purposes.

Certification of Business Use Requirement for Aircraft Exempt From Luxury Tax

If you purchased a new aircraft in 1991 with a sales price of more than $250,000, the 10% Federal luxury tax generally imposed on such a sale will not apply if at least 80% of your use of the aircraft (measured in hours of flight time) will be for business purposes. If you purchased an aircraft that was exempt from the luxury tax **solely** for this reason, you must attach a statement to your income tax return for each of the 2 tax years ending after the date the aircraft was placed in service. On this statement, you must certify that at least

80% of your use of the aircraft during the tax year was in a trade or business. If you fail to make this certification, you must pay a tax equal to the luxury tax that would have been imposed on the sale of the aircraft if the business use exemption had not applied. In addition, interest is imposed on the tax from the date of sale of the aircraft.

If you do not pay the tax when due because you failed to meet this requirement, no depreciation may be claimed on the aircraft for any tax year.

See the instructions for **Form 720,** Quarterly Federal Excise Tax Return, for more information on paying the tax and interest due.

Specific Instructions

Part I.—Election To Expense Certain Tangible Property (Section 179)

Note: *An estate or trust cannot make this election. If you are married filing separately, see section 179(b)(4) for special limitations.*

You may make an irrevocable election to expense part of the cost of certain tangible personal property used in your trade or business and certain other property described in Pub. 534. To do so, you must have purchased the property (as defined in section 179(d)(2)) and placed it in service during the 1991 tax year, or have a carryover of disallowed deduction from 1990. If you elect this deduction, the amount on which you figure your depreciation or amortization deduction must be reduced by the amount of the section 179 expense.

Section 179 property does **not** include: **(1)** property used 50% or less in your trade or business; or **(2)** property held for investment (section 212 property). If you are a noncorporate lessor, the property that you lease to others does not qualify as section 179 property unless:
(1) you manufactured or produced the property; or **(2)** the term of the lease is less than 50% of the property's class life, and for the first 12 months after the property is transferred to the lessee, the sum of the deductions related to the property that are allowed to you solely under section 162 (except rents and reimbursed amounts) is more than 15% of the rental income from the property.

The section 179 expense deduction is subject to two separate limitations, both of which are figured in Part I:

1. A dollar limitation; and

2. A taxable income limitation.

In the case of a partnership, these limitations apply to the partnership and each partner. In the case of an

Cat. No. 12907Y

S corporation, these limitations apply to the S corporation and each shareholder. In the case of a controlled group, all component members are treated as one taxpayer.

Line 1.—The maximum amount of section 179 deduction you can claim is $10,000. If you are married filing separately, your maximum deduction is $5,000, unless you and your spouse elect otherwise. However, the total deduction for both of you cannot be more than $10,000. If you are married filing separately, cross out the preprinted "$10,000" on line 1 and enter in the margin "$5,000" (or whatever other amount you elect, not to exceed $10,000 for both spouses).

Line 2.—Enter the cost of all section 179 property placed in service during the tax year. Be sure to include amounts from any listed property from Part V.

Line 5.—If you placed $210,000 or more of section 179 property in service during the 1991 tax year, you cannot elect to expense any property. If line 5 is -0-, skip lines 6 through 11, enter -0- on line 12, and enter the carryover of disallowed deduction from 1990, if any, on line 13.

Line 6.—

Column (a)—Enter a brief description of the property for which you are making the election (e.g., truck, office furniture, etc.).

Column (b)—Enter the cost of the property. If you acquired the property through a trade-in, do not include any undepreciated basis of the assets you traded in. See **Pub. 551**, Basis of Assets, for more information.

Column (c)—Enter the amount that you elect to expense. You do not have to elect to expense the entire cost of the property. Whatever amount is not elected to be expensed can be depreciated. See line 14 and line 15 instructions below.

To report your share of a section 179 expense deduction from a partnership or an S corporation, instead of completing columns (a) and (b), write "from Schedule K-1 (Form 1065)" or "from Schedule K-1 (Form 1120S)" across the columns.

Line 9.—The tentative deduction represents the amount you may expense in 1991 or carry over to 1992. If this amount is less than the taxable income limitation on line 11, you may expense the entire amount. If this amount is more than line 11, you may expense in 1991 only an amount equal to line 11. Any excess may be carried over to 1992.

Line 10.—The carryover of disallowed deduction from 1990 is the amount of section 179 property, if any, elected to be expensed in previous years, but not allowed as a deduction due to the taxable income limitation. If you filed Form 4562 for 1990, enter the amount from line 13 of your 1990 Form 4562. For additional information, see Pub. 534.

Line 11.—The section 179 expense deduction is further limited to the "taxable income" limitation under section 179(b)(3).

For an individual, enter the aggregate taxable income from any active trade or business computed without regard to any section 179 expense deduction or the deduction for one-half of self-employment taxes under section 164(f). Include in aggregate taxable income the wages,

salaries, tips, and other compensation you earned as an employee. If you are married filing a joint return, combine the aggregate taxable incomes for both you and your spouse. For all other entities, enter the taxable income computed without regard to any section 179 expense deduction. In any case, do not enter more than line 5.

Line 12.—The limitations on lines 5 and 11 apply to the taxpayer, and not to each separate business or activity. Therefore, if you have more than one business or activity, you may allocate your allowable section 179 expense deduction among them. To do so, write "Summary" at the top of Part I of the separate Form 4562 you are completing for the aggregate amounts from all businesses or activities. Do not complete the rest of that form. On line 12 of the Form 4562 you prepare for each separate business or activity, enter the amount allocated to the business or activity from the "Summary." No other entry is required in Part I of the separate Form 4562 prepared for each business or activity.

Part II.—MACRS Depreciation For Assets Placed in Service ONLY During Your 1991 Tax Year

Note: *The term "Modified Accelerated Cost Recovery System" (MACRS) includes the General Depreciation System and the Alternative Depreciation System. Generally, MACRS is used to depreciate any tangible property placed in service after 1986. However, MACRS does not apply to films, videotapes, and sound recordings. See section 168(f) for other exceptions.*

Depreciation may be an adjustment for alternative minimum tax (AMT) purposes. See the appropriate AMT form that you are required to file.

Lines 14a through 14h.—General Depreciation System (GDS).—
Note: *Use lines 14a through 14h only for assets placed in service during the tax year beginning in 1991 and depreciated under the General Depreciation System, except for automobiles and other listed property (which are reported in Part V).*

Determine which property you acquired and placed in service during the tax year beginning in 1991. Then, sort that property according to its classification (3-year property, 5-year property, etc.) as shown in column (a) of lines 14a through 14h. The classifications for some property are shown below. For property not shown, see **Determining the Classification** below.

● 3-year property includes: (1) a race horse that is more than 2 years old at the time it is placed in service; and (2) any horse (other than a race horse) that is more than 12 years old at the time it is placed in service.

● 5-year property includes: (1) automobiles; (2) light general purpose trucks; (3) typewriters, calculators, copiers, and duplicating equipment; (4) any semi-conductor manufacturing equipment; (5) any computer or peripheral equipment; (6) any section 1245 property used in connection with research and experimentation; and (7) certain energy property specified in section 168(e)(3)(B)(vi).

● 7-year property includes: (1) office furniture and equipment; (2) appliances, carpets, furniture, etc. used in residential rental property; (3) railroad track; and (4) any property that does not have a class life and is not otherwise classified.

● 10-year property includes: (1) vessels, barges, tugs, and similar water transportation equipment; (2) any single purpose agricultural or horticultural structure (see section 48(p)); and (3) any tree or vine bearing fruit or nuts.

● 15-year property includes: (1) any municipal wastewater treatment plant; and (2) any telephone distribution plant and comparable equipment used for 2-way exchange of voice and data communications.

● 20-year property includes any municipal sewers.

● Residential rental property is a building in which 80% or more of the total rent is from dwelling units.

● Nonresidential real property is any real property that is neither residential rental property nor property with a class life of less than 27.5 years.

● 50-year property includes any improvements necessary to construct or improve a roadbed or right-of-way for railroad track that qualifies as a railroad grading or tunnel bore under section 168(e)(4). There is no separate line to report 50-year property. Therefore, attach a statement showing the same information as required in columns (a) through (g). Include the deduction in the line 20 "Total" and write "See attachment" in the bottom margin of the form.

Determining the Classification.—If your depreciable property is **not** listed above, determine the classification as follows: First, find the property's class life. The class life of most property can be found in the Table of Class Lives and Recovery Periods in Pub. 534. Next, use the following table to find the classification in column (b) that corresponds to the class life of the property in column (a).

(a) Class life (in years) (See Pub. 534)	(b) Classification
4 or less	3-year property
More than 4 but less than 10	5-year property
10 or more but less than 16	7-year property
16 or more but less than 20	10-year property
20 or more but less than 25	15-year property
25 or more	20-year property

Column (b).—For lines 14g and 14h, enter the month and year the property was placed in service. If property held for personal use is converted to use in a trade or business or for the production of income, treat the property as being placed in service on the date of conversion.

Column (c).—To find the basis for depreciation, multiply the cost or other basis of the property by the percentage of business/investment use. From that result, subtract any section 179 expense deduction and the amount of any enhanced oil recovery credit (section 43). See section 50(c) to determine the basis adjustment for investment credit property.

Column (d).—See the "Note" in the line 14, column (f) instructions below, for an election you can make to use the 150% declining balance method of depreciation (for 3-, 5-, 7-, and 10-year property). If you do not elect to use the 150% method, determine the recovery period from the table below:

In the case of:	The applicable recovery period is:
3-year property	3 yrs.
5-year property	5 yrs.
7-year property	7 yrs.
10-year property	10 yrs.
15-year property	15 yrs.
20-year property	20 yrs.
Residential rental property	27.5 yrs.
Nonresidential real property	31.5 yrs.
Railroad gradings and tunnel bores . . .	50 yrs.

If you elect the 150% declining balance method, you must use the recovery period under the Alternative Depreciation System discussed in the line 15 instructions below. You will not have an adjustment for alternative minimum tax purposes on the property for which you make this election.

Column (e).—The applicable convention determines the portion of the tax year for which depreciation is allowable during a year property is either placed in service or disposed of. There are three types of conventions (discussed below). To select the correct convention, you must know:
(a) when you placed the property in service; and **(b)** the type of property.

Half-year convention (HY).—This convention applies to all property reported on lines 14a through 14f, unless the mid-quarter convention applies. It does not apply to residential rental property, nonresidential real property, and railroad gradings and tunnel bores. It treats all property placed in service (or disposed of) during any tax year as placed in service (or disposed of) on the mid-point of such tax year.

Mid-quarter convention (MQ).—This convention applies instead of the half-year convention if the aggregate bases of property subject to depreciation under section 168 that is placed in service during the last 3 months of your tax year exceeds 40% of the aggregate bases of property subject to depreciation under section 168 that is placed in service during the entire tax year.

The mid-quarter convention treats all property placed in service (or disposed of) during any quarter as placed in service (or disposed of) on the mid-point of such quarter.

In determining whether the mid-quarter convention applies, do not take into account:
● Property that is being depreciated under the pre-1987 rules;
● Any residential rental property, nonresidential real property, or railroad gradings and tunnel bores; and
● Property that is placed in service and disposed of within the same tax year.

Mid-month convention (MM).—This convention applies ONLY to residential rental property, nonresidential real property (lines 14g or 14h), and railroad gradings and tunnel bores. It treats all property placed in service (or disposed of) during any month as placed

in service (or disposed of) on the mid-point of such month.

Enter "HY" for half-year; "MQ" for mid-quarter; or "MM" for mid-month convention.

Column (f).—Applicable depreciation methods are prescribed for each classification of property. For 3-, 5-, 7-, and 10-year property the applicable method is the 200% declining balance method, switching to the straight line method in the first tax year that maximizes the depreciation allowance.

Note: *You may make an irrevocable election to use the 150% declining balance method for one or more classes of property (except for residential rental property, nonresidential real property, any railroad grading or tunnel bore, or any tree or vine bearing fruit or nuts). If you make this election, see "Alternative Depreciation System" below for the recovery period.*

For 15- and 20-year property, and property used in a farming business, the applicable method is the 150% declining balance method, switching to the straight line method in the first tax year that maximizes the depreciation allowance.

For residential rental property, nonresidential real property, any railroad grading or tunnel bore, or any tree or vine bearing fruit or nuts, the only applicable method is the straight line method.

You may also make an irrevocable election to use the straight line method for all property within a classification that is placed in service during the tax year.

Enter "200 DB" for 200% declining balance; "150 DB" for 150% declining balance; or "S/L" for straight line.

Column (g).—To compute the depreciation deduction you may: **(a)** use the optional Tables A through D on page 7. Multiply the applicable rate from the appropriate table by the property's **unadjusted** basis (column (c)) (see Pub. 534 for complete tables); or **(b)** compute the deduction yourself. To compute the deduction yourself, complete the following steps:

Step 1.—Determine the depreciation rate as follows:

1. If you are using the 200% or 150% declining balance method in column (f), divide the declining balance rate (use 2.00 for 200 DB or 1.50 for 150 DB) by the number of years in the recovery period in column (d). For example, for property depreciated using the 200 DB method over a recovery period of 5 years, divide 2.00 by 5 for a rate of 40%.

2. If you are using the straight line method, divide 1.00 by the remaining number of years in the recovery period as of the beginning of the tax year (but not less than one). For example, if there are 6½ years remaining in the recovery period as of the beginning of the year, divide 1.00 by 6.5 for a rate of 15.38%.

Note: *If you are using the 200% or 150% DB method, be sure to switch to the straight line rate in the first year that the straight line rate exceeds the declining balance rate.*

Step 2.—Multiply the percentage rate determined in Step 1 by the property's unrecovered basis (cost or other basis reduced by any section 179 expense deduction and all prior years' depreciation).

Step 3.—For property placed in service or disposed of during the current tax year, multiply the result from Step 2 by the applicable decimal amount from the tables below (based on the convention shown in column (e)).

Half-year (HY) convention		0.5

Mid-quarter (MQ) convention

Placed in service (or disposed of) during the:	Placed in service	Disposed of
1st quarter	0.875	0.125
2nd quarter	0.625	0.375
3rd quarter	0.375	0.625
4th quarter	0.125	0.875

Mid-month (MM) convention

Placed in service (or disposed of) during the:	Placed in service	Disposed of
1st month	0.9583	0.0417
2nd month	0.8750	0.1250
3rd month	0.7917	0.2083
4th month	0.7083	0.2917
5th month	0.6250	0.3750
6th month	0.5417	0.4583
7th month	0.4583	0.5417
8th month	0.3750	0.6250
9th month	0.2917	0.7083
10th month	0.2083	0.7917
11th month	0.1250	0.8750
12th month	0.0417	0.9583

Short Tax Years.—See Pub. 534 for rules on how to compute the depreciation deduction for property placed in service in a short tax year.

Line 15.—Alternative Depreciation System (ADS).—Note: *Lines 15a through 15c should be completed for assets, other than automobiles and other listed property, placed in service ONLY during the tax year beginning in 1991 and depreciated under the Alternative Depreciation System. Depreciation on assets placed in service in prior years is reported on line 16.*

Under ADS, depreciation is computed by using the applicable depreciation method, the applicable recovery period, and the applicable convention. The following types of property **must** be depreciated under ADS:
● Any tangible property used predominantly outside the U.S.;
● Any tax-exempt use property;
● Any tax-exempt bond financed property;
● Any imported property covered by an executive order of the President of the United States; and
● Any property used predominantly in a farming business and placed in service during any tax year in which you made an election under section 263A(d)(3).

Instead of depreciating property under GDS (line 14), you may make an irrevocable election with respect to any classification of property for any tax year to use ADS. For residential rental and nonresidential real property, you may make this election separately for each property.

Note: *See section 168(g)(3)(B) for a special rule for determining the class life for certain property.*

If the property does not have a class life, use line 15b.

Page 3

For residential rental and nonresidential real property, use line 15c.

For railroad gradings and tunnel bores, the recovery period is 50 years.

Column (b).—For 40-year property, enter the month and year it was placed in service, or converted to use in a trade or business, or for the production of income.

Column (c).—See the instructions for line 14, column (c).

Column (d).—Under ADS, the recovery period is generally the class life. However, when looking up the recovery period in Pub. 534, be sure to look under the heading "Alternate MACRS."

Column (e).—Under ADS, the applicable conventions are the same as those used under GDS. See the instructions for line 14, column (e).

Column (f).—Under ADS, the only applicable method is the straight line method.

Column (g).—The depreciation deduction is computed in the same manner as under GDS except you must apply the straight line method over the ADS recovery period and use the applicable convention.

Part III.—Other Depreciation

Note: *Do not use Part III for automobiles and other listed property. Instead, report this property in Part V on page 2 of Form 4562.*

Use Part III for

● ACRS property (pre-'87 rules);

● Property placed in service before 1981;

● Certain public utility property, which does not meet certain normalization requirements;

● Certain property acquired from related persons;

● Property acquired in certain nonrecognition transactions; and

● Certain sound recordings, movies, and videotapes.

Line 16.—GDS and ADS deduction for assets placed in service in tax years beginning before 1991.—For assets placed in service after 1986, and depreciated under post-'86 rules, enter the GDS and ADS deduction for the current year. To compute the deduction, see the instructions for column (g), line 14.

Line 17.—Property subject to section 168(f)(1) election.—Report property that you elect, under section 168(f)(1), to depreciate by the unit-of-production method or any other method not based on a term of years (other than the retirement-replacement-betterment method).

Attach a separate sheet, showing: **(a)** a description of the property and the depreciation method you elect that excludes the property from ACRS or MACRS; and **(b)** the depreciable basis (cost or other basis reduced, if applicable, by salvage value, enhanced oil recovery credit, and the section 179 expense deduction). See section 50(c) to determine the basis adjustment for investment credit property.

Line 18.—ACRS and other depreciation.—Enter the total depreciation attributable to assets, other than automobiles and other listed property, placed in service before 1981 (pre-ACRS), property subject to ACRS, or property that cannot otherwise be

Page 4

depreciated under ACRS. For ACRS property, unless you use an alternate percentage, multiply the property's unadjusted basis by the applicable percentage as follows:

● *5-year property*—1st year (15%), 2nd year (22%), 3rd through 5th years (21%);

● *10-year property*—1st year (8%), 2nd year (14%), 3rd year (12%), 4th through 6th years (10%), 7th through 10th years (9%);

● *15-year public utility property*—1st year (5%), 2nd year (10%), 3rd year (9%), 4th year (8%), 5th and 6th years (7%), 7th through 15th years (6%);

● *15-year, 18-year, and 19-year real property and low-income housing*—Use the tables in Pub. 534.

If you elected an alternate percentage for any property listed above, use the straight line method over the recovery period you chose in the prior year. See Pub. 534 for more information and tables.

Include any amounts attributable to the Class Life Asset Depreciation Range (CLADR) system. If you previously elected the CLADR system, you must continue to use it to depreciate assets left in your vintage accounts. You must continue to meet recordkeeping requirements.

Prior years' depreciation, plus current year's depreciation, can never exceed the depreciable basis of the property.

The basis and amounts claimed for depreciation should be part of your permanent books and records. **No attachment is necessary.**

Line 20.—A partnership or S corporation does not include any section 179 expense deduction (line 12) on this line. Any section 179 expense deduction is passed through separately to the partners and shareholders on the appropriate line of their Schedules K-1.

Line 21—Section 263A Uniform Capitalization Rules.—If you are subject to the uniform capitalization rules of section 263A, enter the increase in basis from costs that are required to be capitalized. For a detailed discussion of who is subject to these rules, which costs must be capitalized, and allocation of costs among activities, see Temp. Regs. section 1.263A-1T.

Part V.—Automobiles and Other Listed Property

All taxpayers claiming any depreciation for automobiles and other listed property, regardless of the tax year such property was placed in service, must provide the information requested in Part V. However, employees claiming the standard mileage allowance or actual expenses (including depreciation) must use Form 2106 instead of Part V. Listed property includes, but is not limited to:

● Passenger automobiles weighing 6,000 pounds or less.

● Any other property used for transportation if the nature of the property lends itself to personal use, such as motorcycles, pick-up trucks, etc.

● Any property used for entertainment or recreational purposes (such as photographic, phonographic, communication, and video recording equipment).

● Cellular telephones (or other similar telecommunications equipment).

● Computers or peripheral equipment.

Listed property does not include:
(a) photographic, phonographic, communication, or video equipment used exclusively in a taxpayer's trade or business or regular business establishment; **(b)** any computer or peripheral equipment used exclusively at a regular business establishment and owned or leased by the person operating the establishment; or **(c)** an ambulance, hearse, or vehicle used for transporting persons or property for hire.

Section A.—Depreciation

Lines 23 and 24.—

Qualified business use.—For purposes of determining whether to use line 23 or line 24 to report your listed property, you must first determine the percentage of qualified business use for each property. Generally, a qualified business use is any use in your trade or business. However, it does not include:

● Any investment use;

● Leasing the property to a 5% owner or related person;

● The use of the property as compensation for services performed by a 5% owner or related person; or

● The use of the property as compensation for services performed by any person (who is not a 5% owner or related person), unless an amount is included in that person's income for the use of the property and, if required, income tax was withheld on that amount.

As an exception to the general rule, if at least 25% of the total use of any aircraft during the tax year is for a qualified business use, the leasing or compensatory use of the aircraft by a 5% owner or related person is considered a qualified business use.

Determine your percentage of qualified business use in a manner similar to that used to figure the business/investment use percentage in column (c). Your percentage of qualified business use may be smaller than the business/investment use percentage.

For more information, see Pub. 534.

Column (a).—List on a property-by-property basis all of your listed property in the following order:

1. Automobiles and other vehicles; and

2. Other listed property (computers and peripheral equipment, etc.).

In column (a), list the make and model of automobiles, and give a general description of the listed property.

If you have more than five vehicles used 100% for business/investment purposes, you may group them by tax year. Otherwise, list each vehicle separately.

Column (b).—Enter the date the property was placed in service. If property held for personal use is converted to business/investment use, treat the property as placed in service on the date of conversion.

Column (c).—Enter the percentage of business/investment use. For automobiles and other "vehicles," this is determined by dividing the number of miles the vehicle is driven for trade or business purposes or for the production of income during the year (not to include any commuting mileage) by the total number of miles the vehicle is driven for any purpose. Treat vehicles used by employees as being used 100% for business/investment purposes if the value of personal use is included in the employees' gross income, or the employees reimburse the employer for the personal use.

Employers who report the amount of personal use of the vehicle in the employee's gross income, and withhold the appropriate taxes, should enter "100%" for the percentage of business/investment use. For more information, see Pub. 917. For listed property (such as computers or video equipment), allocate the use based on the most appropriate unit of time the property is actually used. See Temp. Regs. 1.280F-6T.

If you have property that is used solely for personal use that is converted to business/investment use during the tax year, figure the percentage of business/investment use only for the number of months the property is used in your business or for the production of income. Multiply that percentage by the number of months the property is used in your business or for the production of income, and divide the result by 12.

Column (e).—Multiply column (d) by the percentage in column (c). From that result, subtract any section 179 expense deduction and half of any investment credit taken before 1986 (unless you took the reduced credit). For automobiles and other listed property placed in service after 1985 (i.e., "transition property"), reduce the depreciable basis by the entire investment credit.

Column (f).—Enter the recovery period. For property placed in service after 1986 and used more than 50% in a qualified business use, use the table in the line 14, column (d) instructions. For property placed in service after 1986 and used 50% or less in a qualified business use, you must depreciate the property using the straight line method over its ADS recovery period. The ADS recovery period is 5 years for automobiles and computers.

Column (g).—Enter the method and convention used to figure your depreciation deduction. See the instructions for line 14, columns (e) and (f). Write "200 DB," "150 DB," or "S/L," for the depreciation method, and "HY," "MM," or "MQ," for half-year, mid-month, or mid-quarter conventions, respectively. For property placed in service before 1987, write "PRE" if you used the prescribed percentages under ACRS, If you elected an alternate percentage, enter "S/L."

Column (h).—Caution: See "Limitations for automobiles" below before entering an amount in column (h).

If the property is used more than 50% in a qualified business use (line 23), and the property was placed in service after 1986, figure column (h) by following the instructions for line 14, column (g). If placed in service before 1987, multiply column (e) by the applicable percentages given in the line 18 instructions for ACRS property. If the recovery period for the property ended before your tax year beginning in 1991, enter your unrecovered basis, if any, in column (h).

If the property is used 50% or less in a qualified business use (line 24), and the

property was placed in service after 1986, figure column (h) by dividing column (e) by column (f) and using the same conventions as discussed in the instructions for line 14, column (e). For automobiles placed in service: (1) during your tax year beginning in 1986, multiply column (e) by 10%; or (2) after June 18, 1984, and before your tax year beginning in 1986, enter your unrecovered basis, if any, in column (h). For computers placed in service after June 18, 1984, and before 1987, multiply column (e) by 8.333%.

For property used 50% or less in a qualified business use, no section 179 expense deduction is allowed.

For property placed in service before 1987 that was disposed of during the year, enter zero.

Limitations for automobiles.—The depreciation deduction plus section 179 expense deduction for automobiles is limited for any tax year. The limitation depends on when you placed the property in service. Use Table E on page 7 to determine the limitation. For any automobile you list on line 23 or 24, the total of columns (h) and (i) for that automobile cannot exceed the limit shown in Table E.

Note: These limitations are further reduced when the business/investment use percentage (column (c)) is less than 100%. For example, if an automobile placed in service in 1991 is used 60% for business/investment purposes, then the first year depreciation plus section 179 expense deduction is limited to 60% of $2,660, which is $1,596.

Column (i).—Enter the amount you choose to expense for property used more than 50% in a qualified business use (subject to the limitations for automobiles noted above). Be sure to include the total cost of such property on line 2, page 1.

Recapture of depreciation and section 179 expense deduction.—If any listed property was used more than 50% in a qualified business use in the year it was placed in service, and used 50% or less in a later year, you may have to recapture in the later year part of the depreciation and section 179 expense deduction. Use **Form 4797**, Sales of Business Property, to figure the recapture amount.

Section B.—Information Regarding Use of Vehicles

The information requested in Questions 27 through 33 must be completed for each vehicle identified in Section A.

Employees must provide their employers with the information requested in Questions 27 through 33 for each automobile or vehicle provided for their use.

Employers providing more than five vehicles to their employees, who are not more than 5% owners or related persons, are not required to complete Questions 27 through 33 for such vehicles. Instead, they must obtain this information from their employees, check "Yes" to Question 37, and retain the information received as part of their permanent records.

Section C.—Questions for Employers Who Provide Vehicles for Use by Their Employees

For employers providing vehicles to their employees, a written policy statement regarding the use of such vehicles, if initiated and kept by the employer, will relieve the employee of keeping separate records for substantiation.

Two types of written policy statements will satisfy the employer's substantiation requirements under section 274(d): **(a)** a policy statement that prohibits personal use including commuting; and **(b)** a policy statement that prohibits personal use except for commuting.

Line 34.—Prohibits Personal Use (including commuting):

This policy must meet the following conditions:

● The vehicle is owned or leased by the employer and is provided to one or more employees for use in the employer's trade or business;

● When the vehicle is not used in the employer's trade or business, it is kept on the employer's business premises, unless it is temporarily located elsewhere, for example, for maintenance or because of a mechanical failure;

● No employee using the vehicle lives at the employer's business premises;

● No employee may use the vehicle for personal purposes, other than de minimis personal use (such as a stop for lunch between two business deliveries); and

● Except for de minimis use, the employer reasonably believes that no employee uses the vehicle for any personal purpose.

Line 35.—Prohibits Personal Use (except for commuting). This policy is NOT available if the commuting employee is an officer, director, or 1% or more owner.

This policy must meet the following conditions:

● The vehicle is owned or leased by the employer and is provided to one or more employees for use in the employer's trade or business and is used in the employer's trade or business;

● For bona fide noncompensatory business reasons, the employer requires the employee to commute to and/or from work in the vehicle;

● The employer establishes a written policy under which the employee may not use the vehicle for personal purposes, other than commuting or de minimis personal use (such as a stop for a personal errand between a business delivery and the employee's home);

● Except for de minimis use, the employer reasonably believes that the employee does not use the vehicle for any personal purpose other than commuting; and

● The employer accounts for the commuting use by including an appropriate amount in the employee's gross income.

For both written policy statements, there must be evidence that would enable the IRS to determine whether use of the vehicle meets the conditions stated above.

Line 36.—An automobile is considered to have qualified demonstration use if the employer maintains a written policy statement that:

• Prohibits its use by individuals other than full-time automobile salesmen;

• Prohibits its use for personal vacation trips;

• Prohibits storage of personal possessions in the automobile; and

• Limits the total mileage outside the salesmen's normal working hours.

Part VI.—Amortization

Each year you may elect to deduct part of certain capital costs over a fixed period. If you amortize property, the part you amortize does not qualify for the election to expense certain tangible property or depreciation.

For individuals reporting amortization of bond premium for bonds acquired before October 23, 1986, do not report the deduction here. See the instructions for Schedule A (Form 1040).

For taxpayers (other than corporations) claiming a deduction for amortization of bond premium for bonds acquired after October 22, 1986, but before January 1, 1988, the deduction is treated as interest expense and is subject to the investment interest limitations. Use **Form 4952**, Investment Interest Expense Deduction, to compute the allowable deduction.

For taxable bonds acquired after 1987, the amortization offsets the interest income. See **Pub. 550**, Investment Income and Expenses.

Line 39.—Complete line 39 only for those costs for which the amortization period begins during your tax year beginning in 1991.

Column (a).—Describe the costs you are amortizing. You may amortize—

• Pollution control facilities (section 169, limited by section 291 for corporations).

• Certain bond premiums (section 171).

• Research and experimental expenditures (section 174).

• Qualified forestation and reforestation costs (section 194).

• Business start-up expenditures (section 195).

• Organizational expenditures for a corporation (section 248) or partnership (section 709).

• Optional write off of certain tax preferences over the period specified in section 59(e).

Column (b).—Enter the date the amortization period begins under the applicable Code section.

Column (c).—Enter the total amount you are amortizing. See the applicable Code section for limits on the amortizable amount.

Column (d).—Enter the Code section under which you amortize the costs.

Column (f).—Compute the amortization deduction by: (1) dividing column (c) by the number of years over which the costs are to be amortized; or (2) multiplying column (c) by the percentage in column (e).

Attach any other information the Code and regulations may require to make a valid election. See Pub. 535 for more information.

Line 40.—Enter the amount of amortization attributable to those costs for which the amortization period began before 1991.

Table A.—General Depreciation System
Method: 200% declining balance switching to straight line
Convention: half-year

	If the recovery period is:			
Year	3 yrs.	5 yrs.	7 yrs.	10 yrs.
1	33.33%	20.00%	14.29%	10.00%
2	44.45%	32.00%	24.49%	18.00%
3	14.81%	19.20%	17.49%	14.40%
4	7.41%	11.52%	12.49%	11.52%
5		11.52%	8.93%	9.22%

Table B.—General and Alternative Depreciation System
Method: 150% declining balance switching to straight line
Convention: half-year

	If the recovery period is:					
Year	5 yrs.	7 yrs.	10 yrs.	12 yrs.	15 yrs.	20 yrs.
1	15.00%	10.71%	7.50%	6.25%	5.00%	3.750%
2	25.50%	19.13%	13.88%	11.72%	9.50%	7.219%
3	17.85%	15.03%	11.79%	10.25%	8.55%	6.677%
4	16.66%	12.25%	10.02%	8.97%	7.70%	6.177%
5	16.66%	12.25%	8.74%	7.85%	6.93%	5.713%

Table C.—General Depreciation System
Method: Straight line
Convention: Mid-month
Recovery period: 27.5 years

	The month in the 1st recovery year the property is placed in service:											
Year	1	2	3	4	5	6	7	8	9	10	11	12
1	3.485%	3.182%	2.879%	2.576%	2.273%	1.970%	1.667%	1.364%	1.061%	0.758%	0.455%	0.152%
2-8	3.636%	3.636%	3.636%	3.636%	3.636%	3.636%	3.636%	3.636%	3.636%	3.636%	3.636%	3.636%

Table D.—General Depreciation System
Method: Straight line
Convention: Mid-month
Recovery period: 31.5 years

	The month in the 1st recovery year the property is placed in service:											
Year	1	2	3	4	5	6	7	8	9	10	11	12
1	3.042%	2.778%	2.513%	2.249%	1.984%	1.720%	1.455%	1.190%	0.926%	0.661%	0.397%	0.132%
2-7	3.175%	3.175%	3.175%	3.175%	3.175%	3.175%	3.175%	3.175%	3.175%	3.175%	3.175%	3.175%

Table E.—Limitations for automobiles

		If placed in service—					
Year of Deduction	after: but before:	6/18/84 1/1/85	12/31/84 4/3/85	4/2/85 1/1/87	12/31/86 1/1/89	12/31/88 1/1/91	12/31/90 1/1/92
1st tax year		4,000	4,100	3,200	2,560	2,660	2,660
2nd tax year		6,000	6,200	4,800	4,100	4,200	4,300
3rd tax year		6,000	6,200	4,800	2,450	2,550	2,550
each succeeding tax year		6,000	6,200	4,800	1,475	1,475	1,575

Depreciation Worksheet

Description of Property	Date Placed in Service	Cost or Other Basis	Business/ Investment Use %	Section 179 Deduction	Depreciation Prior Years	Basis for Depreciation	Method/ Convention	Recovery Period	Ratio or Table %	Depreciation Deduction

☆ U.S. GOVERNMENT PRINTING OFFICE: 1992 312-732/54253

Form **4562**	**Depreciation and Amortization**	OMB No. 1545-0172
	(Including Information on Listed Property)	**1991**
Department of the Treasury (o) Internal Revenue Service	▶ See separate instructions. ▶ Attach this form to your return.	Attachment Sequence No. **67**

Name(s) shown on return	Identifying number

Business or activity to which this form relates

Part I **Election To Expense Certain Tangible Property (Section 179)** (**Note:** *If you have any "Listed Property," complete Part V.*)

1	Maximum dollar limitation (see instructions)	**1**	$10,000
2	Total cost of section 179 property placed in service during the tax year (see instructions) . .	**2**	
3	Threshold cost of section 179 property before reduction in limitation	**3**	$200,000
4	Reduction in limitation—Subtract line 3 from line 2, but do not enter less than -0-	**4**	
5	Dollar limitation for tax year—Subtract line 4 from line 1, but do not enter less than -0- . .	**5**	

(a) Description of property	(b) Cost	(c) Elected cost	
6			

7	Listed property—Enter amount from line 26 . . . . **7**		
8	Total elected cost of section 179 property—Add amounts in column (c), lines 6 and 7 . . .	**8**	
9	Tentative deduction—Enter the lesser of line 5 or line 8	**9**	
10	Carryover of disallowed deduction from 1990 (see instructions)	**10**	
11	Taxable income limitation—Enter the lesser of taxable income or line 5 (see instructions) . .	**11**	
12	Section 179 expense deduction—Add lines 9 and 10, but do not enter more than line 11 .	**12**	
13	Carryover of disallowed deduction to 1992—Add lines 9 and 10, less line 12 ▶ **13**		

Note: *Do not use Part II or Part III below for automobiles, certain other vehicles, cellular telephones, computers, or property used for entertainment, recreation, or amusement (listed property). Instead, use Part V for listed property.*

Part II **MACRS Depreciation For Assets Placed in Service ONLY During Your 1991 Tax Year (Do Not Include Listed Property)**

(a) Classification of property	(b) Mo. and yr. placed in service	(c) Basis for depreciation (Business/investment use only—see instructions)	(d) Recovery period	(e) Convention	(f) Method	(g) Depreciation deduction
14 General Depreciation System (GDS) (see instructions):						
a 3-year property						
b 5-year property						
c 7-year property						
d 10-year property						
e 15-year property						
f 20-year property						
g Residential rental property			27.5 yrs.	MM	S/L	
			27.5 yrs.	MM	S/L	
h Nonresidential real property			31.5 yrs.	MM	S/L	
			31.5 yrs.	MM	S/L	
15 Alternative Depreciation System (ADS) (see instructions):						
a Class life					S/L	
b 12-year			12 yrs.		S/L	
c 40-year			40 yrs.	MM	S/L	

Part III **Other Depreciation (Do Not Include Listed Property)**

16	GDS and ADS deductions for assets placed in service in tax years beginning before 1991 (see instructions)	**16**	
17	Property subject to section 168(f)(1) election (see instructions)	**17**	
18	ACRS and other depreciation (see instructions)	**18**	

Part IV **Summary**

19	Listed property—Enter amount from line 25	**19**	
20	Total—Add deductions on line 12, lines 14 and 15 in column (g), and lines 16 through 19. Enter here and on the appropriate lines of your return. (Partnerships and S corporations—see instructions)	**20**	
21	For assets shown above and placed in service during the current year, enter the portion of the basis attributable to section 263A costs (see instructions) **21**		

For Paperwork Reduction Act Notice, see page 1 of the separate instructions.   Cat. No. 12906N   Form **4562** (1991)

Form 4562 (1991)   Page **2**

| **Part V** | Listed Property.—Automobiles, Certain Other Vehicles, Cellular Telephones, Computers, and Property Used for Entertainment, Recreation, or Amusement |

If you are using the standard mileage rate or deducting vehicle lease expense, complete columns (a) through (c) of Section A, all of Section B, and Section C if applicable.

Section A.—Depreciation (Caution: *See instructions for limitations for automobiles.)*

22a Do you have evidence to support the business/investment use claimed? ☐ **Yes** ☐ **No**   **22b** If "Yes," is the evidence written? ☐ **Yes** ☐ **No**

(a) Type of property (list vehicles first)	(b) Date placed in service	(c) Business/ investment use percentage	(d) Cost or other basis	(e) Basis for depreciation (business/investment use only)	(f) Recovery period	(g) Method/ Convention	(h) Depreciation deduction	(i) Elected section 179 cost
23 Property used more than 50% in a qualified business use (see instructions):								
		%						
		%						
		%						
24 Property used 50% or less in a qualified business use (see instructions):								
		%			S/L –			
		%			S/L –			
		%			S/L –			
25 Add amounts in column (h). Enter the total here and on line 19, page 1							**25**	
26 Add amounts in column (i). Enter the total here and on line 7, page 1								**26**

Section B.—Information Regarding Use of Vehicles—*If you deduct expenses for vehicles:*
• *Always complete this section for vehicles used by a sole proprietor, partner, or other "more than 5% owner," or related person.*
• *If you provided vehicles to your employees, first answer the questions in Section C to see if you meet an exception to completing this section for those vehicles.*

		(a) Vehicle 1		(b) Vehicle 2		(c) Vehicle 3		(d) Vehicle 4		(e) Vehicle 5		(f) Vehicle 6	
27	Total business/investment miles driven during the year (DO NOT include commuting miles).												
28	Total commuting miles driven during the year												
29	Total other personal (noncommuting) miles driven												
30	Total miles driven during the year— Add lines 27 through 29												
		Yes	No	Yes	No	Yes	No	Yes	No	Yes	No	Yes	No
31	Was the vehicle available for personal use during off-duty hours?												
32	Was the vehicle used primarily by a more than 5% owner or related person? . .												
33	Is another vehicle available for personal use?												

Section C.—Questions for Employers Who Provide Vehicles for Use by Their Employees
(Answer these questions to determine if you meet an exception to completing Section B. **Note:** *Section B must always be completed for vehicles used by sole proprietors, partners, or other more than 5% owners or related persons.)*

		Yes	No
34	Do you maintain a written policy statement that prohibits all personal use of vehicles, including commuting, by your employees?		
35	Do you maintain a written policy statement that prohibits personal use of vehicles, except commuting, by your employees? (See instructions for vehicles used by corporate officers, directors, or 1% or more owners.) .		
36	Do you treat all use of vehicles by employees as personal use?		
37	Do you provide more than five vehicles to your employees and retain the information received from your employees concerning the use of the vehicles?		
38	Do you meet the requirements concerning qualified automobile demonstration use (see instructions)? . .		

Note: *If your answer to 34, 35, 36, 37, or 38 is "Yes," you need not complete Section B for the covered vehicles.*

| **Part VI** | **Amortization** |

(a) Description of costs	(b) Date amortization begins	(c) Amortizable amount	(d) Code section	(e) Amortization period or percentage	(f) Amortization for this year
39 Amortization of costs that begins during your 1991 tax year:					
40 Amortization of costs that began before 1991				**40**	
41 Total. Enter here and on "Other Deductions" or "Other Expenses" line of your return. . . .				**41**	

*U.S. Government Printing Office: 1991 — 285-329

Form **8716**
(Rev. November 1989)
Department of the Treasury
Internal Revenue Service

Election To Have a Tax Year Other Than a Required Tax Year

OMB No. 1545-1036
Expires 9-30-92

Name		Employer identification number

Please type or print

Number and street (P.O. box number if mail is not delivered to street address)

City or town, state, and ZIP code

1 Check applicable box to show type of taxpayer:
- ☐ Partnership
- ☐ S Corporation
- ☐ Personal Service Corporation (PSC)

2 Name and telephone number (including area code) of person who may be called for information:

3 Enter ending date of the tax year for the entity's last filed return. (A new entity should enter the ending date of the tax year it is adopting.) . . . .

Month	Day	Year

4 Enter ending date of required tax year determined under section 441(i), 706(b), or 1378 . . . . .

Month		Day

5 Section 444(a) Election—Check the applicable box and enter the ending date of the tax year the entity is (see instructions):
- ☐ Adopting ☐ Retaining ☐ Changing to

Month	Day	Year

Under penalties of perjury, I declare that the entity named above has authorized me to make this election under section 444(a), and that the statements made are, to the best of my knowledge and belief, true, correct, and complete.

▶ _____
Signature and title (see instruction G)

▶ _____
Date

Paperwork Reduction Act Notice.—We ask for this information to carry out the Internal Revenue laws of the United States. We need it to ensure that taxpayers are complying with these laws and to allow us to figure and collect the right amount of tax. You are required to give us this information.

The time needed to complete and file this form will vary depending on individual circumstances. The estimated average time is:

Form	Recordkeeping	Learning about the law or the form	Preparing and sending the form to IRS
8716	2 hrs., 23 min.	2 hrs., 35 min.	2 hrs., 44 min.
Schedule H	5 hrs., 59 min.	47 min.	56 min.

If you have comments concerning the accuracy of these time estimates or suggestions for making this form more simple, we would be happy to hear from you. You can write to the **Internal Revenue Service**, Washington, DC 20224, Attention: IRS Reports Clearance Officer, T:FP; or the **Office of Management and Budget**, Paperwork Reduction Project (1545-1036), Washington, DC 20503.

General Instructions

(Section references are to the Internal Revenue Code unless otherwise noted.)

A. Purpose of Form.—Form 8716 is filed by partnerships, S corporations, and personal service corporations (as defined in section 441(i)(2)) to elect to have a tax year other than a required tax year. The election is provided by section 444.

A copy of the Form 8716 you file must be attached to Form 1065 or a Form 1120 series form (1120, 1120A, 1120S, etc.), whichever is applicable, for the first tax year for which the election is made.

B. When To File.—Form 8716 must be filed by the earlier of:

(1) The 15th day of the 5th month following the month that includes the 1st day of the tax year for which the election will be effective, or

(2) The due date (without regard to extensions) of the income tax return for the tax year resulting from the section 444 election.

Items (1) and (2) relate to the tax year, or the return for the tax year, for which the ending date is entered on line 5 above.

See Temporary Regulations section 1.444-3T for more information.

C. Where To File.—File the election with the Internal Revenue Service Center where the entity will file its return. See the instructions for Form 1065 and the Form 1120 series form(s) for Service Center addresses. If the entity is a foreign entity, file Form 8716 with the Service Center in Philadelphia, PA 19255.

D. Effect of Section 444 Election.—If the section 444 election is made, electing partnerships and S corporations must make a required payment of tax as provided by section 7519. Willful failure of an entity to make the required payment may result in the cancellation of an entity's election. See Instruction H for more information on figuring and making the required payment.

Electing PSCs are subject to the limitations of section 280H. Willful failure of any PSC to comply with section 280H

may result in the cancellation of the PSC's election. See Instruction I for more information on section 280H limitations.

E. Acceptance of Election.—After your election is received and accepted by the Service Center, the Center will stamp it "ACCEPTED" and return a copy to you. Be sure to keep a copy of the form marked "ACCEPTED" for your records.

F. End of Election.—Once the election is made, it remains in effect until the entity terminates its election. If the election is terminated, the entity may not make another section 444 election. See section 444(d)(2).

G. Signature.—Form 8716 is not considered an election unless it is signed. For partnerships, a general partner must sign and date the election. If a receiver, trustee in bankruptcy, or assignee controls the organization's property or business, that person must sign the election.

For corporations, the election must be signed and dated by the president, vice president, treasurer, assistant treasurer, chief accounting officer, or any other corporate officer (such as tax officer) authorized to sign its tax return. If a receiver, trustee in bankruptcy, or assignee controls the corporation's property or business, that person must sign the election.

H. Required Payment of Tax.—Partnerships and S corporations (entities) are required to make a payment for each tax year if: (1) an election under section 444 is in effect for the tax year (any tax year that a section 444 election is in effect, including the first year the section 444 election is made, is hereinafter called an applicable election year), and (2) the required payment for the applicable

Form **8716** (Rev. 11-89)

election year (or any preceding applicable election year) exceeds $500. Required payments for applicable election years beginning in 1989 are made on the first-quarter 1990 **Form 720,** Quarterly Federal Excise Tax Return. The instructions for the 1989 Form 1065 or Form 1120S contain a Computation Schedule for Required Payments Under Section 7519 for applicable election years beginning in 1989 (1989 required payments). Instructions for the section 7519 computation schedule give details on making the 1989 required payments, and how to obtain a refund or credit for prior year payments.

Note: *The Instructions for Form 1120S and Form 1065 for tax years beginning after 1989 will indicate how payments are made and refunds are obtained for applicable election years beginning after 1989.*

Also see section 7519 and related regulations for other details.

I. Minimum Distribution Requirements for a PSC.—An electing PSC is subject to the minimum distribution requirements of section 280H for its first applicable election year (and each subsequent applicable election year). If the PSC fails in any applicable election year to make the minimum distributions required by section 280H, the applicable amounts it may deduct for that applicable election year are limited to a maximum deductible amount.

The PSC may use **Schedule H (Form 8716),** Section 280H Limitations for a Personal Service Corporation (PSC), to figure the required minimum distribution and the maximum deductible amount. If the PSC has not made the required minimum distribution, Schedule H must be attached to its income tax return. The PSC should figure its compliance with the provisions of section 280H at the end of each tax year that the section 444 election is in effect. See section 280H and related regulations for other details.

J. Members of Certain Tiered Structures May Not Make Election.—No election may be made under section 444(a) by an entity which is part of a tiered structure other than a tiered structure that consists entirely of partnerships or S corporations (or both) all of which have the same tax year. An election previously made shall be terminated if an entity later becomes part of a tiered structure that is not allowed to make the election. See section 444(d)(3) and related regulations for other details.

Specific Instructions

Line 1.—Check the applicable box in line 1 to show that you are a partnership, S corporation (or electing to be an S corporation), or a personal service corporation.

A corporation electing to be an S corporation that wants to make a section 444 election must make its section 444 election by the time specified in General Instruction B. The corporation is not required to attach a copy of Form 8716 to its **Form 2553,** Election by a Small Business Corporation. However, the corporation is required to state on Form 2553 its intention to make a section 444 election (or a backup section 444 election). If a corporation is making a backup section 444 election (provided for in item Q, Part II, of Form 2553 (Rev. October 1989)), it must type or legibly print the words "BACKUP ELECTION" at the top of the Form 8716 it files to make the backup election. See Temporary Regulations section 1.444-3T for additional information.

Line 2.—Enter the name and telephone number (including the area code) of a person that the Service may call for information that may be needed to complete the processing of the election.

Line 4.—See the Instructions for Form 1065 or a Form 1120 series form, whichever is applicable, and section 441(i), 706(b), or 1378 for a definition of a required tax year and other details.

Line 5.—Enter the ending date of the tax year the entity is electing under section 444. The following limitations and special rules apply in determining the tax year an entity may elect:

(a) New entity adopting a tax year.— An entity adopting a tax year may elect a tax year under section 444 only if the deferral period of the tax year is not longer than 3 months. For a definition of deferral period, see (d) below and section 444(b)(4).

(b) Existing entity retaining a tax year.—In certain cases, an entity may elect to retain its tax year if the deferral period is no longer than 3 months. If the entity does not want to elect to retain its tax year, it could elect to change its tax year under (c) below.

(c) Existing entity changing a tax year.—An existing entity may elect to change its tax year if the deferral period of the elected tax year is no longer than the shorter of: (1) three months, or (2) the deferral period of the tax year being changed.

For example, ABC, a C corporation that historically used a tax year ending October 31, elects S status and wants to make a section 444 election beginning 11-1-89. ABC's required tax year under section 1378 is a calendar tax year. In this case, the deferral period of the tax year being changed is 2 months. Thus, ABC may elect to retain its tax year beginning 11-1-89 and ending 10-31-90, or change it to a short tax year beginning 11-1-89 and ending 11-30-89. However, it may not elect a short tax year beginning 11-1-89 and ending 9-30-90 because the deferral period for that elected tax year is 3 months (9-30 to 12-31), which is longer than the 2-month deferral period of the tax year being changed. After filing the short year return (11-1-89 to 11-30-89), and as long as the section 444 election remains in effect, the corporation's tax year will begin 12-1 and end 11-30.

(d) Deferral period.—If you are electing **to retain** your tax year, the term " DEFERRAL PERIOD" means the months that occur between the beginning of the elected tax year and the close of the 1st required tax year. For example, if you elected to retain a tax year beginning 10-1-89 and ending 9-30-90 and your required tax year was a calendar tax year, the deferral period would be 3 months (the number of months between 9-30-89 and 12-31-89).

If you are electing **to adopt or change** a tax year, the term "DEFERRAL PERIOD" means the months that occur after the end of the elected tax year and before the close of the 1st required tax year. For example, if you elect to adopt a tax year ending September 30, 1989, and your required tax year is a calendar tax year, the deferral period would be 3 months (the number of months between 9-30-89 and 12-31-89).

See section 444(b) and related Temporary Regulations for additional information on the above rules.

**Department of the Treasury
Internal Revenue Service**

Instructions for Form W-2

Wage and Tax Statement

Paperwork Reduction Act Notice.—
We ask for the information on this form to carry out the Internal Revenue laws of the United States. You are required to give us the information. We need it to ensure that you are complying with these laws and to allow us to figure and collect the right amount of tax.

The time needed to complete and file this form will vary depending on individual circumstances. The estimated average time is 30 minutes. If you have comments concerning the accuracy of this time estimate or suggestions for making this form more simple, we would be happy to hear from you. You can write to both the **Internal Revenue Service,** Washington, DC 20224, Attention: IRS Reports Clearance Officer T:FP; and the **Office of Management and Budget,** Paperwork Reduction Project (1545-0008), Washington, DC 20503. DO NOT send the tax form to either of these offices. Instead, see the instructions below for where to file it.

Changes You Should Note

Separate Reporting of Social Security Wages, Medicare Wages and Tips, Social Security Taxes, and Medicare Taxes.—
Beginning in 1991, the wage bases for the two parts of the social security tax (social security and Medicare) are different. Employers can no longer combine and report the withholding as a single amount. The **Form W-2,** Wage and Tax Statement, for 1991 will require employers to separately report the withholding for social security and Medicare.

The wage bases are $53,400 for social security (old age, survivors, and disability insurance) and $125,000 for Medicare (hospital insurance). For social security, the tax rate is 6.2% each for employers and employees. For Medicare, the rate is 1.45% each for employers and employees. In addition, there are changes to the codes for Box 17.

Obsolete Form W-2P.—Form W-2P, Statement for Recipients of Annuities, Pensions, Retired Pay, or IRA Payments, is obsolete. For 1991, payers must report distributions (periodic and total) from pensions, annuities, retirement pay, profit-sharing plans, IRAs, SEPs, and insurance contracts on **Form 1099-R,** Distributions From Pensions, Annuities, Retirement or Profit-Sharing Plans, IRAs, Insurance Contracts, etc. See the separate Instructions for Forms 1099, 1098, 5498, and W-2G, for more information.

Use **Form W-2c,** Statement of Corrected Income and Tax Amounts, to report corrections on Form W-2P for years ending before January 1, 1991.

State and Local Government Employees.—
State and local government employees who are not participants in a retirement program (with certain exceptions) will be subject to social security and Medicare taxes for services performed after July 1, 1991.

Reporting of Taxes for Group-Term Life Insurance Coverage.—Beginning in 1991, employers are required to report on Form W-2 any uncollected social security and Medicare taxes on group-term life insurance in excess of $50,000 provided to former employees (including retirees). (Information on reporting these taxes is included in items (g) and (h) in the instructions for Box 17).

General Instructions

(Section references are to the Internal Revenue Code unless otherwise noted.)

Who Must File Form W-2.—Form W-2 is filed by employers. (See **Circular A,** Agricultural Employer's Tax Guide, or **Circular E,** Employer's Tax Guide. Household employers, see **Form 942,** Employer's Quarterly Tax Return for Household Employees.) If you have 250 or more Forms W-2, see instructions for *Magnetic Media Reporting* on the next page.

When To File.—File Form W-2 with accompanying **Form W-3,** Transmittal of Income and Tax Statements, by March 2, 1992.

If you need an extension of time to file Form W-2, see *When To File* in the instructions for Form W-3.

Where To File.—See Form W-3 for instructions.

Calendar Year Basis.—The entries on Form W-2 must be based on a calendar year.

Taxpayer Identification Numbers.—We use these numbers to check the payments you report against the amounts shown on the employees' tax returns. **When you prepare Form W-2, be sure to show the correct social security number on the form or on magnetic media.**

Persons in a trade or business use an employer identification number (00-0000000). Individuals use a social security number (000-00-0000). When you list a number, please separate the nine digits properly to show the kind of number.

Sole proprietors who are payers should show their employer identification number on the statements they prepare. But if you prepare a statement showing payment to a sole proprietor, give the proprietor's social security number in Box 5 of Form W-2.

Please show the full name, address, and identification number of the payer and the recipient on the form. If you made payments to more than one individual, show on the first line **ONLY** the name of the recipient whose number is on the statement. Show the other names on the second line. If the recipient is **NOT** an individual and the name runs over the first line, you may continue on the second and following lines.

Note: *If your employee has been given a new social security card because of an adjustment to his or her alien residence status, which shows a different name or social security number, correct your records for 1991 and show the new information on the 1991 Form W-2. If you filed Form W-2 for the same employee in prior years under the old name and social security number, file Form W-2c, to correct the name and number. (See Corrections later.) In this case, one Form W-2c can be used to correct all prior years. Advise the employee to contact their local Social Security Administration (SSA) office to ensure their records have been updated.*

Statements to Employees.—Generally, give statements to employees by January 31, 1992. If employment ends before December 31, 1991, you may give copies any time after employment ends. If the employee asks for Form W-2, give him or her the completed copies within 30 days of the request or the final wage payment, whichever is later.

You may give statements to employees on government-printed official forms or on privately printed substitute forms.

Be sure that the statements you provide to employees are clear and legible (especially if using carbons).

A revenue procedure, titled "Specifications for Private Printing of Forms W-2 and W-3" reprinted as **Pub. 1141,** explains the format that must be used on all substitute paper forms. You can get a copy by calling 1-800-829-3676.

Corrections.—Use Form W-2c to correct errors on previously filed Form W-2. Use **Form W-3c,** Transmittal of Corrected Income and Tax Statements, to transmit the W-2c forms to the SSA. Instructions are on the forms.

If you are making an adjustment in 1991 to correct social security tax for a prior year, you must file **Form 941c,** Statement To Correct Information Previously Reported on the Employer's Federal Tax Return, with your **Form 941,** Employer's Quarterly Federal Tax Return, in the quarter you find the error and issue the employee a Form W-2c for the prior year.

Reissued Statement.—If an employee (or recipient) loses a statement, write "REISSUED STATEMENT" on the new copy, **but do not send Copy A of the reissued statement to SSA.**

Earned Income Credit Notification.— You must notify any employee not having income tax withheld that they may be eligible for an income tax refund because of the earned income credit. You can do this by using the official IRS Form W-2 which contains a statement on the back of Copy C concerning the earned income credit. If you use a substitute Form W-2, or you are not required to furnish Form W-2, or if you do not furnish a timely Form W-2 to your employee, you may have to give your employee **Notice 797,** Notice of a Possible Federal Tax Refund Due to the Earned Income Credit (EIC). Get **Pub. 1325** for more information.

Employee Business Expense Reimbursements.— Reimbursements for employee business expenses should be reported as follows:

● Generally, payments made under an accountable plan are excluded from the employee's gross income and are not required to be reported on Form W-2. However, if you pay a per diem or mileage allowance, and the amount paid exceeds the amount treated as substantiated under IRS rules, you must report as wages on Form W-2 the amount in excess of the amount treated as substantiated. The excess amount is subject to income tax withholding, social security tax, Medicare tax, and Federal unemployment tax. Report the amount treated as substantiated (*i.e.,* the nontaxable portion) in Box 17 using code "L."

- Payments made under a nonaccountable plan are reportable as wages on Form W-2 and are subject to income tax withholding, social security tax, Medicare tax, and Federal unemployment tax.

For more information on accountable plans, nonaccountable plans, and amounts treated as substantiated under a per diem or mileage allowance, see Regulations section 1.62-2, Revenue Procedure 89-66, 1989-2 C.B. 792, Revenue Procedure 89-67, 1989-2 C.B. 795, Revenue Procedure 90-15, 1990-1 C.B. 476, Revenue Procedure 90-34, 1990-1 C.B. 552, Revenue Procedure 90-38, 1990-28 I.R.B. 13, and Announcement 90-127, 1990-48 I.R.B. 8.

Sick Pay.—If you had employees who received sick pay in 1991 from an insurance company or other third-party payer, and the third party notified you of the amount of sick pay involved, you must report the following on the employees' Forms W-2:

(a) in Box 9, the amount (if any) of income tax withheld from the sick pay by the third-party payer;

(b) in Box 10, the amount the employee must include in income;

(c) in Box 11, the employee social security tax withheld (6.2%) by the third-party payer;

(d) in Box 12, the amount of sick pay that is subject to employee social security tax;

(e) in Box 14, the amount of sick pay that is subject to employee Medicare tax;

(f) in Box 15, the employee Medicare tax withheld (1.45%); and

(g) in Box 17, the amount (if any) not includible in income because the employee contributed to the sick pay plan. See the instructions for Box 17 for the correct code to use.

You can include these amounts on the Forms W-2 you issue the employees showing wages, or you can give the employees separate Forms W-2 and state that the amounts are for third-party sick pay. In either case, you must show in Box 25 of Form W-3 the total amount of income tax withheld by third-party payers, even though the amounts are includible in Box 9. Also, see the instructions for Form W-3 for more information on third-party sick pay.

Magnetic Media Reporting.—If you file 250 or more Forms W-2, you must report on magnetic media unless you have been granted a waiver by the IRS.

If you are filing Form W-2 using magnetic media, you will also need **Form 6559,** Transmitter Report of Magnetic Media Filing, and **Form 6560,** Employer Summary of Form W-2 Magnetic Media Wage Information.

You can get magnetic media reporting specifications at many Social Security Administration offices or you may write to the Social Security Administration, P.O. Box 2317, Baltimore, MD 21235, Attn: Magnetic Media Group.

Note: *If you file on magnetic media, do not file the same returns on paper.*

Penalties.—A penalty may be imposed if a person either fails to file an information return or files with incorrect information.

The amount of the penalty is based on when the correct information returns are filed. The penalty is as follows:

- $15 for each information return if the correct information is filed within 30 days after the due date with a maximum penalty of $75,000 per year ($25,000 for small businesses, defined later).

- $30 for each information return if the correct information is filed more than 30 days

after the due date but by August 1, with a maximum penalty of $150,000 per year ($50,000 for small businesses).

- $50 for each information return that is not filed at all or is not filed correctly by August 1, with a maximum penalty of $250,000 per year ($100,000 for small businesses).

Exceptions to the Penalty.—In general, the penalty will not apply to any failure that was due to reasonable cause.

In addition, the penalty will not apply to a de minimis number of failures. These failures are information returns that were filed timely but with incomplete or incorrect information and were corrected by August 1. The penalty will not apply to the greater of 10 information returns or 1/2 of 1% of the total number of information returns that are required to be filed for the year.

Definition of Small Business.—A small business is a firm with average annual gross receipts of $5,000,000 or less for the 3 most recent taxable years.

Failure To Provide Employee Statement or Providing Incorrect Employee Statement.—A penalty may be imposed if a person either fails to furnish a payee statement by the due date or fails to include correct information on a payee statement. The penalty is $50 for each failure. The maximum penalty for such failures is $100,000.

Penalties for Intentional Disregard.—Higher penalties of at least $100 per document may be imposed for intentional disregard of the filing, providing payee statements, and correct information return requirements.

How To Complete Form W-2

Copy A of Form W-2 is printed with two forms to an unperforated page. Send the whole page even if one of the forms is blank or void. If you are sending 42 or more Forms W-2, please show subtotals on every 42nd form for the preceding 41 forms to permit checking the transmittal totals.

Since this form is processed by optical scanning machines, please type the entries, if possible, using black ink. Please do not make any erasures, whiteouts, or strikeovers on Copy A. Also, do not use script type. **Make all dollar entries without the dollar sign and comma but with the decimal point (000.00).**

If possible, please file Forms W-2 either alphabetically by employees' last names or numerically by employees' SSNs. This will help SSA locate specific forms if there is a problem processing your submission.

The instructions below are for boxes on Form W-2. If an entry does not apply, leave it blank.

Box 1—Control number.—You may use this box to identify individual Forms W-2. *You do not have to use this box.*

Box 3—Employer's identification number.—Show the number assigned to you by IRS (00-0000000). This should be the same number that you used on your Federal employment tax returns (Forms 941, 942, 943). Do not use a prior owner's number.

Box 4—Employer's state I.D. number.—You do not have to complete this box, but you may want to if you use copies of this form for your state return. The number is assigned by the individual states.

This box is separated into two parts by a dotted line so that you may report two state I.D. numbers if you are reporting wages for two states. If you are only reporting for one state, enter the number above the dotted line.

Box 5—Employee's social security number.—Enter the number shown on the employee's social security card. If the employee does not have a card, he or she should apply for one at any SSA office.

Box 6—Check the boxes that apply.

Statutory employee.—Check this box for statutory employees whose earnings are subject to social security and Medicare taxes but **NOT** subject to Federal income tax withholding. (See Circular E for more information on statutory employees.)

Deceased.—Check this box if the employee is now deceased. If an employee is deceased, you must report wages or other compensation for services he or she performed and that were paid in the year of death to the estate or beneficiary. In addition, such wages received in a year after the year of death may be reportable on **Form 1099-MISC,** Miscellaneous Income. For information on how to report, see Rev. Rul. 86-109, 1986-2 C.B. 196.

Pension plan.—Check this box if the employee was an active participant (for any part of the year) in a retirement plan (including a 401(k) plan and a simplified employee pension (SEP) plan) maintained by you. Also check this box if the employee participates in a collectively bargained plan (*i.e.*, union plan). See IRS Notice 87-16, 1987-1 C.B. 446, for the definition of an active participant. Do not check this box if you are reporting contributions made to a nonqualified pension plan or a section 457 plan.

Legal representative.—Check this box when the employee's name is the only name shown but is shown as a trust account (*e.g.*, John Doe Trust), or another name is shown in addition to the employee's name and the other person or business is acting on behalf of the employee.

Representatives are identified by words such as "custodian," "parent," or "attorney"; sometimes the employee is identified as a minor, child, etc. Do **NOT** check this box if the address is simply in care of someone other than the employee (John Doe, c/o Jane Smith).

942 employee.—For household employers only. See Form 942 instructions for information on when to check this box.

Subtotal.—Do not subtotal if you are submitting 41 or less Forms W-2. If you are submitting **42 or more Forms W-2,** please give subtotal figures for every 41 individual forms. Check the "Subtotal" box on the form that shows the subtotal dollar amounts for the preceding 41 forms and for the last group of forms, even if less than 41 forms. Void statements are counted in order with good statements, **but do not include the money amounts from the void statements in the subtotal figures.** Subtotal statements should always be the last completed form on a page. The subtotal amounts to be shown are:

Boxes 7, 8, 9, 10, 11, 12, 13, 14, 15, 16, 17, and 22. However, in Box 17, subtotal only codes D, E, F, G, and H as one amount. See Box 17 instructions. Also, for Box 16, show one subtotal amount; that is, do not separate distributions from nonqualified plans (uncoded) and distributions from section 457 plans.

Example: *An employer with Forms W-2 for 86 employees should show a subtotal on the 42nd statement, the 84th statement (showing the subtotal for statements 43 through 83), and the 89th statement (showing the subtotal for statements 85 through 88).*

Deferred compensation.—Check this box if you made contributions on behalf of the employee to a section 401(k), 403(b), 408(k)(6), 457, or 501(c)(18)(D) retirement plan. See also instruction "(d)" under Box 17.

Void.—Put an X in this box when an error has been made. **(Be sure the amounts shown on void forms are NOT included in your subtotals.)**

Box 7—Allocated tips.—If you are a large food or beverage establishment, show the amount of tips allocated to the employee. (See the instructions for **Form 8027,** Employer's Annual Information Return of Tip Income and Allocated Tips.) **DO NOT** include this amount in Box 10 (Wages, tips, other compensation), Box 13 (Social security tips), or Box 14 (Medicare wages and tips).

Box 8—Advance EIC payment.—Show the total amount paid to the employee as advance earned income credit payments.

Box 10—Wages, tips, other compensation.—Show in Box 10 (excluding elective deferrals), before any payroll deductions, the following items:

(1) Total wages paid during the year. For example, if the employee worked from December 24, 1990, through January 4, 1991, and the wages for that period were paid on January 7, 1991, include those wages on the 1991 Form W-2;

(2) Total noncash payments (including fringe benefits);

(3) Total tips reported;

(4) Certain employee business expense reimbursements (See *Employee Business Expense Reimbursements* on page 1.); and

(5) All other compensation, including certain scholarships and fellowship grants and payments for moving expenses. Other compensation is amounts that you pay your employee from which Federal income tax is not withheld. If you prefer, you may show other compensation on a separate Form W-2.

Except for section 501(c)(18) contributions, contributions made to deferred compensation arrangements should not be included in Box 10. Also see instructions for Box 17, item "(d)."

Note: *Payments to statutory employees that are subject to social security and Medicare taxes but not subject to Federal income tax withholding must be shown in Box 10 as other compensation. (See Circular E for definition of a statutory employee.)*

Box 11—Employee social security tax withheld.—Show the total employee social security tax (not your share) withheld or paid by you for the employee. The amount shown should not exceed $3,310.80. Include only taxes withheld for 1991 wages.

Box 12—Social security wages.— Show the total wages paid (before payroll deductions) subject to employee social security tax but **NOT** including social security tips and allocated tips. Generally, noncash payments are considered wages. Include employee business expenses reported in Box 10. Also, include contributions to certain qualified cash or deferred compensation arrangements, even though the contributions are not includible in Box 10 as wages, tips, and other compensation. (See Circular E for more information.) Include any employee social security tax, Medicare tax, and employee state unemployment compensation tax you paid for your employee rather than deducting it from wages except for household or agricultural employees. (See Revenue Procedure 81-48, 1981-2 C.B. 623, for details.) **The total of Boxes 12 and 13 should not be more than $53,400** (the maximum social security wage base for 1991).

Box 13—Social security tips.—Show the amount the employee reported even if you did not have enough employee funds to collect the social security tax for the tips. The total of Boxes 12 and 13 should not be more than $53,400 (the maximum social security wage base for 1991). But report all tips in Box 10 along with wages and other compensation.

Box 14—Medicare wages and tips.—The wages and tips subject to Medicare tax are the same as those subject to social security tax (Boxes 12 and 13), except that the wage base for Medicare is $125,000. Enter the Medicare wages and tips in Box 14, but do not enter more than $125,000. Be sure to enter tips the employee reported even if you did not have enough employee funds to collect the Medicare tax for those tips.

If you are a Federal, state, or local agency with employees paying only the 1.45% Medicare tax, enter the Medicare wages in this box. File one Form W-3 for wages subject only to the Medicare tax, and a second Form W-3 for wages subject to both social security and Medicare taxes.

The following is an example of how to report social security and Medicare wages in Boxes 12 and 14. Assume you paid your employee $100,000 in wages. The amount shown in Box 12 (social security wages) should be 53400, but the amount shown in Box 14 (Medicare wages and tips) should be 100000. If the amount of wages paid was less than $53,400, the amounts entered in Boxes 12 and 14 would be the same.

Box 15—Medicare tax withheld.—Enter the total employee Medicare tax (not your share) withheld or paid by you for your employee. The amount shown should not exceed $1,812.50. Include only taxes withheld for 1991 wages. If you are a Federal, state, or local agency, with employees paying only the 1.45% Medicare tax, enter the Medicare tax in this box.

Box 16—Nonqualified plans.—Show the total amount of distributions to your employee from a nonqualified plan or a section 457 plan. This amount should also be included as wages in Box 10.

State and local agencies should separately identify section 457 distributions in this box by using code "G" before the dollar amount. However, if you are reporting a distribution from both a nonqualified plan and a section 457 plan, report it as a single amount in this box and do not identify it by code "G."

Box 17—Complete and code this box for all items described in (a) through (i) below that apply. Do not report in Box 17 any items that are not listed in (a) through (i). Instead, use Box 18 for these items or for any other information you wish to give your employee. For example, union dues, moving expenses, etc., should be reported in Box 18. Also, any retirement plan contributions that are not listed in item (d) below should be reported in Box 18 (for example, section 414(h)(2) contributions).

Use the codes listed below with the dollar amount. The code should be entered using capital letters. Leave one space blank after the code and enter the dollar amount on the same line. Use decimal points but do not use dollar signs or commas. For example, you are reporting $5,300.00 of contributions to a section 401(k) plan. The entry in Box 17 would be: D 5300.00.

(a) You did **not** collect employee social security tax on all the employee's tips. Show the amount of tax that you could not collect because the employee did not have enough funds from which to deduct it. Do not include this amount in Box 11. Use **code A** for uncollected social security tax on tips.

(b) You did **not** collect employee Medicare tax on tips because the employee did not have enough funds from which to deduct it. Enter the uncollected Medicare tax on tips. Do not include this amount in Box 15. Use **code B** for uncollected Medicare tax on tips.

(c) You provided your employee more than $50,000 of group-term life insurance. Show the cost of coverage over $50,000. Also include it in Boxes 10, 12, and 14. Use **code C** for cost of group-term life insurance coverage over $50,000.

(d) Employee contributions were made to a section 401(k) cash or deferred arrangement, to a section 403(b) salary reduction agreement to purchase an annuity contract, to a section 408(k)(6) salary reduction SEP, to a section 457 deferred compensation plan for state or local government employees, or to a section 501(c)(18)(D) tax-exempt organization plan. Check the "Deferred compensation" checkbox in Box 6, enter the total elective deferral (including any excess) in Box 17. Use the following codes for contributions made to the plans listed below.

D—section 401(k)
E—section 403(b)
F—section 408(k)(6)
G—section 457
H—section 501(c)(18)(D)

Note: *The section 457 dollar limitation should be reduced by contributions made to certain other deferred compensation plans. See section 457(c)(2).*

(e) You made excess "golden parachute" payments to certain key corporate employees. Report in Box 17 the 20% excise tax on these payments. Use **code K** for the tax on excess golden parachute payments. If the excess payments are considered as wages, also report the 20% excise tax as income tax withholding and include it in Box 9.

(f) You reimbursed your employee for employee business expenses using a per diem or mileage allowance, and the amount you reimbursed exceeds the amount treated as substantiated under IRS rules. (See *Employee Business Expense Reimbursements* on page 1.) Report the amount treated as substantiated, *i.e.,* the nontaxable portion, in Box 17 using **code L.** In Box 10, show the portion of the reimbursement that is more than the amount treated as substantiated.

Do **NOT** include any per diem or mileage allowance reimbursements for employee business expenses in Box 17 if the total reimbursement is less than or equal to the amount treated as substantiated.

(g) You provided your former employees (including retirees) more than $50,000 of group-term life insurance coverage. Enter the amount of uncollected social security tax on the coverage in Box 17. Use **code M** for uncollected social security tax.

(h) You provided your former employees (including retirees) more than $50,000 of group-term life insurance coverage. Enter the amount of uncollected Medicare tax on the coverage in Box 17. Use **code N** for uncollected Medicare tax.

(i) You are reporting sick pay. Show the amount of any sick pay **NOT** includible in income because the employee contributed to the sick pay plan. If you issue a separate Form W-2 for sick pay, use Box 17 to code the Form W-2 as "Sick pay." Use **code J** for sick pay **NOT** includible as income.

Do **NOT** enter more than three codes in this box. If more than three items need to be reported in Box 17, use a separate Form W-2 or a substitute Form W-2 to report the

Page 3

additional items. If you issue multiple Forms W-2, do **NOT** report the same Federal tax data to the SSA on more than one Copy A. If you use a substitute Form W-2, the form must meet the requirements of Pub. 1141.

Box 18—Other.—You may use this box for any other information you want to give your employee. Please label each item. Examples are union dues, health insurance premiums deducted, moving expenses paid, or educational assistance payments.

Box 19a—Employee's name.—Enter the name as shown on the employee's social security card (first, middle initial, last). If the name has changed, have the employee get a corrected card from any SSA office. Use the name on the original card until you see the corrected one.

Box 19b—Employee's address and ZIP code.—This box has been combined with Box 19a (employee's name) on all copies except Copy A to allow employees' copies to be mailed in a window envelope or as a self-mailer.

Box 22—Dependent care benefits.—Show the total amount of dependent care benefits under section 129 paid or incurred by you for your employee including any amount in excess of the $5,000 exclusion. Also, include in Box 10 on Form W-2 any amount in excess of the $5,000 exclusion. For more information on the amount to report, see Notice 89-111, 1989-2 C.B. 449.

Box 23—Benefits included in Box 10.—Show the total value of the taxable fringe benefits included in Box 10 as other compensation. If you provided a vehicle and included 100% of its annual lease value in the employee's income, you must separately report this value to the employee in Box 23 or on a separate statement so the employee can compute the value of any business use of the vehicle.

Boxes 24 through 29—State or local income tax information.—You may use these to report state or local income tax information. You do not have to use them. But you may want to show the amounts on Copy A if you use copies of this form for your state or local tax returns or as recipients' statements. The state and local information boxes can be used to report wages and taxes on two states and two localities. Keep each state's and locality's information separated by the broken line.

Reducing Discrepancies Between Reports Filed with IRS and SSA

When there are discrepancies between reports filed with IRS and those filed with SSA, we must contact you to resolve the discrepancies. This costs time and money, both for the government and for you, the employer. To help reduce the number of these discrepancies, please:

(1) Reconcile the social security wages, social security tips, Medicare wages and tips, total compensation, advance earned income credit, income tax withheld, social security and Medicare taxes, on the four quarterly Forms 941 to your Form W-3. The amounts may not match for various reasons. If they do not match, you should determine that the reason is a valid one (such as some income tax withheld was reported on Form 1099, or adjustments were made on Form 941c). Please retain your reconciliation. This way, if there are inquiries in the future, you will know why the amounts did not match.

(2) Use Form W-2 for the current year.

(3) File all Forms W-2 with SSA.

(4) Report bonuses as social security and Medicare wages.

(5) Show social security taxes in the box for social security taxes withheld, not as social security wages.

(6) Make sure social security wage amounts for each employee do not exceed the annual social security wage base.

(7) Make sure Medicare wage amounts for each employee do not exceed the annual Medicare wage base.

(8) Do not include noncash wages not subject to social security or Medicare taxes as social security or Medicare wages.

1 Control number	22222	For Official Use Only ▶ OMB No. 1545-0008		
2 Employer's name, address, and ZIP code			6 Statutory employee ☐ Deceased ☐ Pension plan ☐ Legal rep. ☐ 942 emp. ☐ Subtotal ☐ Deferred compensation ☐ Void ☐	
			7 Allocated tips	8 Advance EIC payment
			9 Federal income tax withheld	10 Wages, tips, other compensation
3 Employer's identification number	4 Employer's state I.D. number		11 Social security tax withheld	12 Social security wages
5 Employee's social security number			13 Social security tips	14 Medicare wages and tips
19a Employee's name (first, middle, last)			15 Medicare tax withheld	16 Nonqualified plans
			17 See Instrs. for Form W-2	18 Other
19b Employee's address and ZIP code				
20	21		22 Dependent care benefits	23 Benefits included in Box 10
24 State income tax	25 State wages, tips, etc.	26 Name of state	27 Local income tax 28 Local wages, tips, etc.	29 Name of locality

Copy A   For Social Security Administration   Department of the Treasury—Internal Revenue Service

Form W-2 Wage and Tax Statement 1991

For Paperwork Reduction Act Notice, see separate instructions.

Notice to Employee:

Getting a Refund.—Even if you do not have to file a tax return, you should file to get a refund if Box 9 shows Federal income tax withheld, or if you can take the earned income credit.

Earned Income Credit.—You must file a tax return if any amount is shown in Box 8.

For 1991, if your income is less than $21,245 and you have one qualifying child, you may qualify for an earned income credit (EIC) up to $1,192. If your income is less than $21,245 and you have two or more qualifying children, you may qualify for an earned income credit up to $1,235. Any EIC that is more than your tax liability is refunded to you, but ONLY if you file a tax return. For example, if you have no tax liability and qualify for a $300 EIC, you can get $300, but only if you file a tax return. The 1991 instructions for Forms 1040 and 1040A, and Pub. 596, explain the EIC in more detail. You can get the instructions and the publication by calling toll-free 1-800-829-3676.

Making Corrections.—If your name, social security number, or address is incorrect, correct Copies B, C, and 2. Ask your employer to correct your employment record. If your name and number are correct but are not the same as shown on your social security card, you should ask for a new card at any Social Security office.

If any of the dollar amounts are incorrect, ask your employer for a **Form W-2c,** Statement of Corrected Income and Tax Amounts. If you already filed a return and the information from this Form W-2 was not included, amend your income tax return by filing Form 1040X.

Credit for Excess Social Security Tax.—If more than one employer paid you wages during 1991 and more than the maximum social security employee tax, Medicare tax, railroad retirement (RRTA) tax, or combined social security, Medicare, and RRTA tax was withheld, you may claim the excess as a credit against your Federal income tax. See your income tax return instructions.

Box 6.—If the "Pension plan" box is marked, special limits may apply to the amount of IRA contributions you may deduct on your return. If the "Deferred compensation" box is marked, the elective deferrals shown in Box 17 (for all employers, and for all such plans to which you belong) are generally limited to $7,979 ($9,500 for certain section 403(b) contracts and $7,500 for section 457 plans). Amounts over that must be included in income.

Caution: *The elective deferral dollar limitation of $7,979 is subject to change for 1991.*

Box 7.—For information on how to report tips on your tax return, see the instructions for Form 1040, 1040A, or 1040EZ. The amount of allocated tips is **not** included in Box 10.

Box 16.—Any amount in Box 16 is a distribution made to you from a nonqualified deferred compensation plan. This amount is also included in Box 10 and is taxable for Federal income tax purposes.

Box 17.—If there is an amount in Box 17, there should be a code (letter) next to it. You can find out what the code means from the list below. You may need this information to complete your tax return. The codes are:

A—Uncollected social security tax on tips (See your Form 1040 instructions for how to pay this tax.)

B—Uncollected Medicare tax on tips (See your Form 1040 instructions for how to pay this tax.)
C—Cost of group-term life insurance coverage over $50,000
D—Section 401(k) contributions
E—Section 403(b) contributions
F—Section 408(k)(6) contributions
G—Section 457 contributions
H—Section 501(c)(18)(D) contributions
J—Sick pay not includible as income
K—Tax on excess golden parachute payments
L—Nontaxable part of employee business expense reimbursements
M—Uncollected social security tax on cost of group-term life insurance coverage over $50,000 (former employees only) (See your Form 1040 instructions for how to pay this tax.)
N—Uncollected Medicare tax on cost of group-term life insurance coverage over $50,000 (former employees only) (See your Form 1040 instructions for how to pay this tax.)

Box 22.—The amount in this box is the total amount of dependent care benefits your employer paid to you (or incurred on your behalf). Any amount over $5,000 has been included in Box 10. Also, if you are claiming the credit for child and dependent care expenses, you must use this amount to determine the amount of credit you are able to claim. See the instructions for Form 1040 and 1040A.

Box 23.—This amount has already been included as wages in Box 10. Do not add this amount to Box 10. If there is an amount in Box 23, you may be able to deduct expenses that are related to fringe benefits; see the instructions for your income tax return.

INDEX